Bums

Bums No More

The 1959 Los Angeles Dodgers, World Champions of Baseball

BRIAN M. ENDSLEY

McFarland & Company, Inc., Publishers
Jefferson, North Carolina, and London

Library of Congress Cataloguing-in-Publication Data

Endsley, Brian M.
Bums no more : the 1959 Los Angeles Dodgers, world champions of baseball / Brian M. Endsley.
p. cm.
Includes bibliographical references and index.

ISBN 978-0-7864-3919-5
softcover : 50# alkaline paper ♾

1. Los Angeles Dodgers (Baseball team)—History—20th century.
2. World Series (Baseball) 1959. I. Title.
GV875.L6E63 2009
796.357'640979494—dc22 2009033820

British Library cataloguing data are available

On the cover: pitcher Larry Sherry, left, and center fielder Duke Snider after defeating the Chicago White Sox, 9–3, to win the World Series in game six at Comiskey Park in Chicago on October 8, 1959 (AP Photo)

Manufactured in the United States of America

McFarland & Company, Inc., Publishers
Box 611, Jefferson, North Carolina 28640
www.mcfarlandpub.com

In memory of my mother,
Elizabeth Hanna Endsley,

and to my son,
Jon Brian Endsley

Contents

Preface

THERE HAVE BEEN MANY BOOKS written about the post–World War II Dodgers; their glory days at Ebbets Field in the 1950s; their ascendancy at Chavez Ravine coinciding with the apotheosis of Sandy Koufax in the 1960s; and their accomplishments under Tommy Lasorda in the 1970s and 1980s—capped by Kirk Gibson's epic home run in the 1988 World Series. But surprisingly, the story of the 1959 Los Angeles Dodgers has been neglected. Their near-complete collapse and resurrection in their first two seasons on the West Coast — narrowly escaping the cellar in 1958 before coming out of nowhere to win the 1959 World Series— needs to be re-evaluated.

My interest in the topic comes from personal experience. That season was seared into my memory as a 10-year-old growing up in Southern California. Placed into perspective today, 1959 was a pivotal year in baseball history. In many ways, it marked the end of the post–World War II era and the beginning of a post–modern era.

The book is organized into two parts. Part I describes the Dodgers' descent from the top of the baseball world — Brooklyn, 1955 — to the depths of a seventh-place finish in 1958, their first year in Los Angeles. Part II describes their ascent from a forgotten franchise to 1959 world champions.

The story of the 1959 Dodgers is also one of the great underdog stories. Thus I have attempted to emphasize the rag-tag nature of the team made up of long shots, such as Maury Wills and Larry Sherry struggling for years in the minor leagues before being saved from ignominy by General Manager Buzzie Bavasi, and over-the-hill Boys of Summer from Brooklyn, such as Roger Craig, Gil Hodges, Duke Snider, and Carl Furillo, who dug deep to give us one last triumph. After surviving an historic three-team pennant race, the Dodgers met a team of fellow long shots, the Chicago White Sox, in a truly underdog World Series. The Go-Go Sox were making their first Fall

Classic appearance since the 1919 Black Sox scandal. And this was only possible due to one of the two Yankee "off years" in the Casey Stengel era.

The project presented some research challenges. The 1959 season was 30 years before baseball fans had the benefit of ESPN's instant highlights. But 1959 Dodger fans were blessed with Vin Scully's vivid radio descriptions, which had to hold us until the *Los Angeles Times* arrived early the next morning on the front lawn with box scores, statistics, and in-depth analysis. Sportswriter Frank Finch's contemporaneous coverage, available today through the *Los Angeles Times*' archives, was a key research source. I would like to take this opportunity to acknowledge the invaluable insights provided by Roger Craig, who was kind enough to grant me personal interviews to re-live his greatest season.

Introduction

They called the Mets in 1969 the Miracle Mets, but the Dodgers in 1959 were really the first miracle team

—Vin Scully, 2008

Frustrated in his efforts to replace tiny Ebbets Field with a modern downtown ball park, Brooklyn Dodgers' owner Walter O'Malley moved his team to Los Angeles after the 1957 season. But that was not the only thing New York baseball fans had to grieve over. Baseball could not feasibly support a lone outpost on the West Coast due to the travel burden imposed on the other clubs. O'Malley therefore had conspired with Giants' owner Horace Stoneham to move with him. Two months before the Dodgers' October 8, 1957 announcement, Stoneham, unhappy with the dwindling crowds at the cavernous Polo Grounds, announced that the Giants would move to San Francisco for the 1958 season. 1958 would be the first year since 1882 that New York would be without a National League team.

The year 1958, the Dodgers' first on the West Coast, was a disaster. Tragedy struck early. Catcher Roy Campanella, their rock behind the plate, was left paralyzed from an automobile accident in January. Arriving in Los Angeles without a suitable place to play, they gerry-rigged the Memorial Coliseum, a football-track stadium, into what Casey Stengel would call a "freak ballpark" of grotesque dimensions. Before the season began, the Dodgers made a fateful decision: instead of rebuilding the team with youth, they would go with their aging Boys of Summer to preserve the team's "continuity and tradition." The result was a 7th place finish, their worst since 1944. To make matters worse, Pee Wee Reese, their captain and shortstop since 1940, announced his retirement in the off-season.

The Dodgers faced the 1959 season with little hope for success. The Boys of Summer were either gone or fading fast. Pee Wee Reese and Jackie Robinson had already called it quits. Campy was in a wheel chair. Don Newcombe had been traded the year before. Duke Snider still hadn't recovered from his 1957 knee surgery. Gil Hodges was 35, and it was obvious that Carl Furillo and Carl Erskine were playing on borrowed time. At the age of 22, Sandy Koufax was still an erratic young left-hander. None of the pre-season polls gave the Dodgers a chance to contend for the pennant. The consensus was that the Braves, with a veritable all-star team led by Hank Aaron, Eddie Mathews, Warren Spahn, and Lew Burdette, would win their third consecutive pennant and continue to build a dynasty in Milwaukee.

Due to a chance encounter with Vin Scully over the radio waves in September 1958, the author was fully invested in the Dodgers' fortunes as we approached Opening Day 1959, prepared to suffer with them another painful transition year. But the 1959 Los Angeles Dodgers would shock the baseball world by coming out of nowhere to unseat mighty Milwaukee before going on to win the World Series. In contrast to the powerhouse Brooklyn team that won the Dodgers' first World Championship in 1955, the 1959 team_a rag-tag group of underdogs and has-beens_did in 2 years in Los Angeles what it had taken the Dodgers 75 years to do in Brooklyn.

Prologue: Los Angeles, Tuesday, September 29, 1959, 5:05 P.M.

At this time on a weekday afternoon in L.A., the freeways are jammed with commuters in a cutthroat, lane-hopping frenzy to escape the city for the suburbs— what sociologists will call "white flight." But today there is an unusual feeling of community among these rugged post-war individuals. Perhaps it is because they are all listening to the same voice on their car radios. Vin Scully, voice of the Los Angeles Dodgers, is announcing a baseball game from the Los Angeles Memorial Coliseum.

At the Coliseum on South Figueroa Street, a concrete bowl built for the 1932 Olympics and gerry-rigged for baseball, the Dodgers and Milwaukee Braves are locked in a struggle for Game 2 of their three-game playoff series for the National League pennant. The game has just eclipsed the four-hour mark. It is the bottom of the twelfth inning, there are two outs, the score is tied, 5–5, and the Dodgers' 37-year-old Carl Furillo is in the batter's box. As Milwaukee Braves relief pitcher Bob Rush stares in to catcher Del Crandall for the sign, Furillo's old Brooklyn Dodger teammate, 35-year-old Gil Hodges, cautiously leads off second base. A little man called "Piggy," Joe Pignatano, leads off first base.

Carl Furillo started with the Dodgers in Brooklyn on April 16, 1946, at the age of 24, after a 38-month stint in the military. The 1953 National League batting champion, who played in six World Series against the Yankees, is no longer the Dodgers' regular right fielder with the rifle arm. Making only his 93rd at-bat of the season, he knows his days as a Dodger are numbered. While he led the team with a .290 batting average last year, it was in limited duty. His main job was tutoring 20-year-old Ron Fairly, the former USC Trojan and darling of the local media. Today, Carl, called "Skoonj," entered the game as a pinch-hitter in the bottom of the ninth inning. It was at that moment the author, at the age of ten, had run home from school and turned on the television to see who won the game — only to be shocked by the sight of two things: first, the game was still on; and second, Carl Furillo hit a dramatic sacrifice fly to tie the game at 5–5 and send it into extra innings. Now, at the plate for the third time, although he is behind Rush in the count, one ball and two strikes, Furillo has always been a tough man to strike out, a man who could be counted on to put the bat on the ball in the clutch.

Out at second base, Gil Hodges is also nearing the end of his career. He is still the regular first baseman, leading the team with 25 home runs, but due to injuries, he has been able to play in just 124 games. Hodges broke into the major leagues on October 3, 1943, with the Brooklyn Dodgers at the age of 19. After playing only one game, he was drafted into the U.S. Marines, where he spent the next 29 months fighting the Japanese on Tinian (Mariana Island) and Okinawa, and where he started smoking. He was awarded a Battle Star for his heroism on April 1, 1945 — D-Day on Okinawa.[1] Since returning to baseball after the war, Hodges has been the Dodgers' symbol of quiet strength: a power hitter who hit four home runs in one game in 1950, with hands so big Pee Wee Reese once said, "Gil wears a glove at first because it's fashionable."[2] At this point in his career, Hodges has no speed. But, as the potential winning run less than 180 feet from home plate, the Dodgers must depend on his legs. Fortunately, with two outs he will be off with the crack of the bat.

It has been two years and five days since Carl Furillo and Gil Hodges last played a game together at Ebbets Field in their blue caps with the familiar "B." Last year, their first year in Los Angeles, the Dodgers finished in seventh place, their worst season since 1944. This season they had turned it around, shocking all the experts in the process. Before the season ended in a tie on the last day, the heavily favored Braves, with superstars Hank Aaron, Eddie Mathews, Warren Spahn, and Lew Burdette, were on their way to establishing the next baseball dynasty with their third straight trip to the World Series.

Twenty-seven hours earlier, and 1,700 miles away in Milwaukee, the Dodgers won the first game of the playoff series in a 3–2 cliffhanger to put the Braves in a sudden-death situation today. Now the Dodgers are one hit away from the World Series, one hit away from climbing from seventh place to first in one year. But before we see the climax of this L.A. drama starring the over-the-hill actor team of Hodges and Furillo and a man called "Piggy," we must go back in time — almost four years to the day, to Brooklyn, to relive the view from the top of the world — to understand the depths to which they had descended by the end of their first season in Los Angeles.

Part I

Descent: From Brooklyn Legends to L.A. Has-Beens

Chapter 1

1955: The View from the Top of the World

On September 30, 1955, less than two hours after he was cited for speeding, 24-year-old teen idol James Dean died instantly when he crashed his Porsche 550 Spyder roadster — driving 86 MPH without a seat belt — on U.S. Highway 466 near Paso Robles. He was heading to Salinas, the site of his first film, *East of Eden*, to participate as a driver in a sports car race. His only other films, *Rebel Without a Cause* and *Giant*, would be released posthumously to critical acclaim.[1] Outside a Hollywood restaurant seven days before the accident, when Dean proudly showed fellow actor Alec Guiness his new Porsche which Dean named "Little Bastard" Guiness had warned him, "If you get in that car, you will be found dead in it by this time next week."

* * *

This Is *Next Year*

That same day at Ebbets Field in Brooklyn, with the Dodgers down two games to none to the Yankees in the 1955 World Series after winning the pennant by 13½ games over Milwaukee, Dodger fans were steadying themselves for the inevitable: yet another October collapse. After eight unsuccessful World Series appearances—five against the Yankees since 1941— stoic Dodger fans had adopted the mantra, "Wait till next year!" as a coping mechanism. But today, on his 23rd birthday, left-hander Johnny Podres pulled Brooklyn back from the abyss with a complete-game, seven-hit 8–3 victory. Podres survived a two-run home run by Mickey Mantle over the center-field fence in the second inning before he settled down to subdue the Yankees the rest of the way with a devastating change-up.

Game 4, played October 1 on a bleak gray day at Ebbets Field, was a battle of right-handers: Carl Erskine for the Dodgers and Don Larsen for the Yankees. After New York jumped out to a 3–1 lead, Brooklyn came roaring back to score three in the fourth on home runs by Campanella and Hodges, and three more in the fifth on a tape-measure three-run home run by Duke Snider that cleared the right-field scoreboard and dented the roof of a car in a parking lot on the other side of Bedford Avenue.[2] Snider's blow gave the Dodgers an insurmountable 7–3 lead. Brooklyn reliever Clem Labine got credit for the 8–5 win as he held the Yankees hitless over the final three innings, enabling the Dodgers to tie the Series at two games apiece.

In a controversial move, Walter Alston named 24-year-old rookie right-hander Roger Craig as his starting pitcher for Game 5 on October 2. The *Los Angeles Times* called it "perhaps the longest-shot gamble in Series history."[3] Craig had been in the major leagues for less than three months, but he rose to the occasion in front of 36,796 — the largest crowd in the history of Ebbets Field — allowing four hits and two earned runs over six innings. He left the game in the seventh inning with a 4–2 lead, thanks to two home runs by the incendiary Duke Snider (his third and fourth of the Series) and one by rookie Sandy Amoros, both off Yankees' starter Bob Grim. For the second straight day, Clem Labine came in from the bullpen to pitch the final three innings. This time he gave up only two hits to the save the 5–3 win for Craig and put the Dodgers up three games to two in the Series.

The two teams moved back to Yankee Stadium for Game 6, where 22 hours and 49 minutes after the Dodgers took the Series lead, the Yankees retied it at three games apiece with a 5–1 victory on the strength of Whitey Ford's four-hit complete game. After former Purdue football player Bill "Moose" Skowron ignited a five-run outburst by the Yankees in the first inning with a three-run homer off the Dodgers' Karl Spooner, a 24-year-old sophomore left-hander, the game was effectively over. The Dodgers could manage only one run off Ford, an RBI single by Carl Furillo in the fourth.[4] But after that, the little left-hander from Glen Cove, Long Island, appeared to get stronger, retiring the last six batters in order — the last three on only eight pitches.[5] Across town in Brooklyn, Dodger fans struggled to come to grips with reality: they missed their chance to put the Yankees away in six.

Through the first six games, the 1955 World Series was either tied — or had its lead change —four times. On October 4, tied at three games apiece, it was reduced to a final Game 7 clash between two left-handers. The Dodgers again called on young Johnny Podres. The Yankees, whose three wins were attributable to left-handers— Whitey Ford (two) and Tommy Byrne — again went with Byrne, their 36-year-old veteran. In front of 62,465 mostly hostile Yankee fans, Podres took a 2–0 lead to the bottom of the sixth inning. Manager Walter Alston winced from the Dodger dugout as Billy Martin walked on four straight pitches and Gil McDougald laid down a perfect bunt single. With two on and nobody out, Alston was confronted with an agonizing decision: whether or not to allow his young starter to pitch to Yogi Berra, soon to be named American League Most Valuable Player for the third time and one of the game's great clutch hitters. Berra was already 10-for-22 (.455) in the Series, including a double in the fourth inning off Podres. Not only did Alston stick with Podres, he brought in left-fielder Junior Gilliam to play second base, and replaced him with Sandy Amoros, a left-handed-throwing reserve outfielder from Cuba. Expecting Berra to pull the ball to right field, Amoros was positioned well into left-center, about 150 feet from the left-field foul line. When Berra lifted a high fly ball into the left-field corner, it looked like a sure game-tying double and Podres' ticket to the showers. But with the crack of the bat, the fleet Amoros started a desperate dash for the corner as the baseball continued to slice away from him. With his glove fortuitously positioned on his right hand, he somehow arrived in time to snag the ball a split second before it landed inside the foul line. The right-handed Gilliam would have had to reach across his body to take a back-hand stab at the ball. After narrowly avoiding a collision with the concrete left-field wall, Amoros whirled and threw a perfect strike to cut-off man Pee Wee Reese, who relayed the ball to first baseman Gil Hodges to double up Gil McDougald by inches. The play was a rally-killer for the Yankees. Instead of the game being tied, the go-ahead run at second base with nobody out, and a new Dodger pitcher facing the dangerous Hank Bauer, Podres survived the sixth with his shutout in tact. In the stands, his dad, Joseph Podres, a miner with the day off from the Republic Steel Company, was trying to calm himself when his son gave him a wave of reassurance.

Buoyed by his sixth-inning gift from Sandy Amoros, Podres moved to the bottom of the ninth, still ahead, 2–0. While he quickly induced Bill Skowron to bounce back to the mound and Bob Cerv to pop out to Amoros in left, rookie Elston Howard was trouble. Five months before, the heir apparent to Yogi Berra behind the plate, Howard, an African American, had taken an outfield position to integrate the team. Today, after working the count to two balls and two strikes, he fouled off pitch after pitch after pitch until Podres finally got him to hit a ground ball to shortstop. When Gil Hodges, who drove in both Dodger runs, caught the ball from Pee Wee Reese for the final out, a human hurricane struck the field. At the mound, iron-masked Roy Campanella lifted Podres into the air like a rag doll before they were both submerged under a wave of gray Dodger uniforms.[6]

Two years before, Sir Edmund Hillary from New Zealand reached the summit of Mount Everest, the highest point on earth — 29,035 feet above sea level. But for one day, on October 4, 1955, John Joseph Podres, a 23-year-old Lithuanian ball player from the tiny hamlet of Witherbee, New York, redefined the top of the world as B-R-O-O-K-L-Y-N. Minutes later, upon reflection in the dressing room, he found three words to describe the experience: "Wow! Wow! Wow!"[7] His mother, watching him on her black-and-white television set back home in Witherbee, was so overcome by emotion when the game ended that she could not utter a *single* word.[8]

While groups of dazed Yankee fans milled around the stadium to contemplate what they had just witnessed, across town in the borough of Brooklyn long-suffering Dodger fans released 80 years of frustration. The phone lines, overloaded with calls relating to bet collections, victory dinner reservations, or just plain hysteria, caused the system to crash. Telephone company officials called it the greatest flood since August 15, 1945 (VJ-Day).[9] The delirium quickly spread to the streets, turned white by showers of confetti. Motorcades sounded choruses of screaming horns as they charged up and down Eighty-sixth Street, Fourth and Flatbush avenues, and Ocean Parkway. The pedestrians were not to be outdone. Some clanged cowbells, blew horns, and ignited firecrackers, while others mounted their doorsteps to bang cutlery against pots and pans. Others stuffed pillow cases to form human effigies, added pinstripes and crude "Yankees!" signs, and strung them from lampposts.

In the business district, most offices closed early, since their employees were rendered useless after 3:34 P.M., the official time of the final out and outbreak of mass madness. They simply left their desks and moved into the streets to begin their new job of tying up traffic. Strangers danced with strangers. A UPI reporter struggled to a phone booth to issue a one-line report stating, "I can only say, all hell is breaking loose!"[10]

In an official statement, Borough President John Cashmore promised to order a survey for a new Dodger stadium at Atlantic and Flatbush avenues. In a warning to the rival cities rumored to be interested in his beloved Dodgers, he announced, "They must never leave Brooklyn!" Outside the Dodgers Café on DeKalb Avenue, the crowds spilled out onto the street holding homemade signs, such as "Bums? Champs!" and "Yeah Dodgers!" Approaching total numbness, Joseph Saden, owner of Joe's Delicatessen on Utica Avenue, was so overcome with joy that he set up a sidewalk stand and gave away free hot dogs to passing revelers.[11]

The pandemonium spread. In Miami Beach, Florida, police officers were called to assist a hysterical woman in the middle of a busy intersection. A victim of foul play? No, just another Brooklyn Dodger fan screaming for joy.[12] The next morning, the October 5, 1955, edition of the *New York Daily News* proclaimed:

"This IS Next Year!"[13]

Homecoming Parade Detour—From Main Street to the Induction Center

Four days after he pitched the Brooklyn Dodgers to their first world championship, Johnny Podres returned to a hero's welcome in the tiny Adirondack village of Witherbee. A foot and automotive cavalcade arrived at noon in front of his 75-year-old frame house to mount Podres—transformed from his Brooklyn Dodgers uniform into a coat and tie—atop the back seat of a convertible, a la General Douglas MacArthur. The lead car, holding the 23-year-old blond-haired god and his parents, weeping in gratitude as 3,000 friends and neighbors covered them with confetti, wended its way along Main Street, followed by the second car carrying his sister, Mary, 17, and his three brothers, Walter, 15, Tom, 8, and Jim, 5. The parade ended at the Mineville High School athletic field, where Podres first drew the attention of Brooklyn scouts as a prep phenom. From a speaker's platform, the visibly moved young man spoke in a trembling voice. "I can't find the words to thank you all for the honor you've done me and my family," he said. "Ballplayers make lousy speeches, and I'm no exception. All I can say is thank you for the proudest day of my life."[14] His day was capped off by a telegram of congratulations from New York Governor Averill Harriman.

* * *

On December 1, 1955, Rosa Parks, a 42-year-old black woman rushing home from her job as a seamstress in a Montgomery, Alabama, department store, touched off the civil rights movement with an act of civil disobedience after she boarded the Cleveland Avenue bus. In those days, Montgomery buses were segregated; the first four rows were for whites only. The rear was for blacks, who made up more than 75 percent of the bus system's riders. Blacks could sit in the middle rows only until those seats were *needed* by whites. Then the blacks had to move to seats in the rear, stand, or if there was no room, leave the bus. If whites were already sitting in the front, blacks could board to pay the fare, but they then had to endure the humiliation of disembarking and re-entering through the rear door.

A municipal ordinance gave bus drivers police powers to enforce racial segregation.[15] James Blake, the driver of the Cleveland Avenue bus, demanded that four blacks give up their seats in the middle section so a lone white man could sit. Three of them complied, but Rosa Parks defied him. Recalling the incident in 1987, Mrs. Parks said, "When he saw me still sitting, he asked if I was going to stand up and I said, 'No, I'm not.' And he said, 'Well, if you don't stand up, I'm going to have to call the police and have you arrested.' I said, 'You may do that.'"[16]

Mrs. Parks was arrested, convicted of violating the municipal segregation ordinance and fined $10, plus $4 in court fees. In response, blacks in Montgomery resolved to boycott the city buses. For that purpose they organized a Montgomery Improvement Association (MIA), and drafted an unknown newcomer to Montgomery, 26-year-old Baptist minister Martin Luther King, Jr., as its president. The eloquent and courageous King inspired Montgomery's black community to boycott the buses for more than a year, walking and carpooling rather than riding the buses, enduring police harassment, verbal abuse, and economic retaliation.[17] At the same time, MIA mounted a legal challenge to the state and local Jim Crow laws that had made them second-class citizens on the public bus system. The case, *Browder v. Gayle*, worked its way through the federal court system before it was ultimately decided in the MIA's favor by the U.S. Supreme Court on November 13, 1956.

Jersey City

On the same day Rosa Parks was arrested, Walter O'Malley announced his plans to play seven regular season "home" games in Roosevelt Stadium in Jersey City, New Jersey. As part of his strategy to pressure Brooklyn for a new stadium, he announced, "I have previously stated that it is our present intention to occupy Ebbets Field for only two more years—that is 1956 and 1957." Since the agreement was for three years, it implied that the Dodgers might play the entire 1958 season in New Jersey if the new park was not ready.

While Roosevelt Stadium's seating capacity was only 25,000, compared to 32,111 for Ebbets Field, it had capacity to park up to 7,000 cars, compared to only 500 in Brooklyn.[18]

The Dodgers Lose Podres to the U.S. Navy

The Witherbee fairy tale took a sudden unexpected turn three days after Christmas 1955 when Johnny Podres' draft board reclassified him from 4-F (unfit for duty due to a back problems that periodically affected his pitching) to 1-A (subject to immediate call).[19] Podres was in spring training at Vero Beach, Florida, on March 14, 1956, when he was given five days to report to New York City for induction. On March 19, he was sworn in as a member of the U.S. Navy. He would miss the entire 1956 season.[20]

Chapter 2

1956: Bridesmaids Revisited

Whereas the 1955 Dodgers won the pennant going away after a 22–2 start, as the defending world champions, the 1956 Dodgers had to struggle all year.

A Rough Start

May in Fifth Place

Despite a 7–4 April and Carl Erskine's no-hitter over the Giants at Ebbets Field on May 12, 1956, the Dodgers ended May in fifth place. As the Milwaukee Braves sat atop the National League standings, they appeared ready to replace the Dodgers as the preeminent senior circuit power.

Zim's Rendezvous with a Beanball

In a frightening incident at Ebbets Field on June 23, the Dodgers lost feisty backup shortstop Don Zimmer for the remainder of season. Zimmer suffered a fractured left cheekbone when he was struck in the face by a fastball thrown by Cincinnati Redleg pitcher Hal Jeffcoat. Surgeons repaired his face, but it was feared that a sudden jar could cause him to suffer a detached retina of his left eye. Consequently, he was ordered to wear pin-hole glasses and avoid all physical activity for a minimum of three months. The Dodgers brought up Charlie Neal to take his place as the backup to veteran Pee Wee Reese. Despite the instability at the shortstop position, with an 18–12 June, the Dodgers moved into second place, one game behind Milwaukee as they approached the all-star break.

The Duke Dukes It Out with a Fan

By the end of July, Brooklyn was back in third place, two games behind the second-place Redlegs and four games behind the red-hot first-place Braves. Despite being overtaken by Cincinnati, the Dodgers did not succumb without a fight, as exemplified by Duke Snider on July 17 at Crosley Field. Walking off the field after a 4–3 loss, Snider and a fan named Ralph Baumel exchanged punches after Baumel called him "gutless." The Duke wound up with a bloody lip and Baumel lost two of his false teeth.[1]

Turning Towards Home

Newcombe Wins His 20th Game in August

Led by Don Newcombe, the Dodgers played .667 baseball during August to finish the month in second place, 2½ games behind Milwaukee. In Cincinnati on August 23 — only the 117th game of Brooklyn's 154-game schedule — Newcombe survived home runs by Wally Post, Frank Robinson, and Ed Bailey to record his twentieth win (against only six losses) with a complete-game 6–5 victory over the Redlegs. Pitching every fourth day, Newcombe would still have nine more starts.

On Opening Day 1959, Don Zimmer assumed the shortstop position for the Dodgers after the retirement of Pee Wee Reese the previous winter. (George Brace photograph)

A Hip-Shaking Elvis in a See-Saw September

On Sunday evening, September 9, 1956, 21-year-old Elvis Presley appeared on *The Ed Sullivan Show*. Two years before, he was driving a truck through Tennessee. But tonight, 82.6 percent of the U.S. television audience watched him drive a live audience — composed mainly of hysterical, shrieking teenaged girls— into a frenzy with his fre-

Dodger first baseman Gil Hodges was near the end of his career at age 35 in 1959. He led the team with 25 home runs. (George Brace photograph)

netic sexually provocative hip-shaking performance.[2] For many Americans, it was their first exposure to a disturbing new form of music, known as rock-and-roll. With five number-one singles on the 1956 *Billboard* charts, Elvis (the Pelvis) had already contaminated AM radio. Despite efforts by CBS censors to prohibit the television cameras from shooting Presley below the waist, from the audio, which picked up the wild screams of the young girls in the studio audience reacting to his gyrations, it was clear that the corruption of all the public airwaves was now complete.

* * *

On September 11, 1956, two days after Elvis Presley ignited a cultural revolution, the Brooklyn Dodgers found themselves in a flat-footed tie with the upstart Milwaukee Braves for first place in the National League. It was a seesaw struggle between Milwaukee and Brooklyn the rest of the way with the lead changing hands six times.

After spending 132 days out of first place compared to Milwaukee's 95 days in first, workhorse Don Newcombe clinched the pennant against the Pirates at Ebbets Field on the last day of the season with his 27th victory. The Dodgers won the 1956 pennant by just one game over the Milwaukee Braves and two games over the powerhouse Cincinnati Reds, who hit 221 home runs, including 38 by rookie Frank Robinson. In addition to winning the National League's Most Valuable Player award, Newcombe received the first-ever Cy Young Memorial Award as Major League Baseball's outstanding pitcher. In addition to his boxing exploits, Duke Snider had a career-best 43 home runs.

The End of the Season, and an Era

The 1956 World Series and the Beginning of the Dodger Decline

Casey Stengel's Yankees coasted to another American League pennant — this time by nine games over the Indians— thanks to a rare Triple Crown season by Mickey Mantle. With 52 home runs, 130 RBIs, and a .353 average, he was a near-unanimous choice for Most Valuable Player. The stage was set for another Dodgers-Yankees World Series, the sixth subway series in the last ten Fall Classics. Before the first pitch was thrown, the Yankees were 8–5 favorites to defeat the Dodgers.

On October 3, 1956, a month before the presidential election, President Eisenhower threw out the first baseball before 34,479 at Ebbets Field to open the 1956 World Series. Eight days after he pitched a no-hitter against the Philadelphia Phillies on the same mound, 39-year-old Dodger starter Salvatore Anthony "The Barber" Maglie — who the year before had been one of the most hated men in Flatbush as a member of the New York Giants— survived a first inning two-run home run by Mickey Mantle to pitch Brooklyn to a 6–3 win. The Dodgers got to Yankee starter Whitey Ford with two home runs and a double for five runs in the first three innings.[3] As Brooklyn's bars and grills toasted the name Maglie long into the evening, a storm descended upon the city to wash out the next day's proceedings.

Two days later, Eisenhower's Democratic challenger, former Illinois Governor Adlai Stevenson, appeared as one of 36,217 baseball fans at Ebbets

Field for Game 2. The Dodgers sent Don Newcombe, their 27-game winner, against the Yankees' Don Larsen. But big Newk was roughed up for six earned runs in 1⅔ innings, including a grand slam home run by Yogi Berra that put the Yankees up 6–0 and finished him for the day. Larsen also lasted only 1⅔ innings. After the Yankees blew their 6–0 lead in the bottom of the second, Brooklyn went on to win a 3½-hour, 13–8 slugfest to take a two games to none lead.[4] The Dodgers were now 13–5 favorites with the bookmakers to repeat as world champions.[5]

On October 6, the Series moved to Yankee Stadium for Game 3. Brooklyn's Roger Craig locked horns with New York's Whitey Ford before an enormous crowd of 73,977. In the sixth inning, 40-year-old Enos "Country" Slaughter connected on a three-and-one Craig fastball for a three-run home run to give the Yankees a 5–3 win. Ford pitched a complete game for the Yankees to cut Brooklyn's lead to two games to one.[6] The next day, the Yankees tied the Series two games apiece with a 6–2 win in front of 69,705 at Yankee Stadium on a complete-game six-hitter by Yankee right-hander Tom Sturdivant and home runs by Mickey Mantle and Hank Bauer.[7]

Game 5, on October 8, 1956 at Yankee Stadium, was destined to be a special day in baseball history. The Dodgers' Sal Maglie and the Yankees' Don Larsen each made his second Series start. Mickey Mantle put the Yankees ahead 1–0 with a solo home run in the fourth. He then robbed Gil Hodges of extra bases in the fifth with a back-handed catch while sprinting full-bore into deep left-center field. Through the fifth, sixth, and seventh innings, Larsen, pitching from his new no-windup delivery, still hadn't given up a hit. Like a contagious leper, he sat in solitude on the Yankee bench, as his teammates, frozen by superstition, ignored him. In the eighth, Hodges hit another threatening line drive, this one to the left of third base. Yankee third baseman Andy Carey lunged for the ball and caught it inches off the ground.

The game went to the ninth inning with the Yankees leading, 2–0, and the Dodgers having yet to reach first base. It was dead silence in cavernous Yankee Stadium as Carl Furillo led off for the Dodgers. When he flied out to Hank Bauer in right field, 64,519 fans exploded. When Roy Campanella grounded out to Billy Martin for the second out, a second roar erupted. Now only Dale Mitchell, pinch-hitting for Sal Maglie, stood between Don Larsen and history. After Mitchell ran the count to one ball and two strikes, and he fouled off the fourth pitch, Larsen threw him a fastball aimed at the outside corner. Mitchell thought it was a ball and let it go by. But when plate umpire Babe Pinelli raised his right arm for the third strike, the stadium was in an uproar. Mitchell whirled around to protest Pinelli's call, but it was an exercise in futility. In what would become one of the most memorable scenes in baseball history, 5' 8" Yogi Berra leaped into 6' 4" Don Larsen's arms. Yankees from all directions—infield, outfield, dugout, and bullpen—converged on the mound to pummel Larsen as the umpires fled the field. There had never been a no-hitter in World Series history. But this was a *perfect game*, the rarest of all hitless games, twenty-seven up, twenty-seven down, no one reaching first base. And the Yankees were now up three games to two.[8]

On October 9, the Series returned to Ebbets Field for Game 6. The Dodgers tied it three games apiece as Brooklyn's bullpen ace Clem Labine — in a rare start — shut out the Yankees, 1–0, on seven hits over 10 innings. In one of his last great moments, Jackie Robinson drove in the only run of the game with a single in the bottom of the tenth.[9]

Instead of the highly anticipated classic showdown the next day at Ebbets Field, Game 7 was anticlimactic. The Yankees blanked the Dodgers, 9–0, behind 23-year-old Johnny Kucks' three-hit shutout. Yogi Berra continued his ownership of Dodger starter Don Newcombe with two two-run homers in the first three innings. Elston Howard's solo homer off Newcombe with none out in the top of the fourth ended the 6' 6" right-hander's World Series.[10] The Dodgers suffered their final indignity in the seventh inning when Moose Skowron rocked Roger Craig for another Yankee grand slam homer to make the score 9–0.

Although Berra had three home runs, 10 runs batted in, and a .360 batting average over the seven games, he finished second to teammate Don Larsen as the Series' Most Valuable Player. In a post-season critique of Newcombe's shocking performance — a 19.80 ERA due to being knocked out early in two starts— teammate Sal Maglie attributed his failure to overthrowing. "He was just rearing back and throwing," Maglie said. "When you do that, you can't put the ball where you want it."[11]

After the Dodgers finally broke New York's domination over Brooklyn the prior year, the teams reverted to their familiar pattern. Not only had the Dodgers now lost six of seven World Series with the Yankees, their 1956 collapse — after blowing a two games-to-none lead — would send them into a downward spiral for the next two seasons.

The Dodgers Sell Ebbets Field

On October 30, 1956, 19 days after their World Series defeat, the Brooklyn Dodgers sold Ebbets Field to Marvin Kratter, a real estate developer with plans to eventually build a middle-income residential and commercial community on the land. The Dodgers agreed to lease back the ballpark for three years, through the 1959 season, while the Brooklyn Sports Authority secured a site for a new Dodger stadium.[12]

* * *

A week later, on November 6, 1956, President Dwight D. Eisenhower won reelection by a landslide over Adlai Stevenson. In the Electoral College, Eisenhower won 41 states to only seven for Stevenson and his running mate, Tennessee Senator Estes Kefauver, who had narrowly edged out 39-year-old Senator John F. Kennedy of Massachusetts for the second spot on the ticket. In the popular vote, Ike amassed 35.6 million votes (57.4 percent) compared to Stevenson's 26.0 million (42.0 percent). The Eisenhower landslide was the largest since Franklin D. Roosevelt routed Republican Alfred M. "Alf" Landon in 1936. Richard M. Nixon, who survived a "Dump Nixon" movement at the Republican national convention at San Francisco in August, was swept into a second term as vice president.[13]

The day after the election, the Eisenhower administration claimed a major foreign policy achievement: a United Nations cease-fire in the brief Suez Canal War between Egypt and a coalition comprised of Israel, France, and Great Britain. The crisis erupted back on July 26 when Egyptian President Gamal Abdel Nasser nationalized the canal, which had been controlled by the British and the French since its opening in 1869. The hostilities began on October 29 when Israel — provoked by incessant guerrilla raids from the Gaza Strip — attacked Egypt in the Sinai Peninsula. Pursuant to the coalition plan, the next day the British and French delivered an ultimatum to both sides to stop the fighting and to clear the Egyptian forces from the Canal Zone. When Egypt refused to comply, the British and French dropped paratroopers into the Canal Zone on November 5–6. But the coalition plan did not anticipate the strong opposition of the United States, which arranged for the November 7 U.N. cease-fire and demanded a complete Anglo-French withdrawal.

While the Suez War was a success for the Eisenhower administration, it was a fiasco for the British and the French. After the U.N. General Assembly voted 65–1 for the cease-fire, they had no alternative but to back down and leave. Nasser not only remained in power, but managed to enhance his prestige in the world. The Israelis gained two concessions that would help them in the 1967 6-Day War: the demilitarization of the Sinai with the deployment of U.N. troops along the Egyptian-Israeli border; and a U.S. commitment to keep the Straits of Tiran open to Israeli shipping.[14]

Changes on the South Side of Chicago

Developments on the South Side of Chicago would affect the Dodgers three years later. On December 10, 1956, Grace Comiskey, widow of White Sox owner J. Louis Comiskey, died and left the controlling interest in the club to her daughter, Dorothy Rigney. This came six weeks after Al Lopez was lured away from the Cleveland Indians to replace Marty Marion as White Sox manager for 1957. This would begin a three-year period of success on the

South Side characterized by two consecutive second-place finishes followed by a trip to the World Series.

The Dodgers and the Unthinkable

On December 13, 1956, the Brooklyn Dodgers did the unthinkable. They traded 38-year-old Jackie Robinson to, of all teams, the New York Giants for journeyman left-handed pitcher Dick Littlefield plus $30,000 cash. Feeling stunned and betrayed, Robinson told Giants owner Horace Stoneham that he wanted a few days to think it over before accepting. Stoneham graciously agreed, promising to cancel the trade if Robinson decided to retire. Three weeks later, Jackie Robinson retired after 10 years and a .311 lifetime batting average with the Brooklyn Dodgers. True to his word, Stoneham cancelled the trade. Brooklyn Dodger fans breathed easier. Their beloved Jackie Robinson would never wear a Giants uniform.[15]

Robinson explained his decision to Tim Cohane, sports editor of *Look Magazine*. "After you've reached your peak, there's no sentiment in baseball," Robinson said. "You start slipping and pretty soon they're moving you around like a used car. You have no control over what happens to you. I don't want that."[16] Robinson took a position with Chock Full O' Nuts Foods as vice president and director of personnel in New York City.

* * *

On December 20, 1956, the U.S. Supreme Court's order for integrated buses arrived in Montgomery, Alabama. The order was the result of the Warren Court's decision in *Browder v. Gayle* in which segregation in Alabama's intrastate buses was ruled unconstitutional. Martin Luther King, Jr., and the Montgomery Improvement Association immediately voted to end the 381-day Montgomery bus boycott. In a statement after the vote, King said, "The year-old protest against city buses is officially called off, and the Negro citizens of Montgomery are urged to return to the busses tomorrow morning on a non-segregated basis." The Montgomery buses were integrated the next day.[17]

CHAPTER 3

1957: The Year the Brooklyn Dodgers Died

AFTER SURVIVING A MUMPS OUTBREAK at Vero Beach, the Dodgers closed out their 1957 spring exhibition season in New York on April 14 with a 2–1 win over the Yankees to finish with a 16–17 record.[1]

Opening Day — Ike as Fan in Chief

On Opening Day, April 15, 1957, cameras captured an ebullient President Eisenhower — nearly three months into his second term — as he threw out the first pitch at Griffith Stadium in Washington to open the last post–World War II baseball season marked by relative calm. By the time the World Series ended on October 10, changes were in motion that would transform the game.

In five months Eisenhower would be consumed by the problems at Little Rock. But today, he enjoyed his duties as "Fan in Chief," throwing out the first ball for the fifth consecutive year from his private box behind the Senators' dugout, continuing a tradition that William Howard Taft started on April 14, 1910.[2] Only this year, the president threw out two balls. The first, the ten millionth baseball manufactured by the A.G. Spalding Company since 1876, was snared by the leaping Don Ferrarese, an obscure 6' 3" Orioles pitcher. Ike quickly autographed it and sent it on its way to Cooperstown, then signed a substitute for Ferrarese to keep. The second ball tossed by the 66-year-old right-hander from 1600 Pennsylvania Avenue was caught by Senators outfielder Neil Chrisley, who was allowed to keep it after the president signed it. Plate umpire Ed Rummel then pulled a game ball out of his canvas sack of pre-rubbed specimens and presented it to Senators starter Bob Chakales. Lurking in the background, a smiling, clean-shaven Richard Nixon —

already calculating the days to the November 8, 1960, presidential election — maneuvered in behind Ike to exploit the photo op.

On the field that day were names that would reverberate for decades. Orioles left fielder Dick Williams would win three consecutive world championships as manager of the Oakland Athletics in the early 1970s. Senators center fielder and lead-off man Whitey Herzog would manage the St. Louis Cardinals to the World Series three times in the 1980s. Orioles rookie third baseman Brooks Robinson would win a record 16 Gold Gloves and enter the Baseball Hall of Fame in 1983. Senators third baseman Eddie Yost, who averaged 10 home runs a year, batted in the clean-up spot, while 20-year-old slugger Harmon Killebrew, who would finish his Hall-of-Fame career with 573 home runs, sat on the bench.

Though it was a chilly 53 degrees in Griffith Stadium — balmy to Eisenhower when compared to the Battle of the Bulge weather of December 1944 — the president turned up the collar of his top coat, swigged hot chocolate, munched on peanuts, and soldiered on for the entire game that went 11 innings and 3 hours and 17 minutes. Here was a five-star general who had liberated Europe, headed Columbia University, and won two presidential elections, but who couldn't prevent his Washington Senators from going down to a 7–6 defeat. After the final out, fans only had to look at the standings to see that one the oldest truths in baseball remained incontrovertible: Washington, first in war, first in peace, last in the American League.

The next night at Connie Mack Stadium in Philadelphia, the Dodgers opened the 1957 season as they sent their reigning MVP, Don Newcombe, to the mound against Robin Roberts. It was their first opener since 1946 without Jackie Robinson. While Brooklyn won, 7–6, in 12 innings, ominously, Newcombe — who won 27 games the year before — did not figure in the decision. Clem Labine was the winning pitcher in relief.

The defending NL champion Brooklyn Dodgers played like champions in April and May. With a .605 winning percentage on May 31, they were in second place, two games behind the Cincinnati Redlegs. Then June happened. Two consecutive losses sent Don Newcombe below .500, to 4–6. After a 14–17 June, they continued to sink, falling into fifth place by the July 8–10 All-Star break.

Walter Alston's men rallied, playing .600 baseball in July and August to climb back into second on August 28. They entered September seven games behind Milwaukee, but the month was not kind to the Dodgers. They lost their first four games. By the end of play on Sunday, September 22, they were back in third place, ten games behind the surging Braves. Fortunately, they had the next day off to think about how they would finish the last four games of the season, including their final game at Ebbets Field in 48 hours.

* * *

On September 24, 1957, President Dwight D. Eisenhower ordered federal troops to Little Rock, Arkansas, and federalized the Arkansas National Guard to enforce the racial integration of Central High School. For three weeks, segregationist Arkansas Governor Orval Faubus had defied a federal court order to commence integration. He sent the National Guard to surround the school, ostensibly to maintain law and order. When nine black students, escorted by white and black ministers, appeared on the second day of instruction, the Guard barred them from entering the school, while an angry mob of whites yelled, "Go Home Niggers!"[3]

From the White House, Eisenhower told the nation he acted because the violent defiance of the federal court order had done grave harm to "the prestige and influence, and indeed to the safety, of our nation." He appealed to the people of Arkansas and the South "to preserve and respect the law even when they disagree with it."[4]

The integration issue had been building to a climax since the U.S. Supreme Court in 1954 (*Brown v. Board of Education*) and 1955 (*Brown II*) pronounced that racial segregation in public schools was unconstitutional and must be ended "with all deliberate speed." Eisenhower had seen enough. He called on a unit he learned he could trust to enforce the law and maintain order: the 101st Airborne Division, whose troopers he had said good-bye to with tears in his eyes before they took off for Normandy on the evening of June 5, 1944[5], and federalized the Arkansas National Guard (removing it from Governor Faubus's control). The integration of Central High finally began the next morning when 1,100 federal paratroopers, with bayonets drawn to deter 1,500 angry whites, escorted the nine black students into the school building. It was the first time since Reconstruction that federal troops had been used to protect Southern Blacks.[6]

* * *

"Died — Sept. 24, 1957"

That was text of the hand-written cardboard epitaph placed in the rotunda at Ebbets Field that same evening in Brooklyn, New York, by two distraught Brooklyn Dodger fans, Rosemarie Keegan and Agnes Tolle, after a night game with the Pittsburgh Pirates.[7] Why had such a strange and somber mood descended over the field following a 2–0 victory — a brilliant five-hit shutout by Brooklyn's rookie left-hander Danny McDevitt? Dodger fans were coming to grips with the truth: the Dodgers had just played their last game at Ebbets Field, their home since 1912. Rosemarie and Agnes were part of only 6,702 fans that showed up to say goodbye because their beloved Dodgers could not see fit to give them an official farewell.[8]

Though the Dodgers had not officially announced their move to Los Angeles, everyone knew they were leaving. Gladys Gooding, who had played the pipe organ at Ebbets Field for the past 19 years, ignored the company line and poured out tunes with a farewell motif. At the end of the first inning, when the Dodgers were up, 1–0, she played "Am I Blue?" and "After You're Gone." After the Dodgers scored their final run at Ebbets Field, she played "Don't Ask Me Why I'm Leaving." As the game neared the end, she played "Que Sera Sera" and "Thanks For the Memories."

After the final out, Gladys began to play "May the Lord Bless and Keep You," but a Dodger official cut her off by turning on the recording always played after Brooklyn Dodger games, "Follow the Dodgers." But this was soon silenced, and Miss Gooding was allowed to end her program with "Auld Lang Syne."[9] Groups of heartbroken fans stood arm in arm, some openly weeping.[10] The sense of abandonment was palpable as small groups of fans slowly made their way out of the park that would close its gates forever later that night.

To baseball historian Peter Bjarkman, the Brooklyn Dodger fans seemed to be in a state of denial about the impending loss stating, "As the end came for Brooklyn Dodgers baseball in autumn 1957, most fans— despite all the signs of the past two years— still didn't realize that the demise of their beloved team was quite so near."[11]

"Something Snapped"

The Dodgers spent the last weekend of the season on the road in Philadelphia. On Sunday, September 29, 1957, they played their last game as the "Brooklyn" Dodgers. Their promising 27-year-old right-hander Roger Craig made the final start. Craig was sailing along into the bottom of the sixth inning with a 1–0 lead when, as he would recall fifty years later, "something snapped in my right shoulder."[12] Now pitching tentatively, he gave up a fatal two-run home run to Phillies first baseman Eddie Bouchee. Craig courageously continued for one more inning before the pain forced him out of the game. Twenty-one-year-old Sandy Koufax had to pitch the last inning for Brooklyn.

Not only did Craig lose the game, 2–1, but the shoulder injury he sustained that day in Philadelphia would plague him for the rest of his career. "I was afraid to tell anyone — even my wife," recalled Craig. "When I went to Vero Beach the next spring, it didn't come back. I had a torn rotator cuff, but they didn't know about such things in those days."[13]

Seth Morehead, the Phillies' young left-hander making his first major league start, ended the Dodgers' 1957 season with a complete-game four-hitter, allowing only one unearned run.

1957—A Sorry Season Comes to an End

And a sorry season it was for the Dodgers and their fans. They faded badly down the stretch with an 11–14 September and limped home in third place, 14 games over .500, and 11 games behind the Braves, who won their first National League pennant since 1948, their first since moving to Milwaukee. Although Snider hit 40 home runs and Furillo hit .306 (playing in only 119 games), for the first time in almost a decade, the Dodgers failed to lead the National League in a single offensive category.[14] The Duke tied Ralph Kiner's NL record of forty or more home runs for five consecutive years.[15]

Thirty-eight-year-old Pee Wee Reese, a fixture at shortstop since 1940 but with rapidly declining range, was moved to third base, where he hit only .224. He was forced to share the position with Don Zimmer, who hit .219. After Zimmer had commited an eye-popping 24 errors in only 100 games, Charlie Neal took over as the primary Dodger shortstop in his second year in the major leagues. The shortstop position would continue to be a problem for the Dodgers until mid-season 1959 in Los Angeles.

While the 1957 Dodger pitchers led the league in team strikeouts, shutouts, and fewest runs allowed, the starting pitching was of uneven quality. In only his second season, 21-year-old Don Drysdale emerged as the ace of the staff with a 17–9 record. Twenty-four-year-old Johnny Podres returned from the U.S. Navy to post a 12–9 record, leading the National League in two key categories: six shutouts and a 2.66 earned run average. But the success of the Dodgers' young right-left combination was more than offset by disappointments elsewhere. After his 27–7 Cy Young/MVP season, Don Newcombe, pummeled by 28 home runs, disintegrated to 11–12. Roger Craig, bothered by arm trouble, was a disappointing 6–9 in his third year. And at the age of 41, Sal Maglie could contribute only six wins. Plagued by control problems, 21-year-old Sandy Koufax was an unreliable non-factor at 5–4.

Rampage at Coogan's Bluff

The same day the Dodgers closed out the 1957 season on the road in Philadelphia, at Coogan's Bluff in New York City, the Giants played their last game at the Polo Grounds—a 9–1 thrashing at the hands of Bob Friend and the last-place Pittsburgh Pirates. Six years after witnessing Bobby Thomson's "Miracle at Coogan's Bluff," only 11,606 fans turned out to say goodbye, but they did not go quietly. At the end of play, thousands of fans stormed onto the field to pursue the Giants as they fled across center field to the safety of the clubhouse. Like a tornado, they ripped up and carried away anything on the field, whether movable or not, including the regular and warm-up home plates, the wooden base beneath the main plate, the pitcher's rubber, the bases, and the foam rubber sheathing covering the center-field fence. They smashed the bullpen sun-shelter, gouged out large patches of the outfield grass, carried off telephones, signs, and pried the bronze plaque off the Eddie Grant memorial monument in center field — though police later retrieved it from three youths. With the field stripped clean after an intense half-hour, the rampage was over. The fans, with conflicting feelings of anger, affection, and nostalgia, went home with their souvenirs. The Giants were fortunate to be in their clubhouse.[16]

After 75 years as the New York Giants, including a dismal sixth-place finish in 1957, the Giants were headed for San Francisco to become the second major league team on the West Coast in 1958. Back on August 19 when the board of directors of the National Exhibition Company, the corporation that operated the New York Giants, voted 8–1 to approve the move to San Francisco, Giants owner Horace Stoneham, when asked what forced the decision to move, told reporters, "Lack of attendance. We're sorry to disappoint the kids of New York, but we didn't see many of their parents out there at the Polo Grounds in recent years."[17] Ironically, the 1957 Giants finally abated a trend of declining attendance by outdrawing the 1956 team. But it was too late.[18]

The Announcement

On October 8, 1957, the Brooklyn Dodger fans heard the official announcement that the Dodgers were moving to Los Angeles for the 1958 season. A terse statement was read by a publicist for the Dodgers at 4 P.M. from the World Series press room at the Waldorf-Astoria Hotel:

> In view of the action of the Los Angeles City Council yesterday, and in accordance with the resolution of the National League made October 1, the stockholders and directors of the Brooklyn Baseball Club have today met and unanimously agreed that necessary steps be taken to draft the Los Angeles territory.[19]

After 77 years as the pride and joy of Brooklyn, it was over. Walter O'Malley, president of the Brooklyn Dodgers Baseball Club, did not appear at the announcement.[20]

The Tug of War Ends

Thus ended an epic tug of war between Brooklyn and Los Angeles for the Dodgers that began before spring training of 1957. Provocatively, on February 21, the Brooklyn Dodgers purchased the Los Angeles (Angels) franchise in the Pacific Coast League along with their ballpark, Wrigley Field, from P.K. Wrigley for an estimated $2.5 million.[21] In March, Los Angeles Mayor Norris Paulson led a delegation of city officials to the Dodgers' spring training headquarters in Vero Beach, Florida, to confer in secret with Walter O'Malley and his advisors. After a March 6 meeting in which they proposed to secure a 600-acre tract of land in Chavez Ravine, Paulson and Supervisor Kenneth Hahn emerged to triumphantly announce, "We've got the Dodgers!"[22]

On April 18, the New York City Park Commission countered with an offer of a 78-acre tract of land in Queens as a site for a new ballpark. The site was 12 miles from mid-town, making it more accessible to out-of-town fans than Ebbets Field. O'Malley did not respond.[23]

Things only escalated in May. On May 1, Walter O'Malley arrived in Los Angeles to inspect his Wrigley Field property. Tellingly, he also inspected Chavez Ravine and the Los Angeles Memorial Coliseum.[24] On May 16, New York City Council President Abe Stark suggested that the Dodgers "enlarge" Ebbets Field to a 50,000-seat capacity by closing a street and acquiring additional Land, including a five-acre plot across the street that could house 5,000 cars. O'Malley dismissed the offer by saying he didn't think he was being given "proper support" from the city.[25] A key hurdle was passed on May 27 when the National League club presidents granted permission to the Dodgers and New York Giants to move to California.

The foxy Walter O'Malley would not say "yes" and he would not say "no," but continued to play one city against the other. To Brooklynites, he insisted that "my roots are in Brooklyn," and adamantly held out for a new ballpark site at Atlantic and Flatbush avenues in downtown Brooklyn.[26]

On July 28, the Los Angeles City Council brought in Harold C. McClellan to negotiate with Walter O'Malley on its behalf. The U.S. Department of State had used McClellan as a business consultant to Japanese industry. Offering his services to Los Angeles without pay, McClellan came back with the framework of a deal with the Dodgers, which was presented to the city council in the form of a resolution on September 16. The resolution passed, 10–4, and authorized McClellan and city officials to work with Dodger representatives to draft a "proposed" city ordinance.[27]

On September 20, a plan by Nelson A. Rockefeller to keep the Dodgers in Brooklyn ended in failure. The collapse of the Rockefeller plan ended hopes for a new "Dodger Stadium" on a proposed twelve-acre site at Flatbush and Atlantic avenues. The proposal, submitted to the New York City Board of Estimate, called on the city to sell the site to a Rockefeller corporation for $3 million after acquiring it by condemnation for $8 million plus $1 million for demolition costs. The corporation would then lease the land to the Dodgers rent-free for twenty years, with an option to buy at any time during that period for $3 million plus interest at 2½ percent.

The plan was doomed to failure. New York Mayor Robert Wagner argued that it would require the city to take too great a loss. City Controller Lawrence E. Gerosa called the plan a "giveaway of taxpayers' money for the benefit of a private enterprise."[28] Walter O'Malley rejected the plan, claiming that "any proposal involving $3 million for the land priced the Dodgers out."[29] On the same day the deal collapsed, the Brooklyn Dodgers were eliminated from the National League pennant race with six games left to play in the season.

As September dissolved into October, the momentum seemed unstoppable. The Los Angeles City Council debated the ordinance in an extraordinary session on September 30. The ordinance was placed on the council calendar for action on October 7. Meanwhile, the New York City plan to condemn a slum area in downtown Brooklyn for a new stadium site collapsed when the cost of the project was estimated to be $80 million, despite offers by Nelson Rockefeller to help defray the cost.[30] The National League extended from October 1 to October 15 the deadline for O'Malley to "draft" the Los Angeles territory.

The Los Angeles City Council passed the ordinance by a 10–4 vote on October 7. The ordinance approved the sale of the Chavez Ravine property to Walter O'Malley for the erection of a new baseball stadium. The next day, October 8, the tug of war was over as Walter F. O'Malley notified the National League that he had drafted the Los Angeles territory and made his fateful announcement to move the Dodgers to California.

The Reaction: A Tale of Two Cities

In Brooklyn, the reaction was strangely mixed. The sense of betrayal was summed up by Joseph Sheehan: "In deserting Brooklyn for Los Angeles, the Dodgers will leave an aching void in the Borough of Churches."[31] Others reflected a certain resignation. Gorman Gray, executive vice president and general manager of WOR-TV, which televised the Brooklyn Dodger games, promptly announced that the station would return to its "regular programming schedule."[32]

In Los Angeles, the announcement was cheered by long-suffering baseball fans who had tried—and failed—to bring three different major league teams to their city since 1941.

In the fall of 1941, a deal was nearly completed to bring the perennial doormat St. Louis Browns to Los Angeles, only to have the bombing of Pearl Harbor on December 7 bring the negotiations to a halt. The Browns eventually moved to Baltimore to become the Orioles on September 29, 1953.[33]

Los Angeles next attempted to adopt the Philadelphia Athletics, only to be disappointed. In the words of Mayor Norris Paulson, "Los Angeles was led to the alter only to be jilted," as the A's chose Kansas City on November 8, 1954.[34]

During the 1956 World Series, the lowly Washington Senators "sent out feelers" to Los Angeles. But when city officials invited Senators president Calvin Griffith to Los Angeles to discuss the move, he was forced to decline due to the objections of dissenting shareholders.[35] Los Angeles was still a major U.S. city without a major league baseball team.

* * *

Little Rock wasn't the only crisis for the nation in the fall of 1957. On October 4, 1957, four days before the Dodgers' big announcement of their move to Los Angeles, the Soviet Union made their own big announcement: *SPUTNIK!* They had successfully launched the world's first man-made satellite into orbit around the earth, a steel ball weighing 184 pounds that circled the globe every 92 minutes while emitting a mysterious "beep-beep."

Though President Eisenhower calmly declared that the Russians' achievement did not "raise his apprehensions,"[36] most Americans misinterpreted it as evidence of Soviet superiority in missile development. *Sputnik* ("fellow traveler" in Russian) caused widespread panic — the "Sputnik Alarm" — in the United States. If the Soviets could lob a satellite into orbit, what would stop them from lobbing hydrogen bombs into American cities with intercontinental ballistic missiles?[37] *Sputnik* not only created doubts about the state of the nation's defenses, but about its educational system as well. The Cold War crisis caused by *Sputnik* moved Eisenhower to appoint a President's Science Advisory Committee, establish the National Aeronautics and Space Administration (NASA), and promote passage of a "National Defense Educational Act" by Congress.[38]

On November 3, the Soviets announced the launching of *Sputnik II*, a 1,100-pound satellite carrying a dog named Laika. This tended to prove their previous claim of the successful test of an intercontinental ballistic missile and further stoked American fears that they were now vulnerable to attack. Any rocket capable of placing such an enormous satellite in orbit could surely deliver a nuclear warhead at an intercontinental distance.

By December, after the first American effort to launch a satellite into space failed when the Vanguard rocket carrying it exploded two seconds after takeoff, *Sputnik* had risen to the level of a full-blown national crisis. Not only had the Soviets achieved the distinction of reaching the threshold of outer space first, it was now feared that the United States was two or more years behind them in long-range rocketry.[39]

The State of the Game 1957: Major League Baseball Pre-California

Geographically Challenged

Pre-1958 Major League Baseball was an eastern game. There were two eight-team leagues— none located west of the Mississippi River. Most teams still traveled by train. There were three New York teams: the Giants and Yankees in New York City, and the Dodgers in the borough of Brooklyn. Horace Stoneham and Walter O'Malley signaled their intentions to change that with their announcements of August 19 and October 8, respectively. The national pastime was about to become a truly national game.

Racially Challenged

On the day Jackie Robinson announced his retirement, January 5, 1957, he blasted the three remaining segregated teams, the Phillies, Red Sox, and Tigers, saying, "If 13 major league teams can come up with colored players, why can't the other three?"[40]

On April 22, 1957, when the Phillies sent African American shortstop John Kennedy into the game as a pinch-runner at Ebbets Field in Brooklyn, Philadelphia became the fourteenth team to integrate, leaving the Detroit Tigers and the Boston Red Sox as the sole remaining all-white teams.

A Challenge to the New York Baseball Hegemony from Milwaukee

On October 10, when the Braves defeated the Yankees in the World Series, Milwaukee broke New York's eight-year stranglehold on the world championship — six by the Yankees, and one apiece by the Giants and Dodgers. Twenty-three-year-old Hank Aaron won the National League MVP award. Warren Spahn won 21 games and the Cy Young Award. In their fifth year in Milwaukee, the Braves had emerged as the class of their league and a permanent threat to the New York hegemony.

Ted Williams and Stan Musial: The End of Their Post-War Domination

At the age of 39, after flirting with .400 for most of the season, Ted Williams won the American League batting championship with a remarkable .388 average — 23 points better than the runner-up, Yankee upstart Mickey

Mantle. It was the fifth batting crown for Williams. With a .351 average, Stan Musial won his seventh National League batting championship, at the age of 37. Long before the era of year-round conditioning, Williams and Musial showed no signs of slowing down in their late thirties.

Structurally Challenged—Aging Stadia

With the exception of County Stadium (built in 1953) in Milwaukee, Memorial Stadium (1954) in Baltimore, and Municipal Stadium (1955) in Kansas City, Major League Baseball was built on a deteriorating infrastructure.

In the National League, the Giants were escaping the Polo Grounds (1912) and the Dodgers Ebbets Field (1913). But the Phillies were stuck in Connie Mack Stadium (1909), the Cubs in Wrigley Field (1916), the Cardinals in Sportsman's Park (Old Busch Stadium, 1902), the Reds in Crosley Field (1912), and the Pirates in Forbes Field (1909).

In the American League, the Yankees would continue to play in Yankee Stadium (1923), the Red Sox in Fenway Park (1912), the Indians in Municipal Stadium (the "Mistake by the Lake," 1932), the White Sox in Comiskey Park (1910), the Senators in Griffith Stadium (1911), and the Tigers in Briggs Stadium (1912).

Financially Challenged—Player Salaries

In 1957, 18 years before free agency, Ted Williams was the highest-paid player with an annual salary of $100,000. The major league minimum was a meager $5,000. Nine years before Marvin Miller took over the Major League Baseball Players Association, it was still a toothless organization.

Declining Attendance

For six seasons, 1952–1957, National League attendance was down 13 percent compared with the six seasons following World War II. And this was so despite the Braves drawing more than two million fans for each of the last four years in Milwaukee. Like O'Malley and Stoneham, the other owners began to look west for new markets.

Chapter 4

"A Freak Ball Park"

Where to Play, Walter?

After Walter O'Malley notified the National League on October 8, 1957, that he had drafted the Los Angeles territory and announced to the public that the Dodgers would move to Los Angeles for the 1958 season, that left the question of where the Dodgers would play until the new Dodger Stadium was built. O'Malley was confronted with three alternatives, featuring a minor league crackerbox, Wrigley Field (capacity: 20,500), and two over-sized football stadiums, Los Angeles Memorial Coliseum (capacity: 100,000), or the Rose Bowl (capacity: 100,000).[1]

The Rose Bowl

On the last day of 1957, Walter O'Malley, his wife Kay, daughter Terry, and son Peter were in Pasadena to take in the Tournament of Roses parade and the Rose Bowl game between Oregon and Ohio State. A deal to put the Dodgers in the Rose Bowl for 1958-59 appeared imminent. "The people of Pasadena were kind enough to invite us," O'Malley told reporters, "and I feel very sure we can arrive at an intelligent basis for an agreement to play in the Rose Bowl."[2] The draft of a proposed contract between the Dodgers and the City of Pasadena was on the city manager's desk.[3] Meetings between city officials and a Dodgers task force to iron out the details were scheduled for the first week of 1958. If the deal could be finalized and the revamping of the stadium started by February 1, it could be ready for the April 18 opener with the Giants.

On January 7, while the Dodger task force met with Pasadena city officials, a notice of intent to file an initiative measure to keep the Dodgers out was served on the Pasadena Recreation and Park Board by a local taxpayer group.

Lee Paul, an attorney representing the group, maintained that a 1923 contract prevented the stadium from being used by a for-profit organization.[4] Not only did the Dodgers face the hurdle of a taxpayer initiative, the costs of revamping the Rose Bowl proved to be prohibitive. After weeks of careful study, the Dodgers' engineers concluded that it would take a minimum of $750,000 to transform the stadium into a ballpark meeting major league standards. By January 14, the deal was dead. A joint statement issued by the Dodgers and the City of Pasadena deemed the costs "too large to be amortized over a short-term, two-year lease," and stated that "the alterations would leave physical scars on the Rose Bowl."[5]

With the Rose Bowl out of the picture and time running out, the Dodgers turned their attention to Wrigley Field.

Wrigley Field

Back on October 24, 1957, the Dodgers had moved their offices into tiny Wrigley Field. Built in 1925 for $1.1 million by Cubs owner William Wrigley, Jr., it had been the home of the Los Angeles Angels of the Pacific Coast League from 1925 through 1957. To accommodate the arrival of the Dodgers in 1958, Walter O'Malley transferred his Pacific Coast League franchise to Spokane, Washington.[6]

As a possible temporary solution until Dodger Stadium was built, the park had two major drawbacks. First, it could seat only 20,500, including 18,500 in the covered double-decked grandstand, plus 2,000 in an uncovered single-decked bleacher section in right-center field. There were no seats in left field, only a 15-foot-high concrete wall from the left-field foul pole to dead center field, covered with ivy—intended to replicate Wrigley Field in Chicago.[7] From the tremendous response from the people of Los Angeles to "their" Dodgers, it was evident from the advance ticket sales that the tiny minor league park couldn't handle the business.

The second drawback was the lack of "major league" field dimensions. At first glance, the park appeared normal: 340 feet down the foul lines and 412 feet to dead center field. But these measurements were misleading due to the park's strange angles. The distances from home plate usually increase rapidly from the foul lines toward center, thus forming natural "power alleys." In Wrigley Field, the outfield fences were angled slightly toward the infield instead of away from it. As a result, the power alleys were a cozy 345 feet from home plate, only five feet deeper than down the foul lines, clearly inadequate when compared to the 15 other major league parks.[8]

These drawbacks would be born out in 1961, its only major league season. As the first home of the American League expansion Los Angeles Angels, Wrigley Field yielded 248 home runs, a record that would last 35 years. That year Gene Autry's Angels would barely draw 600,000 fans. The club had to turn away droves of disappointed fans when the mighty 1961 Yankees came to town. Led by Mantle and Maris—with their assault on Babe Ruth's single-season record of 60 home runs—the Bronx Bombers kept the nation enthralled.

In 1958, with a cash outlay of $250,000, O'Malley could add 2,500 seats in right field, upgrade the lighting system, and move the present right-center field bleachers back toward Avalon Boulevard. The Dodgers would not have to pay rent, and would own all the concessions. But with one of the biggest payrolls in the major leagues and facing higher transportation expenses from the move to the West Coast, O'Malley was dubious about being able to make a profit in the tiny park Commissioner Ford Frick had referred to as a "cow pasture."[9] Thus, Wrigley Field was really only a remote contingency as the Dodgers negotiated in earnest with the Coliseum Commission.

The Los Angeles Memorial Coliseum

On January 17, 1958, after several weeks of negotiations among Dick Walsh on behalf of the Dodgers, the city and county of Los Angeles, and the state of California, the parties reached an agreement for use of the Los Angeles Memorial Coliseum for the 1958 and 1959 seasons. By a 9–0 vote, the Coliseum Commission approved Walter O'Malley's fourth proposal:

- For the first 9 home games of each season, after the opening 3-game series, the Dodgers would pay the standard Coliseum rental of 10% of the gate and would not share in the concessions. (This provision for "extra rent" was intended to put the Dodgers on approximately equal terms with the Coliseum's regular tenants, the L.A. Rams, U.S.C., and U.C.L.A.)
- The subsequent games, and the first three games of each year, would be on the basis of a flat rental rate of $200,000 per season, with the Dodgers keeping the concession receipts.[10]

After the negotiations concluded, a beaming Walter O'Malley told reporters, "This ended my longest losing streak."[11]

Baseball in a Concrete Bowl

What Casey Stengel would later call a "freak ball park on the Pacific Coast,"[12] the Coliseum was located ten miles from downtown Los Angeles, adjacent to the University of Southern California. It was built for a mere $900,000 in 1923 for football and track and field, and enlarged for another $900,000 in 1932 for the Olympics.[13]

The first decision for the Dodgers was where to position the field. The Coliseum Commission's initial inclination was to place home plate at the familiar peristyle (east) end. That arrangement, however, would make the outfielders face the afternoon sun. Van Harris, a local contractor, offered a novel solution that was given short shrift by the Coliseum Commission. Harris proposed flying a tethered 50-foot balloon above the field, so positioned as to cast a large shadow around home plate. Fortunately, the Dodgers did not have to resort to the balloon method. By assuring the football tenants that the skin part of the infield would be re-sodded in time for most of their games, O'Malley won his battle to place the baseball diamond in the west end of the oval, which created a strangely misshapen baseball field with grotesque outfield dimensions.

Essentially a football field gerry-rigged with chain-link fences into a baseball park, it was 301 feet down the right-field line, a fantastic 440 feet to right-center, 425 feet to dead center, but only 250 foot down the left-field line, and 320 feet to left-center. Granted, it was a freak, but it was only for two years— and more importantly to Walter O'Malley— it could hold a freakish 94,600 paying customers. Never mind that the most remote seats in right-center field were more than 700 feet from home plate, and that an enormous screen would have to be erected in left field to prevent the wholesale rewriting of the record book for home runs.

The Thing and the Birth of Screeno

On April 4, 1958, workmen completed the erection of a wire barricade to prevent cheap "Chinese" home runs to left field. The 42-foot-high screen was attached to the left-field foul pole at the 250-foot sign, and stretched 140 feet across to a support tower in left-center to neutralize the 320-foot "power alley." Then, for 30 more feet, it was reduced in four "steps" to eight feet. In dead center field, it joined a six-foot chain-link fence that extended across the field to the right-field foul pole.[14] Despite these remedial measures, writers speculated that right-handed sluggers like Gil Hodges could hit 60–70 home runs in the strange park.[15] The leading National League pitchers were soon in an uproar. "It's the biggest farce I've ever heard of," said San Francisco Giants ace left-hander Johnny Antonelli.[16] Pirates ace Bob Friend called the outfield dimensions "ridiculous."[17] The Milwaukee Braves Warren Spahn warned that baseball was being turned into "a hitter's paradise and a pitcher's nightmare."[18] Hall-of-Famer Bob Feller commented, "I think they should let O'Malley pitch on opening day."[19]

The screen would create a new phenomenon: the "screeno." A screeno was a home run in the Coliseum that would have been a pop fly out in any other ballpark. Exasperated pitchers soon referred to the screen as "The Thing."

"I Had to Pitch Different There"

"I had to pitch different there," Roger Craig observed nearly fifty years later, "but my ERA was good there. The right-handed power hitters were all trying to pull the ball over that screen. They liked pitches out over the plate where they could extend their arms. But I pitched them inside with a sinking fastball. Junior Gilliam was a switch-hitter, but he would sometimes hit right-handed against right-handers in the Coliseum. But we all knew it was just 'temporary.'"[20]

Chapter 5

The Dodgers Lose Campy

On January 27, 1958, there was the hint of a thaw in the Cold War, as the United States and the Soviet Union agreed to expand the cultural exchanges between the two superpowers, including the First International Tchaikovsky Piano Competition in Moscow in April.

The next day would be one of the most tragic in baseball history.

* * *

The Stocky Kid from Philadelphia

Roy Campanella was born on November 21, 1921, in Philadelphia, Pennsylvania, of a black mother and an Italian father. He began his baseball career in 1937 with the Bacharach Giants, a Philadelphia semi-pro team. Though he was only 15 years old, he was so impressive that the Baltimore Elite Giants of the Negro National League offered him a place on the team. Still in high school, he played only on weekends to spell veteran catcher Biz Mackey. He quit school the next year to join the team full-time. By 1939, Campanella was the first-string catcher, leading the Giants to playoff wins over the Newark Eagles and the Homestead Grays.

The stocky kid from Philadelphia soon challenged the aging Josh Gibson for the title of leading Negro League catcher. He was voted the MVP in the 1941 East-West All-Star Game. As the result of a dispute with Baltimore owner Tom Wilson, Campanella jumped to the Mexican League in 1942 and 1943, but rejoined the Elite Giants for 1944-1945.

In the fall of 1945, Campanella led a black all-star team in an exhibition series against a squad of white major leaguers managed by Charlie Dressen of the Brooklyn Dodgers. Dressen was so impressed with Campanella that he arranged for him to sign a contract with Brooklyn's Nashua, New Hampshire, Class B farm team run by Buzzie Bavasi and managed by Walter Alston. After winning the 1946 MVP award at Nashua, he made the unusual leap from Class B to Triple-A Montreal of the International League in 1947, where he was again named MVP. Buffalo manager Paul Richards called him "the best catcher in the business — major or minor leagues."

On April 20, 1948, he became the first catcher to break major league baseball's color line when Branch Rickey brought him up to the Brooklyn Dodgers at the age of 26. It was clear that Campanella was ready to take over the catching duties at Ebbets Field. But first, Rickey sent him down to Triple-A St. Paul to integrate the American Association. After he tore the league apart by driving in 39 runs in the first 35 games, the Dodgers recalled him for good on July 1, 1948.

The Rock Behind the Plate

For the next ten years, Roy Campanella was the rock behind the plate for the Brooklyn Dodgers. He soon became the top catcher in the National League, winning three MVP awards, in 1951, 1953, and 1955.

At 5'9" and 225 pounds, the powerfully built "Campy" had amazing power for his size. In 1953 he hit 41 home runs with 142 runs batted in. Then in spring training of 1954, he chipped a bone in the heel of his left hand and damaged a nerve. Unable to grip the bat properly, he was limited to only 111 games that year. Surgery helped him bounce back with 32 home runs and a .318 batting average in the Dodgers' world championship year of 1955. But the problem was chronic, causing him to slump to .219 in 1956 and .242 in 1957.

Even at the age of 36, the Dodgers were counting on his right-handed power for the 1958 season in the Los Angeles Memorial Coliseum with its short left-field screen.[1] Recalling Campanella in 2007, Roger Craig observed, "Roy was a great hitter and would have made a great manager. He had a rapport with all the players."[2]

A Curve He Could Not Handle

That all changed on January 28, 1958, at 3:34 A.M. While returning from a television appearance in New York City, Roy Campanella's rental car skidded on the wet pavement as he went into a dangerous "S curve" a mile from his Glen Cove, Long Island, home. The car flipped over and crashed into a telephone pole. Pinned in the wreckage, Campy lay helpless and moaning.

Fortunately, the sound of the crash awakened Dr. W. Spencer Gurnee, a physician who lived nearby. Dr. Gurnee administered first aid and injected Campanella with a painkiller until help arrived. It took rescue workers 30 minutes to pry open the doors with crowbars to remove him.[3]

Five hours later, he was in surgery. Campy's injury consisted of a fractured dislocation of the fifth and sixth vertebrae at the base of his neck — commonly referred to as a "broken neck." A team of three surgeons performed a laminectomy to repair the fractures and dislocations. Dr. Sengstaken, the head surgeon, said Campanella was lucky to be alive, that the injury would have been fatal if it had occurred "an inch higher."[4] Complicated by the round man's thick neck and heavy muscles, a two-hour procedure turned into a 4½-hour ordeal as his wife and six children waited outside in terror.

The operation was initially deemed a success. Though still paralyzed from his shoulders down, the prognosis was positive. Dr. Sengstaken gave everyone hope, telling reporters that "it was too early to determine when the paralysis would begin to dissipate," but that he "expected recovery to a normal state."[5] He did not even rule out the possibility that Campy might play baseball again. But it was not to be. Tragically, Roy Campanella would never walk again. As a quadriplegic, he would spend the rest of his life in a wheelchair.

The Los Angeles Dodgers' First Crisis

The loss of Roy Campanella was a staggering blow to the Dodgers. "It was a big shock," recalled Roger Craig nearly fifty years later. "It was very devastating to all of us."[6] Just as Yogi Berra was to the New York Yankees, Campanella was an indispensable bulwark in the middle of the Dodger defense. In addition to his power hitting, he was considered the best defensive catcher in the National League — a quick and agile "cat" behind the plate, an expert handler of young pitchers with a powerful, accurate arm that was "poison to base stealers."[7] Ty Cobb once said of him, "Roy Campanella will be remembered longer than any other catcher in the history of baseball."[8]

Eighty days away from their first game in Los Angeles, the Dodgers were in a critical situation. They suddenly had to depend on journeyman catcher Al "Rube" Walker and two youngsters, Joe Pignatano and John Roseboro. For the 1957 Brooklyn Dodgers, Walker had played 50 games behind the plate as the primary backup to Campanella, Pignatano six games, and Roseboro 19 games. And judging by their 1957 performances, they were dismal substitutes for Campanella's bat. Walker batted .181; Pignatano .214; and Roseboro .145.

At first the Dodgers attempted to deal with the crisis by acquisition. But Buzzie Bavasi failed in a desperate attempt to acquire Cincinnati's all-star catcher Ed Bailey. After Walker played his last game on June 15, 1958, to become a Dodger coach, the Los Angeles catching staff was reduced to messieurs Pignatano and Roseboro.

Chapter 6

The 1958 Los Angeles Dodgers: Something Old, Something New

On February 1, 1958, the Cold War competition for space exploration heated up as the United States placed its first space satellite into orbit around the earth. The 30.8-pound *Explorer I* satellite was transported into space by a U.S. Army Jupiter-C four-stage rocket launched from Cape Canaveral, Florida. The bullet-shaped satellite was reported to be "working nicely," orbiting the earth twelve times per day, gathering scientific information about space, and recapturing lost national prestige in the process. In a belated moment of triumph, after *Sputnik* and various failed U.S. attempts, President Eisenhower and a group of scientists made the joint announcement at the Great Hall of the National Academy of Sciences near his vacation retreat in Atlanta, Georgia.[1]

* * *

On February 20, still reeling from the loss of Roy Campanella 23 days earlier, the Dodgers reported to spring training in Vero Beach, Florida, to prepare for their first season in Los Angeles. The Los Angeles Dodgers would be a composite of the old and the new.

The Boys of Summer[2]

After the Dodgers won their only world championship in 1955, the team began to change. Jackie Robinson and Campy were gone. Also gone from the historic 1955 club were Don Hoak (to the Redlegs), Billy Loes (Orioles), Russ Meyer (Red Sox), and Sandy Amoros (back in the minors). Sadly, the Boys of Summer were aging. Going into Opening Day of 1958, Gil Hodges was 34,

Carl Furillo 36, Duke Snider 31, Don Newcombe 31, Pee Wee Reese 38, Carl Erskine 31, and Clem Labine 31.

The Baby Boys of Summer

The Dodgers were loaded with promising young pitchers from the Ebbets Field bullpen. Sandy Koufax was a 19-year-old bonus baby left-hander on the 1955 Brooklyn Dodgers. That meant the Dodgers had to keep him on the big club for two years, even though he clearly needed seasoning in the minor leagues. Twenty-two-year-old right-hander Don Drysdale was now the ace of the staff. Left-hander Johnny Podres, boy wonder of the 1955 World Series as a 23-year-old, was nursing back problems. Twenty-seven-year-old right-hander Roger Craig had struggled through three mediocre seasons in Brooklyn, but still showed promise. Twenty-five-year-old left-hander Danny McDevitt was coming off an impressive 7–4 rookie year.

Journeymen from Brooklyn

Twenty-eight-year-old Gino Cimoli, who took over the center-field position from Duke Snider in 1957, would start there on Opening Day. Twenty-seven-year-old Don Zimmer, a four-year Brooklyn veteran, would take over the shortstop position for the aging Pee Wee Reese.

Big Shoes to Fill Behind the Plate

John Roseboro, a 24-year-old African American player from Ashland, Ohio, would be called on to fill Roy Campanella's shoes by mid-season. A shy man of few words, his teammates, naturally, called him "Gabby." In 2007, Roger Craig recalled Roseboro's contribution: "He did a great job. He could really run for a catcher, and he could block the plate as good as anyone. One time, Daryl Spencer was heading to the plate and Roseboro put a shoulder into him and upended him — just like a football player."[3]

Hey Rook!

The 1958 season marked the brief — and disappointing — major league debut of 22-year-old fireballing right-hander Larry Sherry. He was impressive enough in Grapefruit League work to win a place on the Opening Day roster, allowing only two runs in 24 innings, although his 21 walks were a cause for concern.[4] Mammoth 21-year-old Frank "Hondo" Howard and 27-year-old Norm "Dumbo" Larker would also make their major league debuts.

Roy Campanella's paralyzing accident of January 1958 thrust John Roseboro into the role of principal Dodger catcher with only 19 games of experience. His powerful throwing arm helped to take the Go-Go out of the Sox in the 1959 World Series. (George Brace photograph)

Walter Alston — One Year at a Time

Despite the disappointing third-place finish in 1957, manager Walter Alston, architect of the Dodgers' lone world championship in 1955, was rehired to lead the 1958 Los Angeles Dodgers by signing his fifth consecutive one-year contract.

Walter "Smoky" Alston, from tiny Darrtown, Pennsylvania (population 179), played shortstop and third base for Miami University in Ohio, where he graduated with a bachelor of science degree in education in 1935. He was also a standout guard on the Miami basketball team.[5]

After graduation, he broke into professional baseball as a third baseman for Greenwood of the East Dixie League, where he showed promise with a .326 batting average. But by 1940, he was stuck in the low minors as a player-manager. To supplement his modest minor league salary, he taught high school biology and coached basketball. He worked his way up the Dodger farm system to become manager of the St. Paul Saints of the Triple-A American Association, where he won his first pennant in 1949. After winning another pennant at St. Paul, he took over the Dodgers' Triple-A farm team at Montreal of the International League and won another two

Dodger manager Walter Alston signing a baseball at the Los Angeles Memorial Coliseum. After being hanged in effigy for his team's seventh-place finish in 1958, he was named 1959 Manager of the Year for winning the World Series. (National Baseball Hall of Fame Library, Cooperstown, N.Y.)

pennants and the Little World Series in 1952 and 1953.[6] By then, Alston had attracted the attention of the Dodger front office.

After winning 105 games for the 1953 Brooklyn Dodgers — the sixth-most wins in National League history — and his second consecutive pennant, Dodger manager Chuck Dressen dared to ask team president Walter O'Malley for a two-year contract. O'Malley offered him his customary one-year deal. When Dressen sent him an angry letter, O'Malley, without discussing the matter with his manager, promptly announced that he had "accepted Dressen's resignation."

At a press conference on November 24, 1953, Walter O'Malley introduced Alston as the new Dodger manager for the 1954 season. It was immediately obvious that the quiet, self-effacing Alston represented a sea change from the previous flamboyant Dodger managers, among them the glib and sophisticated Leo Durocher and the peppery, wisecracking Chuck Dressen. Alston described the extent of his major league experience, saying, "Well, I went to bat once for the Cardinals back in '36, and Lonnie Warneke struck me out — that's it."[7] Indeed, Alston's only experience as a major league player was one game as a first baseman for the St. Louis Cardinals in 1936. He would not make the Hall of Fame based on his playing record:

1 at-bat
1 strikeout
2 fielding chances
1 error

In 1954, Alston's first season as Dodger manager, the team finished second to the Giants. But O'Malley didn't blame Alston. Nothing was going to stop the Giants. Willie Mays returned from the U.S. Army to win the National League batting title, leading them to the pennant and a four-game sweep of the Cleveland Indians in the World Series. To make matters worse, Roy Campanella had surgery on his hand, Johnny Podres had his appendix removed, and Don Newcombe struggled after returning from military service. O'Malley rehired Alston for 1955, and was rewarded with the Dodgers' first world championship. Alston was voted National League Manager of the Year. After his manager blew a two-game lead to the Yankees in the 1956 World Series and led the Dodgers to their worst finish in thirteen years the next season, O'Malley was confronted with another tough decision regarding Alston. Again, he stuck with Alston and rehired him to manage the Dodgers for the 1958 inaugural season in Los Angeles. But it would not be easy for the quiet man from Darrtown, Pennsylvania. After winning two pennants and a world championship in Brooklyn, Walter Alston would have to prove himself all over again in Los Angeles.[8]

"He Listened" and "They Listened"

"He listened."[9] That's how Roger Craig would remember Walter Alston's style of managing fifty years later. "In Brooklyn he had some older guys on the team, like Cookie Lavagetto, that he confided in," recalled Craig. "He listened to Jackie Robinson and Pee Wee Reese a lot." And the listening was a two-way street. In hindsight, Craig would further observe, "He was a tough guy who did not have much to say, but when he said something to the players, they listened. The players were afraid of him."[10]

General Manager — Buzzie Bavasi

Emil J. "Buzzie" Bavasi would continue in Los Angeles as executive vice president and general manager of the Dodgers baseball club. Going into the 1958 season — after seven years at the helm — Bavasi had led the Dodgers to four NL pennants, one World Series championship, two second-place finishes, and one third-place showing in 1957.[11]

After the good fortune of making a key contact that enabled him to get his foot in the door, Buzzi Bavasi learned the game in the Dodger farm system from the ground up.[12] Upon graduating from DePauw University in 1939, Bavasi was introduced to Dodgers president Larry MacPhail by then–National League president (and future baseball commissioner) Ford Frick. MacPhail, busy rebuilding the Brooklyn Dodgers, hired Bavasi as the assistant to John McDonald, the team's traveling secretary and publicity director.[13]

In 1940, the raw Bavasi was assigned the task of running the farm team at Americus, Georgia, in the Class D Georgia-Florida League. When his talent-deprived club found itself with only eight men ready to play, Bavasi volunteered to play second base. In 1943, he was promoted to the Class C Piedmont League, where he ran the Durham, North Carolina, club.[14]

Buzzie Bavasi was clearly on his way when World War II intervened. In 1944-45, Bavasi was assigned to an army machine-gun unit that saw heavy action in the Italian campaign. His unit won the Croix de Guerre citation.[15]

Returning to baseball in 1946, Bavasi was put in charge of the Nashua, New Hampshire, club of the Class B New England League. Two of his players would go on to become all-time Dodger greats: Don Newcombe and Roy Campanella. He was recalled to Brooklyn in 1947 to manage the Dodgers' purchasing department.[16]

The next year, 1948, he was back on the diamond as general manager of Montreal in the Triple-A International League. He remained in Montreal until the close of the 1950 National League season, when new Dodger president Walter O'Malley named the 36-year-old Bavasi executive vice president and general manager of the Brooklyn Dodgers baseball club.[17]

Walter F. O'Malley — Renaissance Man

Walter Francis O'Malley was baseball's Renaissance man. In addition to being the principal owner and president of the Dodgers baseball club, he was an engineer, lawyer, pilot, businessman, hunter, fisherman, and grower of prize-winning orchids.[18]

At the time of the Dodgers' move to Los Angeles, O'Malley was 50 percent owner in the team and a partner in two building materials companies, a $6 million advertising agency, a Brooklyn gas company, and on the board of directors of several corporations, including banks and hotels.[19]

His father, Edwin J. O'Malley, was prominent in New York politics, rising to the position of commissioner of public markets. Walter grew up in New York City and went to Jamaica High School and Culver Military Academy. He graduated from the University of Pennsylvania in engineering and went to law school at Columbia and Fordham.[20]

In 1930, at the age of 28, he became a practicing corporate attorney, representing many large New York companies. He became part-owner of one of them, J.O. Duffy Building Materials.[21]

In 1943, Walter O'Malley joined the Brooklyn Dodgers baseball club as an attorney. Within two years he and two others (Branch Rickey and John L. Smith) had acquired 75 percent of the team's stock. In 1950, he ascended from vice president to president of the Brooklyn Dodgers baseball club, succeeding Branch Rickey.[22]

O'Malley — and not Branch Rickey — almost became the man to sign the first black player to a Major League Baseball contract. Early in his career with the club, he went to Havana, Cuba, to sign a Negro shortstop named Silvio Garcia. But the deal fell through when Garcia was unable to get out of his military commitment to the Cuban Army.[23]

Despite his enormous success as a businessman, O'Malley's first love was baseball. Del Webb, former co-owner of the Yankees, said of him, "At heart he has a great love for baseball. I know that he gave up his legal practice for baseball."[24]

While at the time he was accused of making a "land grab" for Chavez Ravine, O'Malley always maintained that he was investing his own money for the good of the game. "The money we made in baseball by the sale of our real estate in Brooklyn, Montreal and Fort Worth is to be invested right back into baseball in the form of a new modern stadium," O'Malley said. "If I'm successful in this effort, we will have made the greatest financial contribution to baseball that has been made by any ball club in the entire history of the game."[25]

Vin Scully — The Indispensable Dodger

Perhaps the most valuable asset the Dodgers brought to Los Angeles was their radio and television broadcaster, Vin Scully. Born Vincent Edward Scully in the Bronx in 1927, he grew up idolizing New York Giants slugger Mel Ott. At the age of eight he told his teacher of his ambition to become a sports announcer. At Fordham University, he played center field on the Rams baseball team for two seasons and broadcast all three major sports on the university's radio station.

From Fordham he sent out about 150 letters to East Coast radio stations, but received only one response, from the CBS Radio affiliate WTOP in Washington, D.C., which hired him as a fill-in. At WTOP he attracted the attention of Red Barber, sports director of the CBS Radio Network, who recruited him for its college football coverage. That fall, Scully so impressed Barber with his account of a college football game under frigid conditions at Fenway Park

Dodgers broadcasters Vin Scully (front) and Jerry Doggett at the Coliseum in 1958. Owner Walter O'Malley would later call Scully "the Greatest Dodger." (National Baseball Hall of Fame Library, Cooperstown, N.Y.)

in Boston that he introduced him to the Brooklyn Dodgers, Barber's summer employer. In 1950, less than a year after graduating from Fordham, Scully joined the immortal Walter Lanier "Red" Barber and Connie Desmond in the Ebbets Field broadcast booth at the age of 23. Red Barber mentored Vin Scully like a father for four years, until Barber left for the New York Yankees after the 1953 season. In 1954, the 26-year-old Scully became the Dodgers' lead broadcaster.

On September 24, 1957, Scully and new partner Jerry Doggett broadcast the Dodgers' last game from Ebbets Field. Six months later, Walter O'Malley — ever the shrewd businessman with a keen sense of value — brought his Scully-Doggett broadcast team with him to Los Angeles. Years later, O'Malley would say, "People will ask me, 'Who is the greatest Dodger?' It's Scully. Without question, he made Los Angeles baseball what it is today. As he literally taught generations of Dodger fans about the nuances of the game and its history, Scully transformed hundreds of thousands of radio listeners and television viewers into loyal team followers."[26]

The author would be one of the converts after a chance encounter with Mr. Scully over the public airwaves near the end of the 1958 season.

The Los Angeles Dodgers Break Camp

Spring training of 1958, the first as the Los Angeles Dodgers, began under a pall with the Campanella tragedy and continued to deteriorate. On February 20, when the pitchers and catchers arrived at Vero Beach, Florida, in unusually frigid weather, Roy Campanella was still paralyzed from the chest down in a hospital in Glen Cove, New York.[27] On March 18, Emmett Kelly, the Brooklyn Dodgers' "bum" clown for 36 years, announced that he would not follow them to California because the Los Angeles Coliseum was "too big for one clown."[28]

The following Monday, March 24, 1958, at 6:35 A.M., 23-year-old Elvis Presley reported to Local Draft Board 86 in Memphis, Tennessee, where he was given a G.I. haircut and assigned U.S. Army serial number 53-310-761. Over the past two years he had sold more than 40 million records and made four movies. Now, as a member of the Second Armored Division's "Hell on Wheels" unit (formerly led by General George Patton), his monthly earnings plummeted from over $100,000 to $83.20. The famous soldier would receive more than 5,000 pieces of mail his first week.[29]

The Dodgers ended their 1958 exhibition season on April 13 with a win over the woeful Cubs in Las Vegas—part of a cross-country exhibition tour—thereby completing the spring with a lackluster 15–16 record.[30] As they flew to San Francisco to face the Giants in the first major league game on the West Coast, the Dodgers faced an uncertain future in a strange city.

Chapter 7

Major League Baseball Comes to California

On April 14, 1958, the United States celebrated its first victory in the Cold War cultural competition when Texan Van Cliburn won first prize in the Soviet Union's First International Tchaikovsky Piano Competition. After obtaining Nikita Khrushchev's approval, the panel of 16 Soviet judges chose Cliburn over eight other contestants, including three Russian pianists and one from Communist China. After receiving a gold medal and 25,000 rubles in cash, Cliburn said, "Thank God it's over! I feel like sleeping for twenty years."[1] But he would still have to give a solo recital in Moscow in four days, an event in which he again rose to the occasion and turned in another triumphant performance. Van Cliburn was a sensation with the Russian audiences who anointed him as their "Malchik (little boy) from the South."[2]

An instant Cold War hero, the 6' 4" 23-year-old pianist from Kilgore, Texas, returned to a ticker-tape parade in New York City.[3]

* * *

On the afternoon of April 15, 1958, a crowd of 23,448 shivering San Franciscans jammed into tiny Seals Stadium to watch baseball's version of high culture: the first major league game played on the West Coast. And an unusual baseball crowd it was to behold. The working stiffs in baseball caps in the right-field bleachers were juxtaposed against an army of businessmen dressed in suits and fedoras interspersed with bejeweled patrons of the San Francisco Opera in the lower box seats. Home of the Seals of the Pacific Coast League since 1931, including the brothers DiMaggio (Vince, Joe, and Dominic), Seals Stadium had one unique feature: there was no warning track for the five-foot concrete walls in left and right field. Adding to the height of the walls was a 10-foot wire screen in left and an 11-foot wire screen in right, thus requiring home runs to clear 15 feet in left and 16 feet in right.[4] The field dimensions were surprisingly long for such a crackerbox ballpark. It was 365 feet down the left field line, 355 feet down the right field line, and 410 feet to center field, where home runs had to clear a 30½-foot scoreboard.

Puerto Rican right-hander Ruben Gomez spoiled the Dodgers' day with a complete-game 8–0 shutout. The Giants roughed up 22-year-old Dodger starter Don Drysdale for six earned runs in less than four innings, including the first major league home run on the West Coast in the fourth inning—a solo shot by Giants shortstop Daryl Spencer.

From the time the Dodgers took the field for pre-game batting practice, the defining characteristic of San Francisco baseball was evident: the wind. A 20-year-old Orlando Cepeda, the eventual National League Rookie of the Year for 1958, introduced himself with an opposite-field home run through a stiff cross-wind that landed in the right-field bleachers. Carl Furillo, unaccustomed to the absence of a warning track, injured his knee as he crashed into the wall in a futile attempt to catch the ball. The great Willie Mays had two hits and two runs batted in to start what was to be one of his greatest seasons.[5]

After the Dodgers squared the series the next day with a 13–1 blowout, thanks to two home runs from Duke Snider and a fine pitching performance from Johnny Podres, the Giants beat Don Newcombe, 7–4, in the rubber game to take the first West Coast series, two games to one. It proved to be a critical defeat in more ways than one. Newcombe injured his shoulder, began drinking heavily, and would be traded at mid-season, never to win a game for the Los Angeles Dodgers.[6]

The transplanted Giant-Dodger rivalry moved to Los Angeles without a break. On April 18, 1958, before a record crowd of 78,672 at the Los Angeles Memorial Coliseum, the Dodgers defeated their arch enemies, 6–5, in the inaugural game in Los Angeles. The Dodgers thereby pulled themselves up to the .500 mark in a rare bright moment in their otherwise disastrous first season in California.

A Parade in L.A.?

Los Angeles had the reputation of a city too blasé to turn out for a parade. But after waiting decades for a Major League Baseball team, the people of Los Angeles were in the mood to celebrate. The April 18 festivities started at 10:30 A.M. with an official civic welcome on the Spring Street steps of City Hall. Gathering for hours, the crowd had swelled to an estimated 5,000. The players were greeted with thunderous ovations as they emerged from a special bus. As they took their seats on the City Hall steps, brightly costumed senoritas from Olivera Street swirled among them.[7]

Coach Charlie Dressen (waving) and manager Walter Alston riding in their Ford Edsel during a welcoming parade through downtown Los Angeles prior to the first game at the Coliseum on April 18, 1958. (National Baseball Hall of Fame Library, Cooperstown, N.Y.)

James "Foghorn" Murphy, on horseback in a Dodger uniform, shouted "Play ball!" through his megaphone as he used to do in San Francisco, where Jack London gave him his nickname. To be historically correct, his original announcement — over 50 years ago — was "Baseball Today!" But on this day, nobody seemed to mind that he blew his lines.

With what must have been a dagger to the hearts of Brooklyn Dodger fans, Walter O'Malley presented Los Angeles Mayor Norris Poulson with the actual home plate ripped from Ebbets Field. "Play Ball!" yelled Foghorn to end the ceremony.

The players, wearing their new Los Angeles Dodger uniforms and rubber shower sandals, flip-flopped two-by-two into convertibles with their names bannered on the sides. In a shiny new 1958 Edsel, Pee Wee Reese and Carl Furillo teamed up as they had for a dozen years in Brooklyn. In a constant deluge of confetti, the motorcade proceeded down Broadway accompanied by Foghorn, its one-man mounted escort. The players were overwhelmed by the size and warmth of the reception. Though the people of Los Angeles had never seen them play, thousands crowded along Broadway to shout greetings of welcome and encouragement. "Hi Duke!" "Next time Newk!" "Coupla homers today, Gil!"[8]

Reminiscent of a royal coronation in downtown London, between Third and Eighth streets, people hung out of Broadway office building windows to see their Dodgers. Nearly lost in the sea of goodwill, one lonely voice presciently yelled, "Stay outta last place!"[9] But he was quickly drowned out by a quick "Play Ball!" from Foghorn.

At Seventh Street and Broadway, the crowd was so dense the motorcade ground to crawl. Opportunistic autograph seekers took full advantage, assaulting the vulnerable Dodgers with pads and pens.

When the procession reached Eighth Street, between Broadway and Hill Street, a bevy of beauties, scantily attired in brief baseball outfits, pitched volleys of toy baseballs to the players. This caused a mad scramble for errant pegs that fell to the street. One young vision of loveliness rode in a golden chariot, pulled by an "ugly giant" in a San Francisco uniform.[10]

Throngs of people jammed the railings of the overhead bridges as the motorcade (sans Foghorn) increased its pace along the Harbor Freeway, heading south toward the Coliseum. When the cars arrived at the Coliseum after 11:30 A.M., the grounds were a seething mass of humanity dressed in Dodger blue. The journey ended as they turned into the parking lot and came to a stop at the tunnel gate. The players got out of their convertibles and triumphantly marched down the tunnel to the Dodger clubhouse beneath the stadium.

Los Angeles had given its welcome. The Dodgers were home.

The Crowd

Bursting with six months of pent-up emotion after the October 8 announcement that they finally had a Major League Baseball team, thousands of fans were lined up at the general admission ticket windows when they opened at 11:00 A.M. Those fortunate enough to buy a $1.50 ticket would be part of the record crowd of 78,762. The crowd not only broke the National League record of 60,747, but also broke the major league record for a regular season single game of 78,382.[11]

The Coliseum Hospital, operated by the Dodgers baseball club, reported ten persons were treated during the game. Four men and four women "collapsed from excitement" before the game was an hour old.[12]

The Opening Ceremonies

The vast Memorial Coliseum was a thrilling sight draped in World Series-style bunting. After both teams had taken batting and infield practice, Johnny Boudreau's band and the "Dodgerettes" entertained the crowd until the formal ceremonies commenced at 1:30 P.M. Hollywood film legend and emcee Joe E. Brown introduced the dignitaries: Governor Goodwin J. Knight, State Attorney General Edmund G. "Pat" Brown, Giants president Horace Stoneham, Mrs. John J. McGraw, Dodgers president Walter O'Malley, Los Angeles Mayor Norris Poulson, San Francisco Mayor George Christopher, Major League Baseball Commissioner Ford Frick, and National League President Warren Giles.

Players on both teams were introduced and stood astride opposite foul lines. A color guard representing all the service branches marched into center field to hoist the American flag atop the familiar arched peristyle entrance as the crowd sang the national anthem.

The loudest, most emotional outburst occurred when Roy Campanella's name was called as a member of the Dodger team. Still paralyzed in New York, Campy was represented by a youthful stand-in, Scoop Remenith of the Toluca Lake Elementary School.

The ceremonies reached a crescendo with a showdown between the mayors. Los Angeles Mayor Norris Poulson took the mound, and San Francisco Mayor George Christopher dug into the batter's box. In a precursor to the real game, Christopher could only manage two foul balls against Poulson.[13]

The Stars Are Out Today

Though the game was played on a sun-drenched afternoon, the stars were already out in force. Packed in the box seats between first and third base was arguably the largest "who's who" gathering ever to witness a Major League Baseball game. Edward G. Robinson and Groucho Marx chomped on their cigars. Jimmy Stewart rushed out to buy his wife a straw hat to shield her from the sun. Ray Bolger elicited howls from the crowd with his army surplus helmet on which he painted, "L.A. DODGER BEANBALL PROTECTOR." Ray's helmet said "HIS," and his wife's said "HERS."

Berkeley alum Gregory Peck, wearing dark glasses and a hat down to his eyebrows, sat provocatively on the Giants side with his young son. *Vertigo* director Alfred Hitchcock took up a seat and a half in section S.

Danny Kaye claimed a priority seat behind the Dodger dugout, "Because, after all, I was born in Brooklyn."[14] That section was an autograph hunter's paradise with such luminaries as Burt Lancaster, Jack Lemmon, Nat "King" Cole, Danny Thomas, the Fords John and Tennessee Ernie, and Gene Autry in his cowboy hat.

Not to be outdone, the politicians made full use of the occasion. California Attorney General Pat Brown tempted fate, and future votes, as he confessed that if he was elected governor in November, he would move to change the name of the San Francisco Giants back to the Seals. Incumbent Governor Goodwin J. Knight pointed to the sky as a helicopter with the streamer "Christopher for U.S. Senator" buzzed the Coliseum.

In the "V.I.P. Gardens," a special temporary section with chairs placed on the playing field, Walter O'Malley held court with his wife and daughter, both dressed from head to toe in Dodger blue. Horace Stoneham, in shirtsleeves, entertained Mrs. John J. McGraw and California's first lady, Virginia Knight.[15]

The Game: An Anti-Climax

The Dodgers won their inaugural game in Los Angeles, 6–5, aided by some bonehead Giants baserunning that cost San Francisco a chance to tie the game in the ninth inning.

With the Giants trailing, 6–4, San Francisco rookie third baseman Jim Davenport opened the top of the ninth inning with a double off the left-field screen. Another Giant rookie, Willie Kirkland, followed with a booming triple off Gino Cimoli's glove in deep center field. Before scoring on the play, Davenport failed to touch third base. Davenport had inadvertently called attention to his mistake as he abruptly stopped short between third base and home, and then sprinted home with what was to be the Giants' fifth run. "My feet tangled, causing me to get off stride," explained Davenport after the game. "I knew I missed the bag and started back. But there was Kirkland coming in, so there was nothing to do but go ahead and hope nobody noticed." But Davenport's counterpart, Dodgers third baseman Dick Gray, did notice the miscue, called for the ball, and stepped on third base. Davenport was called out, and the run was wiped off the scoreboard.[16]

The next batter, Willie Mays, singled home Kirkland with what should have been the tying run. That finished Dodger starting pitcher Carl Erskine, and Clem Labine was called in from the bullpen to get the final two outs to save the victory for Erskine and the Dodgers.

Both starting pitchers were veterans of the New York–Brooklyn rivalry. For Carl Erskine, it was the first victory over the Giants since his epic no-hitter of May 12, 1956, at Ebbets Field. "Oisk" never faced the Giants in 1957. Giants starter Alan Worthington lasted only 4⅔ innings, allowing five runs, seven hits, and walking five to take the loss. After shutting out the Dodgers in his second big league start in 1953, Worthington had now failed to pitch a complete game against them in 11 straight starts.[17]

The Thing

The left-field screen, soon to be dubbed "The Thing" by the players, turned out to be a key factor in the game. In batting practice, the Giants lofted 25 balls over the 42-foot screen attached to the left-field foul pole — a mere 251 feet from home plate. In the real game, big Hank Sauer, who lived a few miles south of the Coliseum in Inglewood, found the distance twice. Sauer hit a "cheap" 275-foot solo homer to tie the game at 2–2 in the fourth inning. Sauer again tied the game, this time 4–4 in the eighth, with a somewhat more "legitimate" solo homer over the screen at the 340-foot sign.

"The Thing" affected both clubs' rookie third basemen (Gray and Davenport). The Dodgers Dick Gray hit the team's first home run in Los Angeles, a 350-foot fly over the screen in the seventh off reliever Johnny Antonelli.

The Coliseum: A Controversial Experiment

The "Great Experiment," Major League Baseball in the Los Angeles Memorial Coliseum, elicited strong feelings in the inaugural game.

The players on both clubs complained that the backgrounds made both hitting and fielding close to impossible. Willie Mays commented, "Those rows of seats go so high, it's awful hard to see anything hit but high flies. Line drives are murder."[18] Herman Franks, Giants coach and acting manager, offered, "The backgrounds are real bad. Those seats in center field should be roped off."[19] Dodger center fielder Gino Cimoli said, "The combination of sun and shirts makes it mighty tough to pick up the ball as it is hit."[20]

"Duke, they killed you"

The outfield dimensions were equally controversial. Duke Snider warned, "The way it is in right field, there won't be many homers for me."[21] That reality was impressed upon Snider before the game by Willie Mays. When Snider walked onto the field for the first time, he encountered Mays, who had just finished taking batting practice. Mays pointed to the distant fence in right, 440 feet away, and said to Snider, "Duke, they killed you!"[22]

"Big leads will mean nothing"

Herman Franks observed, "Big leads will mean nothing, because popfly hitters will be breaking up ball games."[23] On the other hand, the bizarre dimensions were also *penalizing* right-handed batters. After the game, Dodgers coach Chuck Dressen said, "I saw two balls hit the screen that would have been home runs at the Polo Grounds, and I saw two others caught in center field that would have been home runs in Ebbets Field."[24] Ironically, Jim Davenport's lead-off double in the ninth inning would have been a home run in any other NL park. His drive off Carl Erskine was just taking off when it was caught in the mesh monster.[25]

Thus the Coliseum would both giveth and taketh away — as the Milwaukee Braves would learn to their detriment the next year. As manager-philosopher Walter Alston summarized, "Most parks have some background trouble or a short foul line. But good pitchers will pitch good games in the Coliseum, and good hitters will knock the ball out of here."[26]

The Illusion of April 18, 1958

The Dodgers and their new fans experienced the euphoria of winning the first game in Los Angeles, thereby climbing to the .500 level. But it would not last. The 1958 season would be a disaster for the Dodgers, who would eventually finish in seventh place, only two games ahead of the hapless Philadelphia Phillies. It would be their lowest finish since 1944.

CHAPTER 8

May 1958: Welcome to the Cellar

AFTER THE DODGERS AND their new fans experienced the euphoria of winning the first game in Los Angeles, the Giants pounded them, 11–4 and 12–2, to complete the inaugural three-game series at the Coliseum. The team continued to drift, and by the end of April, the Dodgers had fallen into seventh place. At the conclusion of the first homestand on May 7, the Dodgers were 9–13. They got a day off to lick their wounds before facing four straight games with the dreaded Giants— two in San Francisco followed by two in Los Angeles.

A Trip to the Cellar Compliments of Mr. Mays

After being swept, 11–3 and 3–2, in the two games at Seals Stadium, the rivalry moved back to the Coliseum, where, on May 12, the Giants drubbed the Dodgers, 12–3, to drop them into the National League cellar for the first time since July 2, 1948. For the second time in three days, Willie Mays torched Dodger pitching for two home runs and five RBIs— this time including a grand slam.

But Mr. Mays was not done. The next day, May 13, the slaughter at the Coliseum continued as the Giants bludgeoned the Dodgers, 16–9. A meager crowd of 10,507 showed up to watch the Dodger pitchers throw "batting practice" to the Giants, who amassed 26 hits. Getting Willie Mays out was now a virtual impossibility as he went 5-for-5 with yet another two home runs, plus two triples and a single. In the four-game series— swept by the Giants— Mays was 12-for-17 (.706) including:

7 home runs
2 triples
1 double
2 singles
12 runs scored
15 runs batted in

And what about the Coliseum that had drawn the wrath of such pitchers as Johnny Antonelli? The Giants had learned to love it. In their last four games in the concrete oval on South Figueroa, they had crushed the Dodgers, 11–4, 12–2, 12–3, and 16–9.[1]

After the May 12–13 twin blowouts compliments of Willie Mays and the Giants, the Dodgers optioned their promising 22-year-old right-hander Larry Sherry to Triple-A Spokane in the Pacific Coast League. With a 12.46 ERA in five relief appearances, it was evident that the fireballing native of Los Angeles needed "more seasoning."

"I Thought My Career Was Over"

On May 14, 1958, in Chicago, Buzzie Bavasi announced that Roger Craig would be shipped to Triple-A St. Paul in the American Association. With an undiagnosed torn rotator cuff, the big right-hander had pitched only 10⅓ innings with an 8.71 ERA. *Los Angeles Times* baseball reporter Frank Finch dismissed Craig as "of virtually no value this season."[2]

Roger Craig would later remember, "My arm was killing me. I thought my career was over. I had to completely change my way of pitching."[3] He received no encouragement from St. Paul manager Max Macon. "I was devastated when Max Macon told me I would never pitch in the major leagues again," recalled Craig, "but that turned out to be the greatest motivational speech I ever received."[4]

* * *

The same day, 2,500 miles away, Vice President Richard M. Nixon was forced to cut short his turbulent tour of Latin America. In Lima, Peru, Nixon was booed and spat upon as thousands shouted, "Out with Nixon!" and "Death to Yankee Imperialism!" In Caracas, Venezuela, 1,100 U.S. troops had to be called in to protect Nixon and his wife from violent mobs that stoned his car and shattered the windows with melon-sized rocks. As he departed from Caracas to return to the U.S., he had to be protected by a powerful navy task force thirty miles off the coast of Venezuela, consisting of an aircraft carrier with two companies of marines, a missile-armed cruiser, and six destroyers.[5]

Eisenhower had sent Nixon on an 18-day tour of South America for the purpose of improving U.S.-Latin American communications. But Nixon's effect on the crowds soon made the trip counterproductive.[6]

* * *

The Dodgers Wonder: What's Wrong with the Dodgers?

It was mid–May, and the fabled Dodgers were mired in the National League cellar. A frustrated Walter O'Malley cited three reasons for the Dodgers' plight:

First, Campy. "The loss of Campanella was a psychological blow to the team, and a particular blow to the pitching staff he handled so well."

Second, Los Angeles. "The team is trying too hard to make a good impression on a new city. They are 'pressing,' especially in front of record crowds."

Third, the Coliseum. "The team has a 'phobia' about playing in an unorthodox park. Both pitchers and hitters are trying to do unnatural things, such as switch-hitting Junior Gilliam batting right-handed against right-handers in situations where the team needed a home run."[7]

The Duke in a Funk

For the past five consecutive seasons in Brooklyn, Duke Snider had hit forty or more home runs. But on May 14, as the cellar-dwelling Dodgers embarked on a 17-game road trip, he had only one home run. Clearly, Snider's power was neutralized by the Coliseum's dimensions, including 440 feet to right-center field. In fact, no Dodger hit a home run to right field until the right-handed Charlie Neal went the opposite way on May 13.

But there was more to it than just the Coliseum's daunting dimensions. Snider recalled 50 years later that the knee surgery he had in December 1957, before the first game at the Coliseum, was the primary cause of his decline in production. "That was before arthroscopic surgery, and since the knee was never the same, I was never the same hitter," Snider said. "I had to change my whole style. I had to try to be more of a contact hitter, a tough adjustment when you've been a free swinger your entire career."[8]

At the time, General Manager Buzzi Bavasi was unsympathetic with the Duke's plight: "Sure he's unhappy with the Coliseum with its long right field fence. When you get into a park that's not suited to your power, you have to change your style of hitting. That's elementary."[9]

A Reasonable Wager or "Sheer Stupidity"?

Duke Snider had to talk his way into the starting lineup for Game 6 of the 1959 World Series before hitting the decisive home run to clinch the Series for the Dodgers in Chicago. The year before, still hobbled by a 1957 knee surgery, he had slumped to 15 home runs after hitting 40+ in each of the previous five years in Brooklyn. The remote 440-foot right-center-field fence didn't help. (National Baseball Hall of Fame Library, Cooperstown, N.Y.)

Don Zimmer organized his Dodger teammates into a betting pool and was nominated to present an offer to Snider that he could not refuse. The blue syndicate wagered that Snider could throw a baseball over the left-field screen and out of the Coliseum. If the Duke succeeded, his share of the winnings would be $200. At the age of 81, Snider recalled," My first throw went over the screen and reached the top row of seats at the rim. My second throw hit the concrete wall behind the last row of seats. I then told Zimmer, 'This last one is out of here.' But as I released the ball, it slipped out of my fingers and I heard something pop — I had dislocated my elbow."[10] The injury prevented Snider from playing that night. In a sign of their deteriorating relationship, Bavasi characterized the incident as "sheer stupidity,"[11] and fined Snider $200.

On the last day of the season, Snider would succeed in throwing a ball completely out of the Coliseum, thereby winning his $200 back. In a conciliatory move after the season, Bavasi gave him back his $200 fine. Snider analyzed the financial impact of his escapade: "So, I wound up getting $400 out of the deal."[12]

Trying Times for Walter Alston

Walter Alston lamented about the Dodger pitching, saying, "When you have no pitching, you have no ball club. I don't know why we have no pitching. Drysdale and Koufax were set back by military service and are still not in shape. Labine, once our sure-shot reliever, hasn't done a thing. His curve doesn't curve, and his sinker doesn't sink."[13] Unable to take the mound himself, the stoic Alston was condemned to suffer in the dugout.

But it was the shocking decline of Don Newcombe that was the key factor in the demise of the Dodger pitching.

Disaster at Wrigley Field: Newcombe's Days Are Numbered

The Dodgers hit bottom on May 30 when they blew leads of 2–0 and 7–1 to drop a double-header to the Chicago Cubs at Wrigley Field. After the double defeat, the Dodgers were 11 games under .500, hopelessly entrenched in last place, and three games behind the abysmal seventh-place Philadelphia Phillies.[14]

In the second game, Don Newcombe was knocked out in the fourth inning after being staked to a 6–0 lead. Although he was not charged with the loss, it was clear that the big right-hander's days with the Dodgers were numbered. The situation deteriorated as General Manager Buzzi Bavasi fined Newcombe $300 for not being in his room at the Conrad Hilton when a bed check of the players was made at 1:15 A.M. the next morning. Newcombe was now 0–4 for the year, and had failed to complete his last eight starts, dating to September 1957.[15]

* * *

After a dismal 11–17 May performance, the Los Angeles Dodgers finished the month in last place, 10 games behind the league leaders.

Chapter 9

Chavez Ravine: The Big Distraction

As the Dodger players were struggling on the field to escape the cellar at the end of May, the front office was distracted by an existential threat off the field: the specter of Proposition B. Upon closer examination of the ordinance and contract that was passed by the Los Angeles City Council by a 10–4 vote back on October 7, 1957, it was evident that the equities of the transaction were questionable at best.

The City of Los Angeles agreed to do the following:

1. Convey to the Dodgers 300 acres of land in Chavez Ravine (valued at $2,000,000 to $6,000,000), reserving for the city's use a 40-acre plot for public recreational facilities (youth center); the 40 acres to become property of the Dodgers after 20 years;
2. Spend up to $2,000,000 for preliminary grading and road-building, with an additional $2,740,000 of similar work to be provided by the county; and
3. Put into a trust fund for the Dodgers' use for a "youth program" half of any oil revenues obtained anytime in the future from the 300-acre tract and from Wrigley Field.

The Dodgers baseball club agreed to do the following:

1. Convey to the City of Los Angeles Wrigley Field, a 9-acre, 22,000-seat former Pacific Coast League ball park (valued at $2,000,000);
2. Build on the Chavez Ravine tract "a modern stadium seating no less than 50,000;" and
3. Spend not in excess of $500,000 on the 40-acre public recreational facility and $60,000 per year on maintenance of it.[1]

Opponents of the "sweetheart deal" immediately went into action by gathering signatures for a referendum petition to challenge the contract. On November 14, 1957, petitions with 85,000 signatures were filed with the Los Angeles City Clerk.[2] On December 30, 1957, the Los Angeles City Council's

Charter and Administrative Code Committee voted 3–0 to put the referendum on the June 3, 1958, state primary ballot, later named "Proposition B."[3] The validity of the contract between the Dodgers and the City of Los Angeles was now in the hands of the voters. A "yes" vote on Proposition B would confirm the contract, while a "no" vote would nullify it.[4]

Proposition B caught Walter O'Malley by surprise. "I never anticipated a referendum," he recalled more than twenty years later. "In fact, I was completely unaware of the thing they called a referendum because they never had that in New York."[5]

In addition to the hurdle of Proposition B, two taxpayer lawsuits were still pending, asking the Superior Court to block the transfer of the Chavez Ravine land to the Dodgers. The taxpayers argued that the land was restricted to "public use" as set forth in a 1955 deed the City Housing Authority used to convey the land to the City of Los Angeles.[6]

The Big Distraction

When the referendum was placed on the ballot at the end of December 1957, polls showed 70 percent of the electorate favored the contract. Walter O'Malley was content to "remain on the sidelines and not attempt to influence voters."[7] But as June 3 approached, opponents of the deal began to gain ground by calling for a more equitable contract. When support for "yes" on Proposition B had fallen to 52 percent, Los Angeles Mayor Poulson and Walter O'Malley turned to guerilla tactics.

Poulson employed a class-based argument. He suggested that opponents of Proposition B were privileged elites that sought to deprive working-class people of access to Major League Baseball.[8] In his memoirs, Poulson later admitted, "I suggested a scare campaign that would strike home with low-income people who didn't belong to country clubs ... and who wanted big league baseball for entertainment. The referendum, we led them to believe, was a yes-or-no vote for baseball."[9]

Most opponents of Proposition B wanted to keep the Dodgers, but wanted a more even-handed contract. Poulson conspired with National League President Warren Giles to distort the issue of the referendum from a vote on the fairness of the contract to a yes-or-no vote on the Dodgers and major league baseball in Los Angeles. After Poulson convinced Giles to make a public statement, Giles pronounced on May 22, 1958:

> If the vote on the city's Chavez Ravine contract with the Dodgers is refuted by the citizens of Los Angeles, it will be my personal recommendation to our league that we take immediate steps to study ways and means of relocating the franchise in another city. The June 3 referendum ... is more than the Chavez Ravine issue. To me

> it will be an expression by the people of Los Angeles as to whether they want Major League Baseball.[10]

This was essentially a threat. If Los Angeles rejected Proposition B, it would not only lose the Dodgers, but disqualify itself for a future Major League Baseball team.[11]

In his response to Giles' statement, Walter O'Malley publicly attacked the opponents of the contract for the first time. He called John Smith, owner of the San Diego Padres of the Pacific Coast League, "a minor league man who doesn't want Major League Baseball in Southern California."[12] He disparaged the two council members who had opposed the deal from the beginning, stating, "One doesn't understand what it's all about, and the other merely has political ambitions."[13]

* * *

On June 1 in Paris, French government leaders, paralyzed by indecision over the Algeria crisis, returned General Charles de Gaulle to power as premier.

In one of the strangest and most memorable sessions the French National Assembly ever had, it invested the 67-year-old de Gaulle with supreme authority, including six months of full decree "emergency" power, free from Parliamentary interference. After a four-hour debate in which de Gaulle was not even present, the Assembly voted 329–244 to invest de Gaulle as premier. After making their investiture speeches, it was the custom for aspirants to the premiership to follow the debate, take notes, and answer questions put to them. But after making a brief seven-minute speech, de Gaulle showed his contempt for the established system as he strode out of the building before the debate began. In a surreal scene, the debating deputies seemed to be addressing a phantom.[14]

The future French president, Socialist Francois Mitterrand, withheld his support out of concern de Gaulle would become a dictator.[15] In Washington, U.S. officials expressed fear that a de Gaulle regime could lead to a crisis between France and the other nations within the North Atlantic Alliance.[16]

* * *

The Dodgerthon

That night in Los Angeles, two days before the primary election, the Taxpayers' Committee for Yes on B presented a five-hour telethon on KTTV. Eager to broadcast the Dodgers' games, KTTV, a Times Mirror subsidiary, donated production assistance and free airtime to the supporters of Proposition B.[17] The "Dodgerthon" was seen by an estimated 18 million viewers.

The theme was clear: a "yes" vote on Proposition B was the best way to keep the Dodgers in Los Angeles.[18]

In its review of the broadcast, the *Los Angeles Times* called Walter O'Malley, "the cigar-puffing owner of the Dodgers, the star of the Dodgerthon."[19] In the first part of the program from the KTTV studios, O'Malley answered questions from putative "baseball fans." He used the forum to emphasize his intention to stay in Los Angeles. "We have to stay here thirty years to get our money back,"[20] he said. He argued that his stadium in Chavez Ravine would produce $350,000 per year in property tax revenues, compared to the $7,500 per year now generated from the current "scattered land owners."[21]

Though actor Ronald Reagan received second billing eight years before his run for the governorship, his political advocacy skills were on display. He accused the leaders of the "anti-baseball faction" of deception in presenting their arguments to the voters. He called the ballot argument against Proposition B "one of the most dishonest documents I ever read in my life."[22] In typical Reaganesque black-and-white fashion, he said of the opposition, "I have always believed there are two sides to every question, but in this case they are the good side and the bad side."[23] As to the primary issue — the fairness of the contract — Reagan said, "Chavez Ravine has been sitting there in the heart of L.A. for years and nothing has been done with it. Now that a baseball team is to have it, it's worth a lot of money we are told. Sure, Walter O'Malley got a good deal when he was offered Chavez Ravine as a site for his ball park. Any deal to be good must be fair to both sides, not just one."[24] Huh?

Joe E. Brown, comedian, baseball aficionado, and chairman of the Taxpayers' Committee for Yes on B, was the master of ceremonies. Brown announced for the first time that Dodger management would admit for free all blind and deaf persons who wish to attend Los Angeles Major League Baseball games. Additional celebrities who appeared on the Dodgerthon in support of a "yes" vote on Proposition B included Dean Martin, Jerry Lewis, Danny Thomas, George Burns, Groucho Marx, Jack Benny, Ray Bolger, Tom Harmon, Chuck Connors, and Debbie Reynolds.[25]

The second part of the program featured the celebrities convoying by automobile to the Los Angeles International Airport to meet the Dodger team as it arrived from Chicago after beating the Cubs, 1–0. KTTV reported that its switchboard received hundreds of calls — overwhelmingly in favor of Proposition B.[26]

Proposition B Passes

On June 3, 1958, Proposition B, the baseball referendum measure granting the Los Angeles Dodgers the right to build a $12 million stadium in Chavez

Ravine, won voter approval by a margin of 24,293 votes. National League President Warren Giles sent a telegram of congratulations to Los Angeles Mayor Norris Poulson:

> Largely through your efforts, we reached first base in Los Angeles last October [On Oct. 7, 1957 the L.A. City Council voted 10–4 to pass an ordinance approving sale of the Chavez Ravine property to the Dodgers], and the voting umpires have now called us safe. May we now go all the way and score quickly with the early completion of the spectacular stadium planned by the Dodgers.[27]

But Walter O'Malley would not "score quickly" with Dodger Stadium. Certification of the referendum was tied up in litigation for months. The ground-breaking ceremonies for the new stadium would be delayed until May 8, 1959. The issue of Chavez Ravine remained in doubt until October 19, 1959, when the U.S. Supreme Court ultimately upheld the contract.

* * *

The same day in Paris, the French Parliament, under de Gaulle's threats to resign as premier of France, enacted the last of his three "emergency reforms" to reform the state and prevent civil war. Passed by a 350–161 vote in the Assembly, the final measure called for a constitutional amendment to transform the current parliamentary regime into a presidential one with a strong executive. Less than twenty-four hours after he was invested as premier, the imperious general marched to the Assembly podium to deliver his ultimatum to the deputies, who were reluctant to surrender the last of their powers: "Pass the measure or I will immediately resign." The other chamber of the legislature, the Council of the Republic, would promptly agree to the constitutional amendment.[28]

* * *

Throughout the 1958 season, as the Dodgers struggled on the field, Walter O'Malley was forced to focus on the paramount issue facing the Los Angeles Dodgers baseball club: securing the Chavez Ravine agreement. Passing Proposition B and surviving multiple taxpayer lawsuits came first, winning ball games came second.[29]

Chapter 10

The Long Summer of '58

The summer of 1958 saw an escalation of Cold War tensions. On June 7, the United States expelled a Soviet diplomat as a spy. After the State Department charged Soviet Embassy aid Nikolai Korochkin with improper acquisition of classified U.S. Army manuals, he was ordered to leave the country.[1]

On June 28, Cuban rebel forces led by Fidel Castro kidnapped 28 U.S. Marines near the American naval base at Guantanamo Bay, in retaliation for U.S. military support provided to the Cuban dictator, General Filgencio Batista. After scoring two days of propaganda points, Castro released them all, unharmed.[2]

On July 14 — in a violent coup d'état — the Iraqi army executed the three men atop the pro–Western Iraqi government: King Faisal II, the Crown Prince, and the Premier of Iraq. The army had opposed Faisal's efforts to help Jordan and Lebanon quash internal rebellions, and the new Iraqi Revolutionary Cabinet immediately aligned itself with the anti–Western, pan–Arab policies of Egypt's General Gamal Abdel Nasser. The next day, in response to an urgent appeal for military assistance from Lebanese President Camille Chamoun, President Eisenhower sent 5,000 U.S. Marines into Beirut to maintain order. In a statement from the White House, Eisenhower stressed that "we will withdraw our forces as soon as the United Nations has taken further effective steps to safeguard Lebanese independence."[3] The Soviet Union condemned Eisenhower's action as "open aggression" that is "extremely alarming and dangerous to world peace."[4] In Moscow, tens of thousands of Soviet citizens bombarded the United States Embassy with bricks and bottles.[5]

* * *

Mid–1958 was clearly a long, hot summer for U.S. foreign policy, and it would be a long, hot — and futile — summer for the Los Angeles Dodgers. While June started on a positive note for the Dodgers with the passage of

Proposition B in the June 3 primary election, after entering the month in last place, the team continued to disintegrate on and off the field.

Pitching Woes

Their veteran Brooklyn pitchers—Erskine, Labine, McDevitt, Newcombe, and Craig—all continued to have problems adjusting to the Coliseum. Walter Alston was forced to go with a "kiddie corps" of Johnny Podres, Don Drysdale, Sandy Koufax, and Stan Williams. At 25, Podres was the senior member of the group by three years.[6]

Preliminary Injunction

On June 6, Superior Court Judge Kenneth C. Newell issued a preliminary injunction blocking the City of Los Angeles from conveying the Chavez Ravine land to the Dodgers for a baseball stadium site. The judge acted on a taxpayer suit brought by Louis Kirshbaum (*Kirshbaum I*) the previous April 10.

The preliminary injunction prohibited the city from violating any part of the deed restriction imposed by the Los Angeles Housing Authority when it conveyed a major portion of the property to the city in 1955. The restriction limited the use of the land to "public purposes." In addition to *Kirshbaum I*, there were two other taxpayers challenging the validity of the contract between the Dodgers and the City of Los Angeles based on the "public purpose" clause in the deed: Julius Reuben (an attorney suing on his own behalf), and Theresa Steffey (a Chavez Ravine property owner). All three lawsuits were set for trial on June 19.[7]

The Dodgers Sweep the Braves, Set Attendance Record

On June 8, the Dodgers beat the world champion Milwaukee Braves, 12–4, before 57,122 fans at the Memorial Coliseum to sweep a three-game series. It was their fifth consecutive win over the Braves.

Hallelujah! Dodger fans rejoiced as Los Angeles was out of the cellar for several hours after the team won, and the Philadelphia Phillies lost the opener of a double-header with the Cardinals. But the Dodgers slipped back into last place when the Phillies won the nightcap.

Attendance for the three-game weekend series totaled 171,326 (Friday, 54,639; Saturday, 59,365; and Sunday, 57,122), setting a new major league record.

The three-game sweep matched the longest winning streak of the 1958 season for the Dodgers.[8]

The Dodgers Trade Newk

An hour and two minutes before the trading deadline of midnight June 15, the Dodgers traded Don Newcombe to the Cincinnati Redlegs. In return, the Dodgers received burly first baseman Steve Bilko and journeyman relief pitcher Johnny Klippstein.[9]

Newcombe had no advance warning that he was going to be traded from the only team he had played with since arriving in the major leagues in 1949. Earlier in the day, the Dodgers had been pounded by the Pittsburgh Pirates, 12–1, at the Coliseum, with Newcombe absorbing the loss to move his record to a shocking 0–6 for the season. Shocking, since less than two years before, Newcombe had won both the 1956 Cy Young and Most Valuable Player awards with a 27–7 record.[10]

The Dodgers were hoping that the 250-pound Bilko would help them take advantage of the short left-field screen in the Coliseum. He had been a home run–hitting phenomenon for the Angels of the Pacific Coast League, bombing 55 and 56 home runs for the 1955 and 1956 seasons, respectively. But he proved to be a disappointment to the Dodgers for the rest of the season, hitting an anemic .208 with only seven home runs and 18 runs batted in.

A Fourth Taxpayer Lawsuit Is Filed

A fourth taxpayer lawsuit to prevent the City of Los Angeles from conveying Chavez Ravine to the Dodgers was filed on June 17 by Louis Kirschbaum, a garment worker who was already a plaintiff in *Kirshbaum I.* In his second lawsuit (*Kirschbaum II*), he asked the court to pronounce the June 3 referendum void if the land contract was found to be invalid, and for a temporary restraining order preventing certification of the election results until the contract issue was resolved.[11]

Baseball in Court

As the trial of the first three taxpayer lawsuits (*Kirshbaum I, Reuben,* and *Steffey*) began on June 19, the Los Angeles Dodgers relinquished all interest in oil revenues from the Chavez Ravine site. Pierce Works, attorney for the Dodgers, announced to the court, "The Los Angeles Dodgers are in the baseball business and not in the oil business."[12]

On June 25, after a week-long trial, Judge Arnold Praeger dismissed *Steffey*, set *Kirschbaum II* for a July 2 hearing, issued a temporary restraining order preventing certification of the election results, and took *Kirshbaum I* and *Reuben* under submission. The principal arguments in *Kirshbaum I* and *Reuben* were as follows:

1. The Chavez Ravine property was acquired by the City of Los Angeles for "public purposes" only; and
2. The City of Los Angeles usurped its authority for the benefit of a private business (the Los Angeles Dodgers baseball club).[13]

Back to Reality: The Dodgers End June in the Cellar

On June 27, the Dodgers beat the Braves for the seventh consecutive time as Sandy Koufax won, 3–1, in Milwaukee County Stadium. By taking the first two games of a four-game series, the Dodgers were now only ½ game from climbing out of the cellar.[14]

But two days later, Hank Aaron brought them back to reality as the Braves pounded the Dodgers, 10–6, to gain a split in the four-game series, thus burying them again in sole possession of last place. "Bad Henry," as the Dodger pitchers called Aaron, tagged Don Drysdale for a grand slam homer on his way to a 4-for-5, 5-RBI performance. Over the last three games of the series, Aaron punished the Dodgers with three homers, nine hits, and eight runs batted in.[15] Despite Drysdale's sidewinding motion and reputation for knocking down batters, the right-handed-batting Aaron refused to be intimidated, and ultimately hit 17 career home runs off the pitcher.

* * *

Judge Praeger Refuses to Dismiss Kirschbaum II

At the July 2 hearing, attorneys for the City of Los Angeles and the Dodgers sought to have *Kirschbaum II* dismissed on the grounds that it duplicated issues already tried in the other two suits that Judge Praeger took under submission on June 25 (*Kirshbaum I* and *Reuben*). But Praeger refused to dismiss the case, explaining that the cases involve different issues:

- *Kirshbaum I* and *Reuben* charged that the baseball ordinance itself was illegal.
- *Kirshbaum II*, to block certification of the June 3 referendum, sought to avoid a "conflict" which might result from having it certified that the electorate had legally approved an issue which might itself later be ruled invalid.

Consequently, Judge Praeger continued the *Kirshbaum II* temporary restraining order preventing certification of the election results until he ruled on *Kirshbaum I* and *Reuben*.[16]

The Dodgers Pass the Million Mark

On July 3, the Dodgers passed the million mark in attendance as 66,485 fans jammed into the Coliseum to watch a twilight-night double-header with the Cardinals. An estimated 10,000 were turned away when the L.A. Fire Department ordered the turnstiles closed because the swelling crowd was getting too close to a large arsenal of fireworks to be set off at the adjacent American Legion on the Fourth of July. In the first 35 games, the Dodgers had already drawn 1,016,287 people.[17]

Koufax Joins the Injury List

On July 6, the Dodgers added Sandy Koufax to their growing injury list. The 22-year-old southpaw had to be helped off the Coliseum field in the second inning of a game he started against the Cubs when he collided with Chicago's Jim Bolger. Koufax, who suffered a severe ankle sprain and spike lacerations, would be lost to the Dodgers for three weeks. Losing their winningest pitcher, with a record of 7–3, was a blow to the Dodgers. He became the 21st player sidelined during the season.[18]

Baseball in Congress

On July 8, 1958, the American League defeated the National League, 4–3, in the twenty-fifth All-Star Game in Baltimore. Conveniently located next to Washington, D.C., baseball came to Congress the next day to participate in hearings before the Senate Antitrust and Monopoly Subcommittee, headed by Senator Estes Kefauver (D-Tenn.). Kefauver called all-star participants Casey Stengel, Mickey Mantle, Ted Williams, Stan Musial, Robin Roberts, and Ed Yost to the Caucus Room of the Senate Office Building to discuss proposed legislation to exempt baseball from federal antitrust laws.[19]

The legislation initially appeared headed for easy passage. But when Senators owner Calvin Griffith began talking about moving his team out of Washington, D.C., the dynamics of the legislative process changed. One senator insisted on adding an amendment to keep club owners from "thumbing their noses at the public" in shifting franchises from one city to another. Another senator called for vague new language requiring owners to "assume certain responsibilities to the public and to consider the public interest" before moving a franchise.[20]

The Kefauver-Stengel Ballet

After Casey Stengel gave the subcommittee a brief, modest summary of his 48-year career in baseball, Chairman Kefauver asked "the Ol' Perfesser" whether he was "prepared to answer with specificity why baseball wanted the legislation passed."[21] His response was a non-stop super sentence — in Stengelese — moving from the rationale for excluding managers such as himself from the players' pension fund to a discussion on the owners' role in his team's success, saying he thought it was "very interesting to the public or to all of us that it is the owner's own fault if he does not improve his club, along with the officials in the ball club and the players."[22]

After the howls subsided, and Kefauver indicated he thought he hadn't made the question clear, he tried again by asking, "What is the need for the legislation if they (the club owners) are getting along without it?"[23] Stengel, with a broad shrug, palms up, responded, "I didn't ask for the legislation."[24] Kefauver tried again asking, "Are you ready to say there is no need for this legislation?" Stengel provided more tortured logic: "As far as I am concerned, from drawing a salary and from my ups and downs and being discharged, I always found that there was somebody ready to employ you if you were on the ball."[25]

His head spinning, Kefauver thanked "the Ol' Perfesser" and called Stengel's golden boy, Mickey Mantle, to the witness chair for some clarification. When Kefauver asked him whether he had "any observations with reference to the applicability of the antitrust laws to baseball," Mantle responded, "My views are just about the same as Casey's." Kefauver tried to proceed, "Under the reserve clause, of course, they can do anything with you they want to, is that right?" Mantle offered, "I don't think about this stuff very much," touching off a new chorus of laughter.[26]

The subcommittee eventually gave up, and the hearing ended with an autograph session in which senators— reduced to hero worshiping adolescents— asked the players to sign everything from the cast on Senator Robert S. Kerr's injured right arm to copies of the proposed bill to that morning's sports page.[27]

A Judge Praeger Bombshell: The Contract Is Invalid

Stuck in last place on July 14, the Dodgers didn't need the bombshell that Judge Praeger detonated that day in the Superior Court. The contract between the City of Los Angeles and the Dodgers was held to be invalid. In deciding in favor of the taxpayers in *Kirshbaum I* and *Reuben*, Praeger enjoined the City Clerk, Mayor Poulson, and the City Council from executing the contract, enforcing the ordinance, conveying the land, or carrying out the provisions of the deal.[28]

In his opinion, Judge Praeger pronounced the following actions illegal:

1. The donation to a private corporation of land earmarked for a "public purpose."
2. The use of public funds to acquire property to be given to a private corporation (the city already owned 169 of the 300 acres. It acquired them when a public housing project was canceled. It planned to get the remainder of the land through purchase of optional plots or by condemnation).
3. The delegation by the City Council to the ball club of "discretion" over the expenditure of the $2,000,000 preliminary grading money.
4. The delegation by the City Council to the ball club of "discretion" over the expenditure of oil revenues.[29]

Though the Dodgers were stunned by the decision, Walter O'Malley tried to remain hopeful of ultimately being able to acquire the Chavez Ravine property and to build Dodger Stadium. Announcing his intent to appeal, O'Malley told reporters at a Coliseum press conference, "I remain an optimist. I think things will be ultimately resolved in favor of our contract with the city. I had hoped for a favorable ruling now so that the injunction might be dissolved and preparations made to start the grading and construction. But this is just another hurdle that we will have to take in stride."[30]

On July 22, Judge Praeger changed the *Kirshbaum II* "temporary restraining order" preventing certification of the election results to a more restrictive "preliminary injunction."

Malaise and Humiliation on the Road

On July 27, the cellar-dwelling Dodgers looked like a bedraggled and demoralized baseball team as they checked into a Philadelphia hotel lobby at the same time the high-flying second-place San Francisco Giants were checking out. Though the Dodgers had been struggling to escape last place ever since they stopped taking bows before the delirious army of Los Angeles fans and Hollywood stars in April, it was not until this day that they realized the full impact of their lowly state.[31]

Also in the hotel was the Giants' chief scout, Tom Sheehan. One of his principal jobs was to scout the rival clubs to help his team gain an edge for future meetings. When the Dodgers saw Sheehan move toward the airport bus, it was clear that he was leaving town with the team. "Hey, Tom," yelled Dodgers coach Chuck Dressen, "aren't you sticking around to watch us?" Sheehan looked down his long nose and replied, "No, Chuck, I'm not. And listen, brother, when a scout doesn't even stick around to see you play, you know you are really in trouble."

"Why, the big windbag!" exploded Pee Wee Reese, "I can remember when..." But here the Little Colonel closed his eyes and lapsed into silence.[32]

A Noose for Walter Alston

On July 29, Andy Vitalich, an irate service station operator in the Los Angeles suburb of San Pedro, admitted to police that he was responsible for hanging Dodger manager Walter Alston in effigy in front of his business. The crude dummy was dressed in a Little League baseball uniform and had a sign that read: "Mgr. Walt Alston." Vitalich confessed to police, "I did it. I don't think much of that guy as manager."[33]

By the end of July, with the Dodgers still in last place, the air was thick with rumors of the imminent demise of Alston. According to a UPI report, Alston would be gone "within the next ten days."[34]

The Dodgers won the World Series in 1955 and the NL pennant in 1956. But according to *New York Times* reporter John Drebinger, what had happened to them since then — a feeble third in 1957 and their current position stuck in the cellar — was not Alston's fault. Instead, it was the result of a "general crackup" that began in June of 1957 when the Dodger front office started concentrating on "the Great Move to California" and dropped everything else, including the small matter of keeping the manager supplied with playing talent.[35]

Struggling on a road trip with at least four players sidelined, Alston was asked if the litigation-embattled front office was getting him some help. He replied, "I've been trying to get somebody on the phone for four days, but all I get is the operator and she can't help me. I guess we'll just have to do the best we can."[36]

* * *

August was a bittersweet month for the Dodgers. With a record of 17 wins and 14 losses, it was their winningest month of the season. They realized a goal of climbing back into the first division of the National League. They continued to show they could play with the world champion Milwaukee Braves by taking four out of five at the Coliseum, thereby clinching the season series. But they ended the month in a new slide toward the bottom, capped by five straight losses to the Giants in San Francisco.

The City Petitions the California Supreme Court

On August 7, Los Angeles City Attorney Roger Arnebergh petitioned the California Supreme Court for a "writ of prohibition" to prohibit Judge Praeger from trying *Kirshbaum II* in the lower court. Arnebergh hoped that the state's highest court would assume jurisdiction of the case and review the entire controversy, including the validity of the contract. Although the outcome of such a review was uncertain, he considered this to be preferable to the regular appeals process that could have taken more than a year.[37] With the Dodgers' Coliseum lease set to expire after the 1959 season, time was of the essence.

Vote of Confidence: The Dodgers Re-Hire Walter Alston

The Dodgers absolved manager Walter Alston for their sorry season by re-hiring him for the 1959 campaign. The Dodgers traditionally announced their managerial plans at the Major League Baseball winter meetings in December, but General Manager Buzzi Bavasi broke with precedent with his August 14 announcement, stating, "I wanted to give Walter Alston a vote of confidence. I believe he is entitled to one bad year."[38] Alston was always known as a "players' manager," and they voiced their approval. Carl Erskine said of Alston, "He's the same manager today as he was in 1955 when we won the world championship. You can't win with a good jockey on a bad horse."[39]

"The rehiring of Walter Alston was a big factor in our success the following year," Roger Craig would recall. "The players respected him a lot."[40]

The Dodgers Continue to Dominate the Milwaukee Braves

On August 23, the Dodgers pounded the world champion Milwaukee Braves, 10–1, at the Coliseum. Don Drysdale was a virtual one-man team. On the mound, the 22-year-old right-hander pitched a complete-game four-hitter. At the plate, he hit two home runs and drove in four runs. Gil Hodges contributed his 14th career grand slam home run to break his National League record.

The Dodgers thereby won the five-game series with the Braves, four games to one, and improved the season series with the world champions to 13 wins and seven losses. It was the high point of a sorry season for the Dodgers. Realizing a goal of reaching the National League first division, they were now in sole possession of fourth place.[41] But it wouldn't last, as they would soon relapse into a new descent toward the cellar, losing three out of four to the Cincinnati Reds at the Coliseum before running into a meat grinder at Seals Stadium in San Francisco to close out the month.

The Bubble Bursts in San Francisco

On August 31 in Seals Stadium, Sandy Koufax lasted only two-thirds of an inning as the Giants destroyed the Dodgers, 14–2. After rookie catcher Bob Schmidt humiliated Koufax with a grand slam home run in the first inning, it was effectively over.

The Dodgers ended August by losing five out of their last six games, still clinging to a fifth-place tie with St. Louis, seven games under .500, and 15 games behind the leaders.[42]

Chapter 11

September 1958: A Lost Season Comes to an End

THE FIRST DAY OF SEPTEMBER was no kinder to the Dodgers than the first five months. They lost a double-header to the Giants and the six-game series at Seals Stadium, five games to one.

Mr. Mays and the Giants Leave a Love Note at the Coliseum

On September 4, in the last meeting of the season between the two clubs, the Giants humiliated the Dodgers, 13–3, before a meager crowd of 12,441 at the Coliseum. The Dodgers were now mired in sixth place, 16½ games back, and sinking fast.[1] San Francisco took the 22-game season series by an overwhelming 16–6 margin.

There was one consolation for the Dodgers: Willie Mays could no longer torture them. To say good-bye, Mays hit a home run and two singles. It was the twelfth home run of the year off Dodger pitching—one short of the NL record for the most home runs against a single club. Dodger left-hander Danny McDevitt was especially relieved to see Mays leave town. When Mays singled off him in the ninth inning, he was now 9-for-9 against McDevitt for the season: two homers, two triples, two doubles, and three singles.[2]

Disaster at Philadelphia

Back on the road in Philadelphia on September 11 and desperate to avoid being swept by the last-place Phillies, Walter Alston was groping for the right combination as he started six rookies at Connie Mack Stadium. The lineup included: Bob Lillis, shortstop; Ron Fairly, center field; Norm Larker, first base; Frank Howard, left field; and Earl Robinson, third base. But the young Dodgers blew a three-run lead to lose, 4–3. Not only were the Dodgers swept in the three-game series, they also lost a game suspended since July 27, thereby surrendering the season series with the Phillies, 10 games to 12. The Dodgers were now 10 games under .500 and barely hanging on to sixth place as they escaped from Philadelphia and moved on to Pittsburgh to begin a two-game series with the Pirates the next night.[3]

A Chance Encounter with Vin Scully

While channel-surfing on an old wooden AM radio on September 12, 1958, in Los Angeles, the author had a chance encounter with Vin Scully as he broadcast a night game between the Dodgers and the Pirates from Forbes Field in Pittsburgh. It must have been the sound of the large crowd that made the author stop searching for Chuck Berry and listen to the sportscaster-poet speaking in a new language with such terms of art as "bang-bang play," "sacrifice," and "brush-back pitch," from a strange new world ruled by arbiters in black suits with such dignified titles as "Augie" (Donatelli), "Jocko" (Conlon), and "Shag" (Crawford). Even though he had never seen — or heard — a major league game before, there was something utterly compelling about that voice that painted a picture in the listener's mind of Bob Skinner at the plate "waving the wood back and forth," Ron Kline on the pitcher's mound staring in to get the sign from the catcher, "Maz" (Bill Mazeroski) performing his Nureyev-esque moves around second base while looking like a chipmunk with that enormous wad of tobacco lodged in his cheek, and a young Roberto "Bob" Clemente — before he was recognized as "The Great One" — making one of his prodigious throws from right field all the way to home plate on the fly to cut down a Dodger baserunner foolish enough to challenge his arm. The descriptions were so compelling that the sportscaster-poet-storyteller held the nine-year-old transfixed for the remainder of the game, and created another life-long Dodger fan.

The Dodgers won that game, 7–3, as Roger Craig, making his first start of the year and his first appearance in a Dodger uniform since being recalled from Triple-A St. Paul in the American Association, pitched a seven-hit complete game to break the Dodgers' three-game losing streak. Duke Snider, who was fined by Buzzie Bavasi for playing a round of golf that morning — for breaking a club rule of "no golf on a game day" — showed no ill effects as he pounded Pirates pitching for four hits, including a double, homer, and two singles, and four runs batted in.

* * *

Earlier that day in Little Rock, Arkansas, Governor Orval Foubus ordered the closing of four Little Rock high schools for the 1958-1959 academic year. His action was an angry response to the U.S. Supreme Court's unanimous decision in *Cooper v. Aaron* in which the court refused to grant the Little Rock Board of Education a 2½-year delay in the desegregation of Central High. The four Little Rock high schools would reopen — fully integrated — in the fall of 1959.[4]

* * *

Hondo Homicide Averted in Cincinnati

September 16 in Cincinnati was a baserunner's worst nightmare come true. In the sixth inning of the second game of a double-header with the Redlegs at Crosley Field, Duke Snider was leading off third base with the 6' 7" 250-pound Frank Howard standing less that 90 feet away at the plate with a bat in his hand. Snider was rendered helpless when Howard, whom his teammates called "Hondo" after the John Wayne film character, pulled one of Tom Acker's fastballs and rifled it directly at him. The ball struck Snider's right shoulder and then his right ear with a glancing blow, dropping him "as if he'd been shot by an elephant gun." A hush fell over the crowd as everyone in the park feared he was dead as he was carted off the field on a stretcher.[5]

Later at the hospital, where he was taken for precautionary x-rays, medical personnel must have questioned Snider's sanity when he told them, "I saw the ball coming off Howard's bat and I tried to duck into it so that I would take the blow on my plastic helmet."[6] Though he survived, Duke Snider was lost for the rest of the season. Hondo was not charged.

The Dodgers Collapse on the Final Day

On September 27, the 1958 season mercifully came to an end. The story of the Dodgers' last game of the season at the Coliseum was representative of their first year in Los Angeles— one of ineptitude and frustration.

With a 4–3 lead and sixth place wrapped up going into the ninth inning, the Dodgers collapsed in a heap as the Chicago Cubs batted around to score four runs on five hits and two Dodger errors that resulted in a heart-breaking 7–4 defeat. Roger Craig gave up all four earned runs to take the loss. Craig, who had won his last two starts since being recalled from the minors, came in from the bullpen to pitch two scoreless innings before his ninth-inning collapse.

The debacle dropped the Dodgers into seventh place in the National League standings with a record of 71 wins and 83 losses. It was the first time since 1944 they had played below .500 and finished lower than third place.[7] It was Walter Alston's lowest finish since he started managing professionally at Class C Portsmouth, Ohio, of the Mid-Atlantic League in 1940. Though the Dodgers were 10–15 for the month of September, they narrowly escaped finishing in the cellar thanks to a season-ending nose dive by the Philadelphia Phillies.

1958: The Lost Season

The older players looked out of place at the Coliseum as they tried in vain to adjust to the odd dimensions that caused their skills to disappear prematurely.[8] The offense — the toast of the league in Brooklyn — sputtered in the concrete bowl. As a team, the Los Angeles Dodgers finished last in the National League in several key offensive indices, including batting average, .251; hits, 1,297; and on-base percentage, .317.

With a .312 average in only 327 at-bats, Duke Snider was the only Dodger to hit over .300. Due to the 440-foot power alley at the Coliseum, his home run production plunged to 15 after five straight seasons with more than 40. Gil Hodges, who some had predicted would break Babe Ruth's single-season home run record with the cozy left-field screen in the Coliseum, hit a modest 22 home runs to tie Charlie Neal for the team lead.

At age 40, team captain Pee Wee Reese spent most of the season on the bench, and finished with a .224 average in just 59 games. Don Zimmer became the primary shortstop, batting .262 with 17 home runs, but made a glaring 23 errors in 114 games.

The Dodger pitchers tanked along with the hitters. They gave up a league-leading 173 home runs, including 101 at the Coliseum. Stocked with their usual assortment of wild young fireballers, their 855 team strikeouts led the National League for the tenth straight year, but there was a downside: they also had the most wild pitches (70) and the highest walks and hits per innings pitched ratio (WHIP 1.47). At 9–7, 22-year-old Stan Williams was the only Dodger starter to break .500. Sandy Koufax was 11–11, Johnny Podres 13–15, and Carl Erskine 4–4. After a 1–7 start, Don Drysdale recovered to finish with a 12–13 record. At the plate, he hit seven home runs, one in every 9.4 at-bats. Ace reliever Clem Labine (6–6) was second in the National League with 14 saves.

On the plus side, young catcher John Roseboro rose to the occasion after the loss of Roy Campanella, hitting .271 with 14 home runs. And despite their seventh-place finish, the Dodgers drew 1,845,556 new fans to the Los Angeles

Memorial Coliseum, an increase of more than 800,000 from their last year at Ebbets Field.

As expected, the Milwaukee Braves coasted to their second consecutive National League pennant, finishing eight games ahead of the Pittsburgh Pirates. Milwaukee played under .500 against only one club: the Los Angeles Dodgers. With a 14-games-to-8 advantage, it was evident that the Dodgers were not intimidated by the mighty Braves— a fact they would store away for next season.

The San Francisco Giants finished a surprising third, thanks to a Hall-of-Fame season by Willie Mays (who finished with a career-high .347 batting average, just shy of Richie Ashburn's .350 in the race for the NL batting title), a Rookie-of-the-Year performance by Orlando Cepeda, and a team .305 batting average and, 43-homer orgy on Dodger pitching.

A Bitter Pill

Fifty years later, 81-year-old Carl Erskine, the winning pitcher of the Dodgers' first game in Los Angeles, reflected on the catastrophe that was the 1958 season: "The Boys of Summer were really past our peak, and it was tougher for us to go to L.A. and try to reprove ourselves with all those new fans thinking we would be the same players we had always been. Finishing seventh that first year was a *bitter pill*."[9]

Chapter 12

Whither the Milwaukee Dynasty?

In 1988, the *Sporting News* named the 1957-58 Milwaukee Braves as the 12th greatest team of all-time.[1] After the Braves clinched their second consecutive National League pennant on September 21, 1958, the word "dynasty" began to be heard around the baseball world. Although the Braves were favored to repeat as world champions against the New York Yankees in the 1958 World Series, the remainder of baseball season would take some strange twists before it concluded in Milwaukee on October 9. Before turning to the 1958 Fall Classic, we will trace the history of the Milwaukee Braves, from doormat refugees from Boston in 1953 to world champions in 1957.

1953: Major League Baseball Comes to Milwaukee

After finishing in seventh place in 1952, the Boston Braves moved to Milwaukee to play the 1953 season in the elegant new County Stadium. The core of the 1953 Milwaukee Braves was made up of holdover stars from Boston (third baseman Eddie Mathews, shortstop Johnny Logan, and pitchers Warren Spahn and Lew Burdette), plus such new players as first baseman Joe Adcock (obtained from the Brooklyn Dodgers), catcher Del Crandall, and center fielder Billy Bruton.

Paced by Mathews' 47 home runs and Spahn's 23 wins (both tops in the National League), the Braves were the "surprise team" of 1953. With starters Spahn, Burdette, Johnny Antonelli, and Bob Buhl, the Braves had a world-class pitching staff that led the senior circuit with 14 shutouts and a 3.30 ERA. The 1953 Braves won 28 more games than the year before to climb from seventh to second place, 13 games behind the Brooklyn Dodgers. They drew 1,826,297 fans to County Stadium compared to 792,394 in 1952 in the dilap-

Pure elegance—the swing of Eddie Mathews. (National Baseball Hall of Fame Library, Cooperstown, N.Y.)

idated Braves Field, the largest one-year increase in baseball history until the 1958-1959 Los Angeles Dodgers.[2]

1954: Henry Aaron and the Second Base "Problem"

Second base had been a nagging problem for the Braves since the early 1950s. But after the 1953 season, Milwaukee compounded the problem by sending six players (outfielders Sid Gordon and Sam Jethroe, and pitchers Max Surkont, Curt Raydon, Fred Walters, and Larry Lasalle) and $100,000 in cash to the Pittsburgh Pirates for second baseman Danny O'Connell. To fill the void in left field created by the departure of Gordon, the Braves sent another $50,000, pitchers Johnny Antonelli and Don Liddle, catcher Ebba St. Claire, and infielder Billy Klaus to the New York Giants for aging outfielder Bobby Thomson and catcher Sammy Calderone.

The Bobby Thomson deal became a disaster for the Braves when he broke his ankle in a March exhibition game and was lost for most of the 1954 season. To rub salt in Milwaukee's wounds, Johnny Antonelli won 21 games for the Giants on their way to a world championship. But there was a silver lining: to replace Thomson, the Braves brought up a 20-year-old second baseman-turned-outfielder named Henry "Hank" Aaron. The Braves finished a disappointing third in 1954, but Aaron, their rookie right fielder, began his Hall-of-Fame career, batting .280 with the first 13 of his 755 home runs.[3]

The great Henry Aaron watching one of his 755 home runs. (National Baseball Hall of Fame Library, Cooperstown, N.Y.)

1955-1956: Bridesmaids to the Dodgers

By 1955, the Milwaukee Braves were a virtual all-star team. Unfortunately, 1955 was the year of the Brooklyn Dodgers. While the Braves had standout starting pitching with Spahn, Burdette, Buhl, and Gene Conley (a 6'8" right-hander who played basketball for the Boston Celtics in the off-season), the Dodgers had a better bullpen. Sophomore manager Walter Alston led the Dodgers to their first world championship after winning the National League by 13½ games over the second-place Braves.

Although the Braves were so confident that they made no trades after the 1955 season, they still had weaknesses, including a lack of team speed (seventh in stolen bases), the second base "problem" (Danny O'Connell was a disappointment), and a weak bullpen. By late July of 1956, the Braves were in first place with a 5½-game lead over the Dodgers. But the Dodgers surged in August, and by September, it was a see-saw pennant race down to the final weekend. The Dodgers clinched the National League pennant on the final day of the season, with the Braves again finishing in second place, this time only one game behind.

The 1956 season was a frustrating year for the Milwaukee Braves. Aaron won his first NL batting title (.328), Burdette led the league in ERA (2.70) and shutouts (6), Spahn was second in wins (20) and ERA (2.78), and Buhl had a career-high 18 wins. As a team, they had the best ERA, the third-best scoring offense, and the second-best slugging percentage, but still no pennant.[4]

1957: Finding the Missing Piece — In Red

The Braves finally solved their second base "problem" on June 15, 1957, when they traded Danny O'Connell, Bobby Thomson, and Ray Crone to the New York Giants for second baseman Red Schoendienst. The deal, put together by Milwaukee General Manager John Quinn, was closed exactly six hours before the trading deadline of midnight, June 15.[5] A perennial all-star, Schoendienst had played 11 years with the St. Louis Cardinals before being traded to the Giants in 1956. This proved to be the missing piece of the puzzle for the Braves, as the 34-year-old redhead gave them an unbeatable lineup — batting .309, hitting in 25 straight games, and leading all NL second basemen in fielding percentage.[6]

With the addition of Schoendienst, everything fell into place. Rookie Wes Covington was a sensation, stepping into Bobby Thomson's left-field position with 21 home runs in only 96 games. Henry Aaron had 44 home runs, 132 runs batted in, and a .322 batting average to win the NL Most Valuable Player award. Twenty-six minutes before midnight on September 23, he clinched the pennant with a dramatic eleventh-inning home run against the Cardinals at County Stadium.[7] Spahn won the Cy Young award with 21 wins after languishing with a 8–7 record at the All-Star break; Buhl won 18, and Burdette 17. The Braves' bullpen was greatly improved with the addition of hard-throwing right-hander Don McMahon. The Braves won the National League by eight games over the second-place St. Louis Cardinals, and broke their own league attendance record with 2,215,404 fans— their fourth straight year eclipsing the two million mark.[8]

The night the Braves clinched the pennant, manager Fred Haney attempted to distribute the credit widely: "A team effort, desire and the determination of every man won for us."[9] But a Milwaukee pitcher, requesting anonymity, was more realistic, stating, "Without Red, I don't know where we would have finished."[10] "That goes for me too," said an anonymous infielder. "Just by talking to me, Schoendienst got me out of a batting slump."[11] The Milwaukee Braves were loaded with talent, but they needed someone to take charge. Albert "Red" Schoendienst filled the bill.

When the Braves met the Yankees in the 1957 World Series, it was the first time since 1946 that a team west of New York (Red Schoendienst and the St. Louis Cardinals) had represented the National League in the Fall Classic. The 1957 Series came down to a seventh-game showdown between Lew Burdette (pitching on two days rest because Spahn had the flu) and Don Larsen (who had pitched a perfect game against the Dodgers in the last World Series). Series MVP Burdette pitched his third seven-hit victory of the Series and second straight shutout to give the Milwaukee Braves their first world championship.[12]

The Missing Piece: Red Schoendienst plugged the Braves' hole at second base to propel them into the World Series in 1957 and 1958. But he would miss all but five games (three at-bats) in 1959 due to tuberculosis. (National Baseball Hall of Fame Library, Cooperstown, N.Y.)

1958: Another Pennant and an October Setback

Despite being heavy favorites to win the 1958 National League pennant, the world champion Milwaukee Braves had to overcome adversity to repeat. Injuries caused manager Fred Haney to constantly juggle his lineup. Young phenom left fielder Wes Covington, who injured his knee in a spring exhibition game, did not play until May 2. Center fielder Billy Bruton did not return from knee surgery until late May.

The second base "problem" again reared its ugly head. Red Schoendienst missed one-third of the season, and was otherwise sub-par, due to tuberculosis that was not diagnosed until after the season. Backup second baseman Mel Roach blew out his knee on August 3, and missed the rest of the year.

Hank Aaron got off to an unusually slow start. At the end of May, the reigning National League MVP was hitting only .230 with six home runs.[13] He came on strong in the summer to turn in another outstanding season: 30 home runs, 95 runs batted in, and a .326 batting average.

The 1958 Braves would score almost 100 fewer runs, hit 32 fewer home runs, and hit for a lower team average than the year before, but they made up for the decline in offense with the best pitching in baseball. Roommates Spahn (22–11) and Burdette (20–10) were tied for the league's best winning percentage at .667. The off-season trade for veteran Cubs starter Bob Rush turned out to be a key acquisition. When starters Buhl (5–2) and Gene Conley (0–6) were sidelined with arm troubles, Rush stepped into the breach to post a 10–6 record. In addition, youngsters Joey Jay (7–5), Juan Pizarro (6–4), and rookie Carlton Willey (9–7, with a league-leading four shutouts) performed ably as spot starters.[14]

On July 30, Spahn beat the Dodgers and Sandy Koufax, 4–3, to put the Braves in first place to stay. It was the first time Spahn had beaten them since September 25, 1951 when he was a "Boston" Brave. It was also the first time the Braves had *ever* beaten Koufax after suffering four losses over three seasons. That historic game was a turning point — the start of a six-game winning streak, including a four-game sweep of the second-place Giants that left San Francisco five games behind on August 3. The pennant race was for all intents and purposes over, as the Braves played .655 (38–20) baseball for the August-September stretch drive.[15] The Braves clinched the National League pennant in game number 150, on September 21 in Cincinnati.

* * *

On September 30, 1958, the U.S. Atomic Energy Commission reported that the Soviet Union had resumed test explosions of nuclear weapons in the Arctic. Before the two detonations — of moderate to high yield — north of the Arctic Circle, the Soviets had suspended testing for six months. The U.S. and the Soviet Union were due to begin test ban talks in Geneva on October 31. The U.S. State Department announced that the Western powers were willing to suspend nuclear tests for one year after October 31, provided the Soviets did not conduct further tests after the talks began. Americans held their breath.[16]

* * *

On October 1, 1958, the Milwaukee Braves met the New York Yankees in a rematch of the 1957 World Series. The Yankees ran into the Spahn-Burdette express on a cold day at County Stadium. The Braves won the opener, 4–3, in 10 innings. Warren Spahn, who pitched all 10 innings, gave up only eight hits, including a solo home run by Bill Skowron and a two-run homer by Hank Bauer. When Spahn threw the first pitch, the temperature was 52 degrees. But when Ryne Duren, in relief of New York starter Whitey Ford, gave up the winning hit to Bill Bruton in the bottom of the tenth, the temperature had dropped into the low 40s.[17]

The next day it was Lew Burdette's turn to humiliate the Yankees. Burdette's three-run home run in the bottom of the first gave the Braves a 7–0 advantage. With a 13–2 lead, Burdette took a three-hitter into the ninth inning. He completed the game, but not before the Yankees got to him for two home runs—a solo home by Hank Bauer and a two-run shot by Mickey Mantle, his second homer of the game—to make the final score 13–5. By the end of October 2, roommates Spahn and Burdette had staked the Braves to a two games-to-none lead. Milwaukee looked like a sure bet to repeat as world champions. As the teams used the next day to travel to New York, for Game 3, the odds on the Braves winning the Series jumped from 6-to-5 to 11-to-5.[18]

On October 4 in front of 71,599 at Yankee Stadium, Hank Bauer drove in all four runs in the Yankees' 4–0 win in Game 3. The 36-year-old ex–Marine knocked in the game's first two runs with a single in the fifth off Braves starter Bob Rush. He then hit a two-run home run off Don McMahon in the seventh. It was Bauer's third home run in three games. Yankee starter Don Larsen shut out the Braves for the first seven innings on six hits. Ryne Duren no-hit the Braves over the final two innings to complete the shutout.[19]

More than 71,500 watched Warren Spahn shut out the Yankees, 3–0, on two hits at Yankee Stadium in Game 4 to give Milwaukee a three games-to-one lead in the Series. Yankee starter Whitey Ford was victimized by poor defense. Shortstop Tony Kubek let a ball go through his legs in the sixth inning, allowing the game's first run to score. In the eighth, young Yankee left fielder Norm Sieburn lost Johnny Logan's ball in the sun for a ground-rule double. Ed Mathews promptly drove him in with a legitimate double.[20]

Going into Game 5 on October 6, the Braves were one game away from being the first National League team to win consecutive World Series since the 1921-1922 New York Giants. But Bob Turley kept the Yankees alive as he out-pitched Lew Burdette to shut out the Braves, 7–0, in Yankee Stadium and send the Series back to Milwaukee.[21] After losing three games to Burdette in the 1957 Fall Classic and Game 2 four days before, the Yankees finally solved him. Gil McDougald was the hitting star with a solo home run in the third and a two-run ground-rule double in the sixth.[22]

Still up three games-to-two, the Braves only needed to win one of the last two games at home. On October 8, in Game 6, manager Fred Haney went with Warren Spahn (on two days rest) against Whitey Ford. Spahn pitched well for nine innings, and the tiring left-hander gamely took the ball to pitch the tenth inning of a 2–2 tie. Gil McDougald finished him with a lead-off home run, and the Yankees scored an insurance run off reliever Don McMahon to take a 4–2 lead. In the bottom of the tenth, the Braves fought back with one run and had runners on first and third with two out. But Stengel brought in Turley from the bullpen to retire pinch-hitter Frank Torre on a pop-up to end the game. With a 4–3 victory over the great Warren Spahn,

Left: **Due to a violent collision with Norm Larker at second base, Braves shortstop Johnny Logan was knocked out of the pivotal second 1959 playoff game with the Dodgers in the 7th inning, causing Felix Mantilla to take over his position. (National Baseball Hall of Fame Library, Cooperstown, N.Y.)** ***Right:*** **Fidgety Lew Burdette won a league-tying 21 games for the 1959 Milwaukee Braves. (National Baseball Hall of Fame Library, Cooperstown, N.Y.)**

the Yankees had battled back from a three games-to-one deficit to tie the Series and force a Game 7 the next day.[23]

On October 9, for the second straight year, the World Series between the Braves and the Yankees would be reduced to a Game 7 duel between Don Larsen and Lew Burdette. Burdette (like Spahn the day before, pitching on only two days rest) rose to the occasion, pitching brilliantly for $7\frac{2}{3}$ innings. He gave up two unearned runs in the second, both caused by errant underhand tosses to him from first baseman Frank Torre, ironically, the National League's top fielder at his position for 1958. Clinging to a 2–2 tie in the top of the eighth with two out and nobody on base, Burdette suddenly lost his command. Yogi Berra doubled off the right-field wall, and Elston Howard bounced a single through the middle to score him and give the Yankees a 3–2 lead. Even after Andy Carey lined a sharp single off Eddie Mathews' glove, Fred Haney stayed with the laboring Burdette and allowed him to face the dangerous Moose Skowron with two runners on and a chance to break the game open. After Burdette and Skowron fought a battle of fastballs and curves to a two-and-two draw, Burdette made the fatal decision to throw him a

The fearsome middle of the 1959 Milwaukee Braves lineup. Henry Aaron (left) had one of the greatest seasons in NL history: .355 batting title, 39 home runs, and 400 total bases. Eddie Mathews (center) led the majors with 46 home runs. Joe Adcock contributed 25 homers despite having two disqualified. (National Baseball Hall of Fame Library, Cooperstown, N.Y.)

changeup. As the 1957 World Series MVP watched the ball disappear over the left-center-field fence, it was too late to rethink his pitch selection. Skowron's devastating three-run home run made it 6–2 Yankees.[24] Too late to make a difference, Haney brought in Don McMahon to strike out Tony Kubek and end the inning.[25]

Bob Turley, who had entered the game in the third inning in relief of Larsen, held the Braves scoreless in the eighth and ninth innings, and was credited with the victory. His clutch 6⅔-inning, two-hit performance was Turley's third straight appearance in the Series. With two wins and a save, Turley was named the Most Valuable Player of the 1958 World Series for his 16⅓ innings of work in four games.[26]

* * *

The Milwaukee Braves had entered the 1958 World Series brimming with confidence, having won two consecutive pennants, both by eight games. But after their collapse was complete on October 9, 1958, the cries of "Break up the Braves!" subsided. Once lost, confidence would prove to be surprisingly elusive for Milwaukee. The Braves would take the same star-studded team into 1959, but they would have to struggle with a new problem: doubt.

The 1958 World Series showed the Braves were too dependent on Spahn and Burdette, who were pressed to start six of the seven games. They were badly out-hit by the Yankees. "We scored 17 runs in the first two games and 25 for the Series. That's it in a nutshell," recalled Warren Spahn.[27] The Milwaukee home run machine broke down, producing only three in seven games, compared to the Yankees' ten. Top Brave sluggers Aaron, Mathews, Covington, and Adcock failed to hit a single ball out of the park. Johnny Logan hit .120, and Eddie Mathews hit .160.

It would be a difficult off-season for the Braves. Not only would they have to live with a World Series disaster, they would be forced to absorb a blow in the form of some devastating news about their red-headed second baseman.

PART II

Ascent: From Seventh Place to World Champions

Chapter 13

Restless Winter

The winter of 1958-1959 saw a nearly 20 percent increase in the size of the United States with the addition of Alaska as the 49th state. A foreign policy crisis would erupt 90 miles off the shore of Florida, featuring a revolution in Cuba. "The Day the Music Died"— February 3, 1959 — would claim the lives of Buddy Holly, Richie Valens, and J.P. "Big Bopper" Richardson when their small plane crashed in an Iowa cornfield.[1]

* * *

It would be a restless winter for the Los Angeles Dodgers. Their new fans felt let down after they had turned out in numbers approaching two million, only to be rewarded with a seventh-place finish. As a shrewd businessman, Walter O'Malley knew he could not sustain that kind of support without improving his product. *Los Angeles Times* sports editor Paul Zimmerman summed it up the day after the 1958 season ended when he wrote, "After the fashion in which the Dodgers slipped to the depths this year and the manner in which their new-found fans supported them in spite of the horrible slump, it is not too much to expect of Walter O'Malley and his staff that they start regrouping their faltering forces immediately."[2]

Reflecting on his team's disappointing performance, Walter O'Malley confessed that the Dodger management had made a mistake in deciding to let their new fans see the legendary Brooklyn old-timers instead of starting a youth movement during the first year in Los Angeles. The Dodgers knew they had to remedy the situation in the offseason. But before they began taking the appropriate steps, the baseball world was stunned by the news from St. Louis concerning the Milwaukee Braves' second baseman.

A Blow to the Braves

On November 18, 1958, a mere 40 days after their World Series collapse, the Braves received another blow when Red Schoendienst was diagnosed with tuberculosis.[3] For most of the season, he had been plagued with colds and respiratory infections that never seemed to completely clear up. He missed 48 games, and eventually became so weak that he had to choke up more and more on the bat. He batted .262 for the season with only one home run.[4] Toward the end of the campaign, he began to complain of chest pains. On September 22, the day after the Braves clinched the pennant, and nine days before the start of the World Series, he had a chest x-ray taken. To the Braves' relief, it proved negative. He played brilliantly in all seven games of the Series. As the leadoff man, he batted .300 with nine hits, including three doubles and a triple. In Game 4, he saved Warren Spahn's shutout by making a sensational leaping catch to rob Yogi Berra of a run-scoring hit.

The chest pains persisted. In late October, he had another x-ray taken in St. Louis. This one reflected a definite change. After two positive tests, Dr. Raymond T. Martin diagnosed him with tuberculosis, the infection located in the right lung. Schoendienst was immediately admitted to Mount Saint Rose Hospital in St. Louis. The prognosis was bleak, raising the possibility that his career could be over. He would be in the hospital for at least four months, and it would be at least a year before he could resume a normal active life.[5] He would ultimately have part of his right lung surgically removed. On February 19, 1959, a tubular portion of his right lung was removed in a three-hour operation at Mount Saint Rose Hospital. Although Schoendienst had recently signed a contract with Milwaukee, hospital director Dr. William A. Werner said not only was it unlikely he would play in 1959, but that his doctors remained uncertain about 1960.[6]

Schoendienst would be sidelined for all but five token appearances—including three at-bats—in 1959.[7] "That really hurt the Braves," Roger Craig would recall in 2007. "He was a great player."[8]

The Braves Pursue Junior Gilliam

When he received the shocking news about his second baseman, Braves manager Fred Haney said, "The Braves could still win the National League pennant again without Red Schoendienst, but we might have to trade to do it."[9] Thus began the Milwaukee Braves' pursuit of the Dodgers' Jim Gilliam.

Jim Gilliam started his baseball career as a batboy for the Baltimore Elite Giants, a Negro National League team starring a roly-poly catcher called "Campy." By the time he was 16, Gilliam was in the Elite Giants' starting lineup.

As the youngest player on the team, Gilliam was nicknamed "Junior."[10] In 1951, the Brooklyn Dodgers purchased Gilliam and Joe Black from the Elite Giants for $11,000, in what Buzzie Bavasi would later call "the best deal I ever made."[11]

Bavasi refused to cave in to the pressure from Braves General Manager John McHale for Gilliam. "The Braves are the team to beat," Bavasi said at the time, "so why should we help them by dealing Gilliam? Junior is three men-in-one. He hits both ways, he can play infield or outfield, and he's probably the best lead-off hitter in baseball."[12] Junior Gilliam would be a key player for the 1959 Los Angeles Dodgers with a league-leading 96 walks, 23 stolen bases, 91 runs scored, and a .282 batting average as their lead-off hitter. On defense, the versatile Gilliam solved a chronic Dodger infield problem by playing third base.

The Braves' failure to acquire Gilliam would haunt them during the 1959 season. Fred Haney would be forced to platoon seven different men at second base, including such marginal players as Felix Mantilla, Chuck Cottier, Johnny O'Brien, Casey Wise, and Bobby Avila. *Los Angeles Times* sports editor Paul Zimmerman would later say, "The Braves probably would have coasted to their third straight pennant with Gilliam."[13]

Looking back over his career, Buzzie Bavasi would say of Gilliam, "Funny thing about Gilliam: he was on the trading block every year since we got him. It gives me great pleasure to report that we never even came close. I'd hate to think what our record would have been without him."[14]

The Dodgers Shoot for the Moon

On December 4, 1958, the Dodgers made a trade that would help reverse their fortunes. They sent outfielder Gino Cimoli to the St. Louis Cardinals in exchange for outfielder Wally Moon and young pitcher Phil Paine. Years later, Buzzie Bavasi would sum up the importance of the trade, saying, "If ever there was a pennant deal in the whole history of baseball, it had to be the one for Wally Moon."[15] Nearly fifty years later, Roger Craig would recall, "The trade for Moon was a big factor in 1959."[16]

Cimoli was a personal favorite of General Manager Buzzi Bavasi. But Bavasi did not let that interfere with his better judgment.[17] In hindsight, Bavasi explained his reasoning, "I realized I was giving up a good player in Cimoli, and that Moon's elbow was a question mark. But Moon had had four fine seasons with St. Louis before he was hurt and I just couldn't believe that he was through. Besides, he used to murder our pitchers."[18] It was a classic case of "if you can't get him out, sign him up."

The right-handed-batting Cimoli hit .293 for the 1957 Brooklyn Dodgers.

But during the 1958 season, when he began to be platooned, the disgruntled Cimoli had told Alston to "play me or trade me." For 1958, in 109 games, the 29-year-old Cimoli hit just .246 and managed only nine home runs despite the cozy left-field screen in the Los Angeles Coliseum. At Major League Baseball's winter meetings in Washington, D.C., the Dodgers were clearly looking for someone to provide more pop and less popping off.

At 28, the left-handed-batting Moon had a rare off-year in 1958 in which he batted only .238 with seven home runs. After the aggressive Moon injured his elbow crashing into a wall at mid-season, he rode the bench as Cards manager Freddie Hutchinson played Curt Flood and Joe Cunningham. Moon had been the Rookie of the Year in 1954 and averaged .298 for his first four seasons.[19]

As Walter Alston analyzed the Dodgers' new acquisition, he noted, "Moon isn't a great defensive outfielder, but I know he can play left field in the Coliseum. He's aggressive, he can run, and what I like most about him is his power." It was evident the Dodgers were looking to create a new aggressive style of play.[20]

With the St. Louis Cardinals, Wally Moon had the reputation for coming through under pressure. When he broke in as a raw rookie in 1954, the Cardinals had just traded St. Louis favorite Enos "Country" Slaughter to the Yankees. When Moon was announced to bat for the first time on Opening Day, the fans chanted, "We want Slaughter! We want Slaughter!" Moon answered by hitting a home run in his first major league at-bat.[21]

Wally Moon, M.S. for "Moon Shots"

Trading the right-handed-hitting Gino Cimoli for the left-handed-hitting Moon — a graduate of Texas A&M with a master of science degree in education — was controversial. Right field in the Coliseum was a graveyard for fly balls in 1958. But not only would Moon bring speed and aggressiveness, he would develop a new swing for lofting "Moon Shots" over the left-field screen. "We knew from the way he hit us in St. Louis that he could hit the ball to left field," Roger Craig recalled, "but he learned to 'inside-out' the ball to hit that left-field screen. And he worked at it all day long in batting practice."[22] Moon explained how he adapted his swing for his new environment: "I decided to shoot for the screen with what I call a calculated slice. It's simply a matter of bringing your hands closer to your body and slightly delaying your swing. You keep the bat cocked for a split second after the hands have begun to move, and at the last possible moment you flip the barrel of the bat at the ball."[23] Moon's new "inside-out" swing would produce results for the Dodgers in 1959.

The Dodgers Lose Their Captain

On December 18, 1958, the Dodgers' 40-year-old team captain Harold "Pee Wee" Reese announced his retirement as a player, and accepted a job as a Los Angeles coach for 1959.

Reese had been the Dodgers' shortstop since before World War II. After two years in the minors with the Louisville Colonels in the Red Sox organization, Brooklyn Dodgers General Manager Larry MacPhail purchased "The Little Colonel" to replace legendary Leo Durocher as the Dodger shortstop for the 1940 season. Interrupted by three years in the military during World War II, Reese spent his entire 16-year career with the Dodgers. He played in seven World Series and was chosen for nine all-star teams.

Wally Moon, acquired in a key trade with the Cardinals the previous December, brought a new aggressive style of play to the 1959 Dodgers. He developed an inside-out swing to loft "Moon Shots" over the left-field screen at the Coliseum, contributing 19 home runs and a .302 batting average. (George Brace photograph)

Reese was the regular Dodger shortstop until 1957, when injuries forced him to turn the position over to Charlie Neal. He played in only 59 games and batted .224 in his final season of 1958, as Don Zimmer took over shortstop and Charlie Neal moved to second base.[24]

The loss to the Dodgers was difficult to measure. Though his skills had eroded, his field leadership was irreplaceable. Through years of ownership changes, roller-coaster pennant races, playoff debacles, and the storm of racial integration, he was their one constant, their anchor. He was the peacemaker between factions—black and white, northern and southern, regular and bench. Pee Wee Reese was the glue that held the Dodgers together. He stayed in the clubhouse for hours after every game talking baseball, teaching, unifying the team.[25]

After their descent to seventh place in their first year in Los Angeles without their rock behind the plate, the Dodgers now faced the 1959 season without their leader on the field.

* * *

The New Year broke with disturbing news from Cuba. On January 1, 1959, bearded Cuban revolutionaries, led by rebel leader Fidel Castro, took over the capital city of Havana. Dictator Fulgencio Batista resigned as president of Cuba and fled with 400 members of his regime to exile in the Dominican Republic.[26] Three weeks before, Major Ernesto "Che" Guevara led rebel forces in the decisive battle at Las Villas, 150 miles from Havana. It was there that Guevara defeated the last remnants of Batista's army. Castro proclaimed Dr. Manuel Urrutia, a former judge of Cuba's Urgency Court, as provisional president of Cuba. Urrutia named Fidel Castro Ruz, the 32-year-old lawyer and leader of the revolution, as head of the armed forces.[27] Castro, who promised to immediately restore the constitutional guarantees suspended by Batista during the two-year rebellion, claimed to have no interest in power, stating, "Power does not interest me, and I will not take it. From now on, the people are entirely free."[28]

The western world initially welcomed Castro's victory over the cruel and corrupt Batista regime. Six days after Castro's takeover of Havana, and after his assurances that the new Cuban government would honor its international agreements, the U.S. State Department sent a letter of recognition to President Urrutia.[29]

Move in the Fences!

On January 9, 1959, Duke Snider received a belated Christmas present when the Dodgers announced their decision to shorten the center-field and right-center-field fences in the Los Angeles Memorial Coliseum. The distance from home plate to dead-center field was reduced from 425 feet to 410 feet. The right-center-field "power alley" was cut down from a near-impossible 440 feet to a more-humane 385 feet.

General Manager Buzzie Bavasi explained the rationale for the changes: "Except for left field, which we can't do anything about, the new measurements are an approximate average of the other seven parks in the league."[30]

Of Snider's 15 home runs hit in 1958, only six were hit at the Coliseum. The chain-link fence in right field proved to be his nemesis. He failed to clear it, hitting three out to dead center and three over the 42-foot screen in left.

Of the 193 home runs hit at the Coliseum in 1958, the Dodgers hit 92 and their opponents clubbed 101. Only eight homers were hit to right field, including five by the Dodgers: Charlie Neal (2), Norm Larker (2), and John Roseboro (1).[31]

Good News from the California Supreme Court

On January 13, 1959, the California Supreme Court unanimously upheld the contract between the City of Los Angeles and the Los Angeles Dodgers for the construction of a new stadium in Chavez Ravine. The 21-page opinion written by Chief Justice Phillip S. Gibson and joined by the six other justices pronounced the contract valid as serving a proper "public purpose."

The court thereby granted the Writ of Prohibition sought by the City of Los Angeles to prevent Judge Praeger and the Superior Court from:

1. enforcing a preliminary injunction enjoining the carrying out of the contract; and
2. taking further action to enjoin certification of the June 3, 1958, referendum in which the voters ratified the contract.

A jubilant Walter O'Malley announced that "of course" the Dodgers were pleased with the decision, and that work would start within 30 days in Chavez Ravine in order to have his new stadium ready for the opening of the 1960 season.

But not all parties to the controversy were in a mood to celebrate. Opposing counsel Phil Silver told reporters, "I am going to file a petition for a hearing before the United States Supreme Court!"[32]

CHAPTER 14

A Voice in the Wilderness

ON MARCH 18, 1959, President Eisenhower signed a bill from Congress making Hawaii the 50th state. At the same time, he commissioned a new 50-star American flag with the stars arranged in nine alternate staggered rows of five and six stars each, making it the twentieth different design since the United States was formed.[1]

* * *

Spring Training 1959: The Experts Predict More of the Same

Before the 1959 season began, no one gave the Dodgers a chance. UPI polled 50 baseball experts, asking them to predict the pennant winners. Not one picked the Los Angeles Dodgers to win the National League pennant. The Dodgers were picked to finish fifth behind Milwaukee, San Francisco, Pittsburgh, and Cincinnati.[2] *New York Times* sportswriter John Drebinger also picked the Dodgers to finish fifth,[3] and the oddsmakers on Broadway picked them to finish sixth, 25–1 to win the pennant.

A Lone Voice in the Wilderness

There was one unusual "expert" who went against the tide: Peter Hurkos, one of the foremost psychics of the twentieth century. Hurkos was a former Dutch house painter whose life was changed when he fell 35 feet from a ladder and suffered a brain injury from a fractured skull in 1941. After three days in a coma, he regained consciousness to discover that he had developed psychometry: the ability to see past-present-future associations by touching objects. After his fall, he gained worldwide acceptance as a psychic by working on famous cases involving missing persons and murder victims, such as "The Boston Strangler Multiple Murders," which he cracked by pressing a photograph of a victim against his forehead.[4]

In February 1959, *Parade Magazine* hired Hurkos to visit Major League Baseball's spring training camps to use his gift to predict the pennant winners. Hurkos had never seen a baseball game. After being cajoled into actually watching a Grapefruit League game, he asked White Sox manager Al Lopez, "When you see somebody with a stick knock with the ball, he runs away like crazy and then another guy runs to another corner. For what?"[5]

When practicing psychometry, Hurkos would focus for about ten minutes on his subject. Such intense bursts of concentration, during which he would break out in a sweat, left him exhausted. Consequently, he refused to switch on his psychic "current" more than three times per day.

In St. Petersburg, Florida, Milwaukee Braves catcher Del Crandall was getting dressed after an exhibition game. Hurkos, who had never heard of Crandall or the Braves, came into the clubhouse to observe him. After several minutes of strenuous concentration while observing Crandall try on different neckties, Hurkos staggered out into the fresh air, overcome with psychic radiations. "This is a magic team," he said. "Perfectionists, I get a terrific feeling Milwaukee will be at the top most of the year. But in the last days they will lose the flag to the Los Angeles Dodgers." In light of the Dodgers' seventh-place finish in 1958 and the experts' dismal forecast for 1959, rational people did a double-take. But Hurkos was even more certain after sitting between Duke Snider and Clem Labine on the Dodger bench in Tampa to feel their "radiations."[6]

* * *

On February 16, 1959, in Havana, Fidel Castro, despite his previous public denunciations of power, took over direct control of the Cuban government. After Premier Jose Miro Cardona was forced to resign along with his cabinet, Castro assumed the premiership. His 27-year-old brother, Raul Castro, replaced him as commander of the armed forces.

The 32-year-old Castro reassured the Cuban people that he did not aspire to be president, and maintained that provisional President Urrutia and the cabinet had approved a new law lowering the minimum age for president from 35 to 30. He said the executions of former members of the Batista regime as "war criminals" would continue. According to Castro, the death penalty would be applied against anyone who attempted to establish a tyranny.[7]

* * *

Alston in Florida: From Sober to Optimistic

Two days later, and 300 miles west of Havana, when Walter Alston arrived at Dodgertown in Vero Beach, Florida, with the pitchers and catchers on February 18, 1959, he was not as enthusiastic as the Dutch psychic. Speaking to reporters at the opening press conference, he did not once utter the word "pennant." "I'm not going to say anything specific about where I expect the club to finish," he said. "I've got to think we're better than a seventh-place club, but last year you'll recall, I thought we had the best pitching in the National League — but it didn't work out that way."[8]

Alston promised to impose the discipline lacking on the team in the distraction-filled opening season in Los Angeles. "There was too much horsing around last year for the good of the club, and we're going to do all we can to correct it."[9] The mild-mannered ex–school teacher could be as tough as a Marine drill sergeant when the circumstances required it. He handed out several fines in 1958, including two for the "playboy antics" of bachelors Don Newcombe and Johnny Podres, who were temporarily blinded by the bright lights of Chicago. Drawing on his teaching skills as a disciplinarian of children, he had to fine Duke Snider, who the Dodgers were counting on to hit baseballs out of the Coliseum, for trying to *throw* one out of the concrete oval.[10]

Seven weeks later, on April 9, 1959, when the Dodgers completed their 1959 exhibition game schedule atop the National League with an unexpected 13–10 record, Alston's outlook had changed. "The Dodgers have made me optimistic," he told reporters two days before Opening Day. "Everybody has worked harder this spring. The general attitude is much better than it was last year."[11] To Alston, the 1959 Dodgers were a new team, a team on a mission. "That seventh-place finish undoubtedly hurt the pride of a team that's been up in the race for so many years," Alston said.[12] But exhibition games do not make a baseball season. In two days, when the Dodgers opened the regular season against the reigning National League MVP Ernie Banks and the Chicago Cubs at Wrigley Field, they would begin the real test.

Back to the Minors

The previous September the Dodgers recalled Roger Craig from St. Paul after his American Association–leading 17 losses. His shoulder had improved and he made three starts for the Dodgers, posting a 2–1 record. But on March 30, 1959, after only one spring training appearance and with another sore arm, he was cut from the roster and sent down to the Pacific Coast League along with fellow pitcher Bob Giallombardo. "Buzzie Bavasi told me I was optioned to Spokane," recalled Craig. "Spokane manager Bobby Bragan told me I was going to pitch on Opening Day, so Giallombardo and I drove together all the way from Vero Beach to Spokane. My wife was pregnant at the time."[13]

Three days later, on April 2, 1959, the Dodgers sent inconsistent right-hander Larry Sherry to Triple-A St. Paul in the American Association.[14] But Sherry would show immediate signs of improvement as he won his first three minor league starts, striking out 26 batters in 26 innings.

Plucking Sam Jones from the Cardinals before the 1959 season was a key acquisition for the Giants. "Sad Sam" tied Spahn and Burdette for the NL lead with 21 wins and took the ERA title with a 2.82 mark. (National Baseball Hall of Fame Library, Cooperstown, N.Y.)

The Giants Get Sad Sam

Just as the Dodgers' December acquisition of Wally Moon from the Cardinals would prove to be a key move, the Giants made their own trade with St. Louis that would make them a sure-fire pennant contender. As spring training was winding down on March 25, they acquired 33-year-old flame-throwing right-hander "Sad Sam" Jones from the Cardinals. In 1958, Jones won 14 games, led the league with 225 strikeouts in 250 innings, and was second to the Giants' Stu Miller in ERA, 2.88 to 2.47. Known as one of the game's true characters—chomping on a perpetual toothpick while on the mound—Sad Sam did not come cheap. The Giants had to give up first baseman Bill White, who went on to become a perennial all-star and National League president in 1989.

After ranking fourth in 1958, the Giants' pitching staff suddenly looked like a candidate to be considered best in the National League. In December, they acquired right-hander Jack Sanford from the Phillies. Though he had a mediocre 10–13 year in 1958, Sanford had been Rookie of the Year in 1957 with 19 wins. Giants manager Bill Rigney now had a well-balanced starting staff: three top right-handed starters in Stu Miller, Sam Jones, and Jack Sanford, and two top left-handers in Johnny Antonelli and Mike McCormick. With improved pitching, combined with their established offensive firepower, the Giants were in position to challenge Milwaukee.

Chapter 15

Spring Roller Coaster: April in First, May in Despair

In the spring of 1959, the United States would experience the duplicity of Cuban Premier Fidel Castro. Armed with 100 cases of "good-will rum," he arrived in Washington, D.C., on April 15 to cries of "Viva Castro" from about 1,500 Cuban refugees at National Airport.[1] The stated purpose of his 11-day unofficial visit was "to better understand the United States." In a speech before the Senate Foreign Relations Committee, Castro attempted to ease U.S. fears by declaring, "The July 26 movement is not a Communist movement. We have no intention of expropriating U.S. property, and any property we take we'll pay for."[2]

A month later in Havana, he signed an agrarian-reform decree that effectively outlawed the $300 million U.S. direct foreign investment in Cuban sugar. Under the new law, no corporation could own land in Cuba unless all stockholders were Cuban. If U.S. sugar companies did not sell out within a year, their land would be expropriated, and they would be paid from $15 to $45 per acre, barely one-fourth what the land was worth before the revolution.[3]

* * *

April: The Dodgers Hit; The Dodgers Win

The Dodgers carried their spring training success into the regular season. Despite a cold start (their April 10 opener was snowed out in Chicago, and Don Drysdale was drubbed, 6–1, by the Cubs the next day at Wrigley Field in 42-degree weather), the Dodgers turned to a baseball fundamental to produce a solid April: they hit the baseball. For the month, the Dodgers hit .282 as a team, compared to .239 in April 1958. Six Dodgers hit over .300: Moon (.352), Neal (.338), Fairly (.324), Demeter (.317), Furillo (.316), and Snider (.314).[4] With Duke Snider's knee reducing his mobility, the Dodgers relied on an obscure minor leaguer, Don Demeter, to play center field, and moved Snider to right. Surprisingly, Demeter became their top run producer with six home runs (2nd in NL) and 21 RBIs (1st in NL).

Moon Brings Aggressiveness

In addition to being the Dodgers' top hitter (.352), Wally Moon made the team more aggressive on the bases. On the last day of April, Moon was thrown out trying to steal home. Moon explained the reasoning behind his risk-taking style, saying, "This is a running ball club, and I noticed in the last few games that the opposing outfielders' heads are popping up when ground balls are hit to them with men on base. They're so concerned with the runners that they take their eyes off the ball. That will produce some errors and some runs for L.A."[5]

Drysdale's Strong Start

Don Drysdale anchored the Dodger pitching for the month of April. After losing the opener in the cold in Wrigley Field, Drysdale (3–1) reeled off three straight wins. Johnny Klippstein (3–0) picked up three wins in relief. Hard-luck Sandy Koufax (0–0) had three starts and three no-decisions.

After a dismal (6–16) record against the Giants in 1958, the Dodgers took two out of three from San Francisco in their first series— ending April 22 — at the Coliseum. Don Demeter won the second game in the 11th inning with his third home run of the game.

Off to a Good Start

With an 11–6 record, the Dodgers ended April in a virtual tie for first with Milwaukee. Of their first seven series, they won five and split two.

	W	*L*	*Pct.*	*
Milwaukee	9	4	.692	—
Los Angeles	11	6	.647	—
San Francisco	9	7	.563	1½

*Games behind leader

May: A Losing Month Precipitates a Crisis

After winning or tying every series in April, the Dodgers lost their first two series in May — on the road in Cincinnati (3 games to 1) and in Milwaukee (2 games to 1).

A-A-R-O-N Spells Trouble

The Dodgers were 1–4 for the month of May with the defending NL champion Milwaukee Braves. They lost a three-game series in Milwaukee, two games to one. In the second game, Drysdale went 11 innings for a no-decision before Henry Aaron doubled off Clem Labine (0–3) in the 16th to beat the Dodgers three minutes before the 1:00 A.M. curfew in a 4-hour, 47-minute game.[6]

Led by a torrid Aaron, who was having a career year, the Braves then swept a two-game series at the Coliseum. Aaron had two home runs and four RBIs off Danny McDevitt in the first game as Buhl shut them out, 6–0, before 73,898.[7] In the second game, Burdette needed only 84 pitches to beat Drysdale and the Dodgers, 8–3, in front of 49,347 fans. Aaron — by then batting .484 — hit his third homer of the series against Drysdale.[8]

Roy Campanella Night May 7—The Dodgers, Yankees, and 93,103 Fans Honor Campy

In an unusual bifurcated "double-header," the Dodgers played an official league day game in San Francisco, flew down to Los Angeles for a night exhibition game with the New York Yankees to honor Roy Campanella, before flying right back to San Francisco to resume their four-game series with the Giants.

In the afternoon, big right-hander Stan Williams pitched the Dodgers into third place with a complete-game 2–1 victory over the Giants at Seals Stadium. Norm Larker hit a two-run homer in the fourth inning off an 0–2 pitch from Giants starter Jack Sanford to account for the Dodgers' only runs. Larker replaced Gil Hodges in the first after he injured his neck while running out a 405-foot triple.

The great Willie Mays was a one-man show for the Giants, but committed a fatal blunder late in the game. Of the six hits given up by Williams, Mays ripped him for a single, double, and triple, stole two bases, and scored the Giants' only run. But in the eighth inning while Williams was walking him intentionally with two runners on base, Mays impulsively tried to hit a wide pitch and fouled out to end the rally. The San Francisco fans showered him with boos.[9]

That evening in Los Angeles, a record crowd of 93,103 jammed into the Memorial Coliseum to watch the Los Angeles Dodgers and New York Yankees pay tribute to Roy Campanella in an exhibition game.[10] The crowd shattered the former major league attendance record of 86,288, set October 10, 1948, in the fifth game of the World Series between the Cleveland Indians and the Boston Braves in Cleveland's Municipal Stadium.[11] Los Angeles Fire Department observers estimated that at least 15,000 people were turned away after the crowd overflowed onto the playing field. When 10,000 general admission tickets went on sale before the game, a "near riot" ensued as 30,000 fans converged on two ticket windows at the peristyle end of the Coliseum. Ticket sales had to be stopped three times so that police could push back the people. The Los Angeles Police Department dispatched 43 motorcycle officers, all available squad cars, and dozens of foot patrolmen to maintain control—all this for Roy Campanella, a player Californians had never seen play.[12]

Roy Campanella received a thunderous ovation when his old pal, Pee Wee Reese, wheeled him out to second base for the pre-game ceremonies. A visibly moved Campy told the hushed crowd, "I want to thank each and every one of you from the bottom of my heart for the wonderful tribute, and I thank God that I'm here, living, to be here to see it."[13]

At the end of the fifth inning, Campy was again wheeled to the center of the infield for a unique tribute. The Coliseum was pitched into darkness as house lights were turned off. Master of ceremonies Vin Scully then asked each person in the multitude to light a candle of hope with a match or cigarette lighter. It was a stunning sight. For a full minute the cavernous bowl became a mass of flickering fireflies. When the lights came back on, Roy Campanella received a final ovation of love and support.

The game, won by the Yankees, 6–2, meant nothing to either team.[14] To participate, the Dodgers interrupted their important four-game series in San Francisco with the Giants, and the Yankees gave up two off-days.

In addition to the travel burden, the Dodgers incurred an additional unforeseen cost. In the seventh inning, Dodger outfielder Carl Furillo, batting .300 for the season, was called on to pinch-hit against fireballing Yankee right-hander Ryne Duren. Duren was an intimidating presence on the mound, squinting through Coke-bottle-lens glasses, with a near-100 MPH fastball, and a reputation for wildness. One of Duren's wayward missiles struck Furillo in the ribs, putting him out of action for more than a month, not to return until June 11.[15]

Mid-Month Roller Coaster

From May 7 to May 12, the Dodgers went on a modest run, winning five games out of six. They went on to take three of the four games from the

Giants at Seals Stadium, and swept a two-game series from the Phillies at the Coliseum to complete a four-game winning streak. On May 12, the anniversary of their descent to the cellar in 1958, the Dodgers even moved into first place by a half-game over the Milwaukee Braves. But the Dodgers then did an immediate about-face, losing five straight to the Pirates, Braves, and Reds to drop back to fourth place on May 18, 4½ games behind the first-place Braves, who would remain at the top of the National League standings for the rest of May.

May 26—A Dark Night for Lefties

On May 26, a cold Tuesday night at Seals Stadium in San Francisco, the Dodgers and Giants collided for the fifth consecutive day. This was common in the pre-expansion era, since each of the eight teams in the National League would play one another 22 times over the 154-game season. The second-place Giants had just dropped the Dodgers into fourth place by taking two out of three over the weekend at the cavernous Los Angeles Coliseum. And the Dodgers had been lucky to salvage game one, 2–1, in 13 innings Friday night, thanks to a marathon complete game by Don Drysdale, who threw 172 pitches over 3 hours and 34 minutes.

Monday night, the bitter rivalry moved to tiny Seals Stadium, where Dodger left-hander Johnny Podres halted his team's slide with a brilliant two-hit, 8–0 shutout supported by two home runs and four runs batted in by Gil Hodges. But that still left the Dodgers in a third-place tie with the Pirates, 3½ games behind the league-leading Milwaukee Braves and a half-game behind the Giants as the enigmatic 23-year-old left-hander, Sandy Koufax, took the mound for the Dodgers against the Giants' "junkman," Stu Miller.

Koufax had already made four ineffective starts, resulting in no-decisions. Tonight he was on his game, turning in one of the best pitching and batting performances of his young career. The first Giant run he allowed was unearned—the result of bad luck. When he walked Willie Mays with two out in the first, he coaxed reigning National League Rookie of the Year Orlando Cepeda to pop up. But Mays scored as Dodger second baseman Charlie Neal dropped the ball. The Dodger left-hander made his only mistake in the fifth, as journeyman shortstop Andre Rodgers made Koufax pay with a solo home run. Despite coming into the game with only one extra-base hit in his four-year career, Koufax hit two doubles and scored the Dodgers' fourth and final run in the sixth. By then it was clear, this was his night.

Koufax appeared to be getting stronger as he entered the bottom of the ninth with a 4–2 lead. He had blown away 10 Giants on strikes, including six of the last nine batters he faced. He struck out the dangerous Cepeda, the

Giants' lead-off batter, to move to within two outs of his first victory of the season. Ominously, he issued his third walk to left fielder Jackie Brandt. He then got Felipe Alou on a pop foul, but more bad luck intervened as Dodger catcher Joe "Piggy" Pignatano failed to make the play behind the plate. Given new life, the clutch-hitting Alou blooped a single to left, putting the tying runs on base with one out. The Koufax misfortunes continued as he failed to get the call on a close 3–2 pitch to second baseman Daryl Spencer, thereby loading the bases. Lacking confidence in Sandy Koufax at this stage in his career, Dodger manager Walter Alston panicked, and brought in veteran right-handed reliever Art Fowler to face right-handed-hitting catcher Bob Schmidt. With Koufax finally gone, Giants manager Bill Rigney countered by sending up dangerous left-handed pinch-hitter Leon Wagner. Fowler got ahead in the count as his first pitch was a called strike, but his next pitch produced a most unwelcome sound familiar to all pitchers: the sickening "crack" of wood colliding with horsehide. "Daddy Wags" connected with a fastball, launching a towering drive high over the 378-foot sign before it disappeared deep into the right-field bleachers.[16]

Orlando Cepeda was NL Rookie of the Year in 1958. The Baby Bull hit .317 with 27 home runs for the 1959 Giants. (National Baseball Hall of Fame Library, Cooperstown, N.Y.)

It was a shattering blow to Koufax and the Dodgers. Instead of recording his first win — an 11-strikeout victory — Sandy Koufax's first 1959 decision was transformed into a devastating loss. A Dodger win would have given them a two-game sweep on the road against the Giants and propelled them into second place. But as the result of one swing of the bat, they remained mired in fourth place.

Sandy Koufax was not the only National League pitcher to suffer a crushing defeat on this night. Some 1,700 miles away in Milwaukee, fellow left-hander Harvey Haddix would make baseball history before succumbing to his own cruel fate in the 13th inning at County Stadium.

As a rookie with the St. Louis Cardinals in 1953, Harvey Haddix appeared headed for greatness with a 20–9 record, including six shutouts. Since Haddix looked even smaller than his actual 5' 9" and 160 pounds, his Cardinal teammates nicknamed him "the Kitten" because of his physical resemblance to former Cardinal pitcher Harry "the Cat" Brecheen.[17] Now at the age of 33, he was a drifting journeyman, pitching for his fourth different team in four years. Some said that he had lost the "zip" on his fastball.[18]

When the Pirates arrived in Milwaukee a few hours before the game, their scheduled starter, Haddix, was suffering from cold and flu symptoms. He checked into the hotel and went straight to bed. After a few hours of sleep, he attempted to rally and arrived at County Stadium only to find severe weather, including threatening skies, gusty winds, and flashes of lightning in the distance.[19]

Harvey Haddix would be facing the most powerful lineup in baseball, featuring such renowned sluggers as Hank Aaron, Eddie Mathews, Joe Adcock, Wes Covington, Andy Pafko, and Del Crandall. The reigning National League champion Braves, currently in first place by three games over San Francisco, had feasted on Haddix during his career, beating him four consecutive times. Haddix had not pitched a complete game against them in eight starts, since September 14, 1956. But it soon became evident that Haddix was enjoying a turnaround of historic proportions against his nemesis.

By the end of the fifth inning, Haddix was aware that he was pitching a no-hitter, but he thought he might have walked a batter.[20] His teammates provided no confirmation of a perfect game, as by tradition and superstition, they ignored him in the Pirate dugout.

In the bottom of the seventh, a steady drizzle caused many of the 19,194 fans to head for cover. But the determined Haddix ignored the conditions and again retired the Braves in order, including the dangerous duo of Mathews and Aaron.[21]

In the top of the ninth, the Pirates desperately tried to give Haddix a run. After Lew Burdette retired the lead-off batter, Dick Schofield, Bill Virdon singled. The Braves' fidgety right-hander then got Smoky Burgess to fly out. Rocky Nelson, playing first base in place of long-ball hitter Dick Stuart, singled Virdon to third base. The left-hand-hitting Bob Skinner, Pittsburgh's leading hitter the year before with a .321 average, came to the plate needing a hit to give Haddix a chance to be the winning pitcher. But the Braves had their infield positioned perfectly for Skinner, who hit a sharp grounder directly at first baseman Joe Adcock. Adcock did not have to move as he fielded the ball and stepped on the bag for the third out. Harvey Haddix would enter the bottom of the ninth with a perfect game, but without a chance to win.[22]

It was impossible for Haddix to have forgotten the last time he entered the ninth inning with a no-hitter, on August 5, 1953. On that day Richie Ashburn of the Philadelphia Phillies ruined the Cardinal rookie's no-hitter with a lead-off single. But tonight he overcame any negative thoughts, and again retired the Braves in order.[23]

By the end of regulation, Haddix had retired all 27 batters he faced over nine innings— a perfect game. But perfect wasn't good enough; he had achieved only a tie. In the opposite dugout, Braves ace right-hander and 1957 World Series MVP Lew Burdette was also pitching brilliantly, surviving multiple hits to shut out the Pirates through nine innings. Thus, it was still a scoreless tie after nine.

Haddix continued to mesmerize the Braves, pitching inning after inning of perfect baseball until he had completed a staggering 12 frames: 36 batters up, 36 batters down. No pitcher in history had ever gone more than nine innings without allowing a baserunner, nor had anyone ever pitched more than 10⅔ hitless innings in a single game.[24] There had been only seven perfect games in major league history, including Don Larsen's masterpiece in the 1956 World Series. There had not been a perfect game pitched in the National League since 1880. Burdette, who eventually gave up a total of 12 hits, continued to deftly pitch out of trouble, throwing his own remarkable shutout through 13 innings. After 12 perfect innings, Pirates manager Danny Murtaugh suggested to Haddix that he retire for the evening and allow the Pittsburgh bullpen to take over. But Harvey talked him out it; he was determined to complete the game.

Despite the little left-hander's resolve, things finally came to a head in the bottom of the 13th inning. Young Braves second baseman Felix Mantilla, who had replaced Johnny O'Brien in the eleventh and was destined to play a crucial role in Milwaukee's fortunes at the end of the season, was the lead-off batter. Haddix thought he had struck him out looking, but home plate umpire Vinnie Smith refused to give him the call. On the next pitch, Mantilla hit a routine ground ball to Pirate third baseman Don Hoak. Hoak fielded the ball cleanly but threw wildly to first base, where first baseman Rocky Nelson could not scoop it out of the dirt. Hoak's throwing error destroyed the perfect game and allowed Mantilla to reach first base, making him the first Braves baserunner. Desperate for a run, Braves manager Fred Haney had the eventual 1959 home run champion, Eddie Mathews, lay down a sacrifice bunt to advance Mantilla, the potential winning run, to second base. Haddix, who still had an unprecedented 12-inning no-hitter, then intentionally — and wisely — walked Henry Aaron, who entered the game with a frightening .453 batting average.

And the Holocaust Was Complete

With two on and one out, and slugging first baseman Joe Adcock coming to the plate, those remaining of the initial 19,194 fans at chilly and damp

County Stadium were about to witness one the most bizarre endings in baseball history. After taking ball one, Joe Adcock connected with what Harvey Haddix later called his only bad pitch of the night, a hanging slider, and drove it over the right-center-field fence.[25] In his autobiography, *I Had a Hammer*, Hank Aaron describes what unfolded, "Adcock hit a long drive to deep right center that I knew was not going to be caught. When I saw Felix cross home plate to end the game, I stepped on second base, and turned back toward the dugout. What I hadn't realized was that ball cleared the fence for a home run. Adcock kept running, but when he passed me on the bases, he was called out."[26]

The chaotic scene on the field became clear in retrospect. Adcock, who thought he had hit a game-winning three-run home run, was declared out by head umpire Frank Dascoli, and awarded only a double after he passed Aaron between second and third. The jubilant Aaron, after seeing Mantilla score the winning run and not seeing the ball clear the right-field fence in the darkness of poorly lit County Stadium, cut across the diamond without touching third base. His run was permitted to count, however, after Fred Haney, the stage director of this baseball comedy, sent him back onto the field to touch third base and then home plate. Adcock's run was nullified—his fourth home run of the season erased from the record book. He would "lose" another home run at the Los Angeles Coliseum in the heat of the September pennant race.

Harvey Haddix's performance of May 26, 1959, in Milwaukee has been called the greatest baseball game ever pitched. He needed only 104 pitches to complete 12 perfect innings. Until the twelfth inning, he was never behind a single batter in the count. But the thirteenth turned into a cascading tragedy for Haddix. After 12 perfect innings—in a matter of minutes—he lost the longest perfect game in history; he lost the longest no-hitter in history; he lost his shutout; and finally, he lost the game. It was as if F. Scott Fitzgerald was describing Harvey Haddix's fate 24 years before it happened when he wrote the haunting last line of the penultimate chapter of *The Great Gatsby*: "And the holocaust was complete."[27]

In a strange twist of fate, after Haddix retired 36 Braves batters in a row, the Milwaukee Braves had escaped with a 2–0 win. Thanks to a nearly unnoticed 13-inning, 12-hit shutout by Lew Burdette, they maintained their three-game lead over the Giants, and increased their lead to 4 1/2 over the two teams tied for third that had both suffered heartbreaking losses—the Pirates and the Dodgers.

* * *

A Cold Warrior Laid to Rest

If May 26 was a dark night for left-handers, the next day was a dark day for the United States in its Cold War battle with Communism. On May 27, Secretary of State John Foster Dulles was laid to rest at Arlington National Cemetery. Three days before, a bulletin from Washington announced: "MR. JOHN FOSTER DULLES DIED QUIETLY IN HIS SLEEP AT 7:49 E.D.T. THIS MORNING."[28]

The tragic figure of young Braves second baseman Felix Mantilla. Fate forced him to move to shortstop for the last five innings of the final playoff game with the Dodgers. His wild throw in the 12th inning cost Milwaukee a chance for its third straight NL pennant. (George Brace photograph)

At the age of 71, Secretary of State John Foster Dulles had lost his own two-year battle with cancer. President Eisenhower, who had been heavily dependent on Dulles' counsel in foreign policy matters for the past six years, remarked, "It is like losing a brother."[29] The death of Dulles marked the end of a dangerous era in post–World War II international relations. He was the principal architect of America's Cold War policy. With a messianic zeal, he accused the Democrats of being "soft on Communism," and threatened to use nuclear weapons to meet Soviet aggression.[30]

At Gettysburg, Pennsylvania, President Eisenhower told the nation:

> John Foster Dulles is dead. A lifetime of labor for world peace has ended. His countrymen and all who believe in justice and the rule of law grieve at the passing from the earthly scene of one of the truly great men of our time.
>
> Throughout his life, and particularly during his eventful six years as Secretary of State, his courage, his wisdom, and his understanding were devoted to bettering relations among nations. He was a foe only to tyranny.
>
> Because he believed in the dignity of men and in their brotherhood under God, he was an ardent supporter of their deepest hopes and aspirations. From his

life and work, humanity will, in the years to come, gain renewed inspiration to work ever harder for the attainment of the goal of peace with justice.[31]

* * *

Bavasi Calls for "Drastic Action" as the Dodgers Hit Bottom

A three-game series at the Coliseum with the Cubs at the end of May marked the low point in the season for the Los Angeles Dodgers. After Drysdale won the first game on May 27 with a complete-game five-hitter with 11 strikeouts, things fell apart for the Dodgers. They dropped the final two games of the series, falling to a fourth-place tie with the Pittsburgh Pirates. Walter Alston called for a "team shakeup" after three Cubs pitchers struck out 14 Dodgers in the second game.[32] In the third game, after the Dodgers committed five errors (including three by shortstop Bob Lillis), Buzzie Bavasi called for "drastic action."[33]

Even after they swept a two-game series with the Cardinals at the Coliseum on the last two days of the month, the Dodgers still had a disappointing 14–17 record for May. It would be their only losing month of the season. After a promising April, they ended May dispirited and mired in fourth place, five games off the pace. To prevent a repeat of their 1958 disaster, the Dodgers' options were clear: change or parish.

	W	*L*	*Pct.*	*
Milwaukee	28	16	.636	—
San Francisco	26	19	.578	2½
Pittsburgh	24	21	.533	4½
Los Angeles	25	23	.521	5

*Games behind leader

Chapter 16

The Summer of '59: Bavasi's Miracle

During the summer of 1959, the main battleground of the Cold War moved to Moscow. In what *New York Times* reporter James Reston — present at the scene — called "perhaps the most startling personal international incident since the war," Vice President Richard Nixon and Soviet Premier Nikita Khrushchev engaged in their famous "kitchen debate."[1] Nixon was formally opening the American National Exhibition when the heated exchange erupted in a model American kitchen. The verbal confrontation of one-upmanship covered such subjects as the merits of washing machines, the free exchange of ideas, summit meetings, rockets, threats, and ultimatums.

Nixon showed Khrushchev a model built-in washing machine. Unimpressed, Khrushchev dismissively said, "We have such things." Nixon explained, "What we want to do is to make easier the life of our housewives." Khrushchev responded by saying that in the Soviet Union, they did not have "the capitalist attitude toward women," suggesting that discrimination and exploitation of women did not occur under Communism.[2]

In the course of their increasingly fast and furious exchanges, witnessed by hundreds of newspaper reporters and photographers, Khrushchev and Nixon each accused the other of trying to indirectly threaten his country. After a lengthy speech in which Khrushchev told Nixon, "You don't know anything about Communism except the fear of it," former U.S. Senator Nixon accused him of "filibustering."[3]

At the end of his 11-day visit on August 1, Nixon appeared on Moscow TV to address the Soviet people. Sitting gravely in a simple straight-backed chair, he read from a manuscript placed on a table before him. After beginning pleasantly by ad-libbing an apology for pre-empting a popular comedy show, Nixon launched into a Cold War diatribe: the Russian people were being kept in the dark about U.S. aims and proposals for peace; the Soviet policy of "peaceful coexistence" would only lead to "two hostile camps," and offered as an alternative "one world" with freedom to choose economic and political systems; and Soviet attempts to export Communism had caused the U.S. arms build-up.

Nixon concluded his television address by saying, "Mr. Khrushchev predicted that our grandchildren in the U.S. would live under Communism. Let me say that we do not object to his saying this will happen. We only object if he tries to bring it about. And this is my answer to him. We do not say that your grandchildren will live under capitalism. The very essence of our belief is that we will not try to impose our system on anybody else."[4] Before leaving Moscow, Nixon—overstepping his bounds—issued an invitation to Khrushchev to visit the United States, much to President Eisenhower's chagrin.[5]

* * *

Due to the genius of General Manager Buzzie Bavasi, the summer of 1959 would see the transformation of the Los Angeles Dodgers from also-rans to legitimate pennant contenders.

June: Drastic Action Pay Off

Dodgers General Manager Buzzie Bavasi took his first "drastic action" on the first day of June. On June 1, in a desperate attempt to strengthen their problem-ridden infield, the Dodgers swapped shortstops with their Spokane farm club. They optioned Bob Lillis to their Pacific Coast League team and purchased the contract of Maury Wills, a 26-year-old journeyman minor leaguer and father of five who was hitting .313 with 25 stolen bases in 48 games at Spokane. Lillis, 29, was batting .229 in only 48 at-bats for the Dodgers and had committed four errors in his last two starts.[6]

Wills joined the team in Milwaukee on June 5.[7] The next day he replaced the Dodgers' principal shortstop, Don Zimmer, who had a .202 batting average and a limited range that caused him perpetual injuries from having to dive for balls. It would be an inauspicious beginning to a storied career, with Wills going 0-for-4 at the plate and committing two errors in the field. Only baldness prevented Walter Alston from pulling his hair out.

A 9-Year Struggle with Rejection

The June 6, 1959, debut of Maury Wills was the culmination of a nine-year struggle to climb to the major leagues. A native of Washington, D.C., he was a standout in baseball, football, and basketball at Cardozo High School. After graduation in 1950, he turned down nine football scholarships, including Ohio State and Syracuse, to pursue a professional baseball career. He went to a New York Giants tryout camp where he was rejected as a pitcher. Dodger scout Rex Rowan signed Wills to a contract with the Hornell club of the Class D Pony League. He began in 1951 as a "mop-up" pitcher, but it soon became evident that his future was at shortstop. He soon developed a "good field, no hit" reputation in the minor leagues, where he struggled for the next eight years.

Although he hit a modest .253 at Triple-A Spokane in 1958, Wills was "conditionally purchased" by the Detroit Tigers. When he reported to spring training in 1959, the Tigers had already acquired a proven big league shortstop from the Washington Senators named Rocky Bridges. Consequently, the Tigers returned him to Spokane to avoid paying his purchase price of $35,000. It was at Spokane that his manager, Bobby Bragan, helped him make a breakthrough as a switch-hitter. "I'm a natural right-handed batter. Bragan was the first manager to let me try switch-hitting, and I think it paid off," recalled Wills.[8]

Maury Wills was a 26-year-old rookie with a wife and five kids when he was brought up from the minors on the first day of June 1959. He soon took over the shortstop position from the fiery Don Zimmer. (George Brace photograph)

The Wills-Zimmer Wars for Shortstop

After watching Wills go 1-for-12 at the plate in four games, Walter Alston returned Zimmer to shortstop on June 11. Dodger coach Pee Wee Reese told Bavasi, "Buzzie, you've made your first big mistake. You should not have brought that kid up. He'll never make it."[9] Thirteen games later, on June 22, with Zimmer hitting .194 and hobbled by a bruised left ankle, Wills got another chance. Again, Wills didn't perform up to expectations, resulting in he and Zimmer sharing the shortstop position for the remainder of June.[10]

Carl Erskine Retires

On June 15, Carl Erskine asked Buzzie Bavasi to put him on the "voluntary retired" list. At the age of 32, the author of two no-hitters and the holder of the then–World Series record for the most strikeouts for a single game, Erskine's career came to a sudden end.[11] "Several times this season I've made up my mind to quit, but didn't do it," Erskine explained to reporters. "But I realize now that I can no longer help the club."[12] Erskine was 0–3 in 10 appearances. His mind was probably made up the day before in Pittsburgh when he failed to finish the first inning of his last start, getting pounded for five hits and four runs, as the Dodgers dropped a double-header and fell to fifth place.[13]

Sadly, Erskine needed only 28 more days to qualify for the players' ten-year pension. Thus ended Erskine's career with the Dodgers that began in 1948. Buzzie Bavasi announced that a right-handed pitcher would be called up from the Dodgers' farm system.

"Now He's a Pitcher"—The Resurrection of Roger the Dodger

Bavasi took his next drastic measure on June 16 when the Dodgers replaced Carl Erskine by purchasing the contract of Roger Craig from Spokane. Roger Lee Craig of Durham, North Carolina, had been banished to the Triple-A St. Paul Saints the prior year because of a torn rotator cuff—what at the time was diagnosed as tendonitis in his pitching shoulder. With the Saints, he had the ignominious distinction of being the losingest pitcher in the American Association with 17 defeats. He made a game attempt to make the club the following spring, but was returned to the minors on March 31, 1959. The prevailing view was that Roger Craig was washed up.

Had it not been for Erskine's retirement, it is doubtful that Craig would have played a part in the Dodgers' 1959 season. His current performance at Spokane was mediocre: six wins, seven losses, with a 3.28 ERA in 96 innings. But, fortuitously, he had attracted the attention of Buzzie Bavasi by throwing a three-hit shutout the day before Erskine retired. Craig would return to the Dodgers with a career 25–24 major league record. Arriving in Brooklyn during the summer of 1955, the rangy 6' 4" right-hander had dazzling stuff. By 1956 he was a mainstay of the starting rotation. But his rotator cuff injury, sustained at the end of 1957, changed all that. By 1958, he was being shunted between the big club and the minor leagues.[14]

On June 18, 1959, Roger Craig was a man on a mission of redemption. He loaded his wife and three young children into his car and drove 1,300 miles, from Spokane to Los Angeles, so he could be in uniform that same night for the Dodgers' game with the Milwaukee Braves. While initially assigned to the bullpen, Craig was brimming with optimism. "I know I can win if they let me pitch. I'm throwing real good and I'm ready to start," Craig told reporters.[15]

Roger Craig at Wrigley Field, where he won the last game of the 1959 season to force a playoff with the Milwaukee Braves. Upon being recalled from the minors that June, he drove his wife and three kids all the way from Spokane to L.A. to rejoin the Dodgers for a key game the same night at the Coliseum. Craig would become the Dodgers' stopper, posting an 11–5 record. (George Brace photograph)

Roger the Dodger received his chance to start on June 19 against the Cincinnati Reds. He came through with a complete-game, 6–2 victory, aided by Duke Snider's two home runs and four runs batted in. Craig kept the dangerous fastball-hitting Reds off-balance by relying on his slider and curveball. "That's the best game I ever saw him pitch for us," observed Walter Alston. "He was a thrower before, but now he's a pitcher."[16] Craig's inspiring comeback performance was just what the Dodgers needed as they tenaciously clung to fourth place.

Koufax Ignites a Seven-Game Win Streak

The Dodgers entered their June 22 game with the Phillies in fourth place, 3½ games behind the league-leading Milwaukee Braves. But that night at the

Coliseum, Sandy Koufax turned in a season-changing performance. His 6–2 complete-game victory ignited a seven-game Dodger winning streak that lifted Los Angeles into second place, one game behind the Braves. His 16 strikeouts established a major league record for a night game. It was the fourth consecutive win for Koufax (4–1), and his first complete game after eight previous starts.

Five days later, Koufax gave the Dodgers their sixth straight win with a 3–0, six-hit shutout of the Pirates in only 1 hour and 59 minutes at Forbes Field in Pittsburgh.

Giants Come to Town, Spoil the Party

The Giants snapped the Dodgers' win streak and ended the month of June on a sour note as they swept a brief two-game series at the Coliseum. Though the Giants pushed the Dodgers back into third place, with a league-leading 18–12 record for the month of June, the Dodgers had gained 3½ games on Milwaukee.

	W	*L*	*Pct.*	*
Milwaukee	42	31	.575	—
San Francisco	43	33	.566	½
Los Angeles	43	35	.551	1½
Pittsburgh	39	37	.513	4½

*Games behind leader

July: Larry Sherry Brings a New Slider and a Big Heart

Buzzie Bavasi's drastic measures continued into July with the recalling of Larry Sherry from the minor leagues—but not before he lost a long-distance phone battle with scout Johnny Corriden. In early June, Bavasi had told Corriden to find him another relief pitcher. A week later, when Corriden called Bavasi to tell him he had found Larry Sherry—a player Bavasi didn't think was ready—he told Corriden, "Take another look at him." An angry Corriden told Bavasi, "If you want to be bull-headed and stubborn, all right. I'll take another look. But it'll be the same!"[17]

At the end of June, with the Dodgers still in critical need of a relief pitcher, Corriden called Bavasi to report, "I took another look at Sherry and nothing's changed. Besides, you've got to take him *now.*" When a surprised Bavasi asked, "Why now?" Corriden explained, "Because I just bought him a plane ticket to Los Angeles!"[18]

Journey to the Major Leagues on Two Club Feet

On July 2, with Johnny Podres sidelined with a bad back and the Dodger pitching staff otherwise showing signs of coming apart at the seams, Larry Sherry was recalled from St. Paul. It was another desperate move by Bavasi since Sherry had a mere 6–7 record for the Triple-A Saints. But the Dodgers had their hopes riding on another key fact: he had just started and completed three straight games.

Underdog at Birth

Larry Sherry's is a compelling story that began when he was born in 1935 with club feet. He had to undergo corrective surgery at six weeks old, and had to wear foot braces and orthopedic shoes during his childhood.[19]

1959 World Series MVP Larry Sherry was recalled from the minors in July 1959. He became the star of the Dodger bullpen, winning the first playoff game with the Braves in Milwaukee before winning two games and saving two others in the Series. (George Brace photograph)

When he reported to the Dodgers on the Fourth of July in Chicago, he was 6' 2" tall and weighed 200 pounds. But in 1949 when he entered Fairfax High School in Los Angeles, he was only 5'1" and barely weighed 100 pounds. His baseball coach, Frank Shaffer, recalled Sherry as a freshman: "He was a lanky, clumsy kid. He had little coordination and was terribly slow. But, oh, how he tried — he tried awfully hard. He wanted to play second base, so we let him. If you had to pick out one reason why Larry finally made it, it would simply have to be hard work."[20]

At Fairfax, he played lots of basketball, which helped to develop his coordination. In fact, Sherry went on to become an all-city basketball player. "By the end of his sophomore year, he had become a pretty good second baseman," noted Shaffer.[21]

Accidental Pitcher

Fate intervened to cause the intersection of Larry Sherry with the pitcher's mound. Coach Shaffer remembered the circumstances: "Early in his senior year, Larry injured his ankle. In addition to being our second baseman, he was our batting practice pitcher. He had a pretty good curve, so I talked him into trying pitching. He developed so fast that, by the end of the season, he was our number one starter."[22] Remarkably, Sherry threw a no-hitter and led the team to the finals of Los Angeles city championship tournament.

Six-Year Climb to the Majors

Although Larry Sherry was talented enough to sign a professional contract immediately upon graduation from high school, the 18-year-old had a steep hill to climb before reaching the major leagues. He had a dazzling fastball, but it was rendered ineffective by an often companion trait: wildness. His wildness would plague him during his six seasons in the minor leagues. While he steadily advanced through the ranks of the Dodger farm system, leading various leagues in strikeouts, he often suffered from debilitating spells of not being able to find home plate.[23]

The 1958 spring training exhibition season appeared to be a breakthrough for Sherry. He was clearly the most effective Dodger pitcher, allowing only two earned runs in 25 innings. But when the regular season started, he had a heartbreaking relapse of wildness and was unable to get anybody out. With an eye-popping 12.46 ERA in five relief appearances, he was shipped out to Triple-A Spokane. A demoted and demoralized Sherry couldn't get his game under control there either, and ended up with a disappointing 6–14 record and a 4.91 ERA.[24]

The Slider and the Rebirth of Larry Sherry

After the 1958 season, Sherry went to the Venezuela Winter League to try to conquer his wildness. It was there, with the help of his brother, Norm, a catcher in the Dodgers' minor league system, that he learned a revolutionary new pitch: the slider. The slider did wonders for him. It was a perfect complement to his fastball and curve. "The slider gave me more confidence," recalled Sherry.[25] With confidence came better concentration; with concentration came control.

Second Chance

Reporting to the Dodgers in Chicago on July 4, 1959, Larry Sherry received a second chance to make the major leagues. Alston called on him to start the opening game of a double-header at Wrigley Field. He pitched seven solid innings, allowing only four hits and no earned runs. But two defensive lapses by the Dodgers caused the Cubs to score two unearned runs off him, and his major league return was turned into a bad-luck 2–1 loss.

On July 12 in Cincinnati, Alston gave Sherry another chance to start. He pitched 8⅔ innings, but gave up three home runs to the powerhouse Reds, who hung another 4–3 loss on him. Seven days later in Los Angeles, he was given a third opportunity to start against the cellar-dwelling Philadelphia Phillies, but he lasted just 3⅓ innings for a no-decision. After three starts, Larry Sherry was 0–2, and there were rumblings that Buzzie Bavasi had made another mistake.

Things finally began to turn around for Sherry on July 23 in Los Angeles. In his fourth start — against the Cubs at the Coliseum — he achieved his first major league victory with a workmanlike seven-hit, three-run performance over 7⅓ innings, with Don Drysdale coming in from the bullpen to pitch the final 1⅓ innings to earn the save.

Sherry lasted only one inning in his next start in Pittsburgh on July 28. Fortunately, the Dodgers rallied to win the game, 9–4, and he escaped with another no-decision.

Wills Wins the Shortstop Wars

Maury Wills finally took over the shortstop position on July 4 in Chicago. At that point, Don Zimmer's batting average had plummeted to .175. In two consecutive double-headers at Wrigley Field, the Dodgers took three out of four from the Cubs to go into the first All-Star break in third place, one-half game behind the deadlocked Giants and Braves.[26]

Dodgers Sweep Braves in Milwaukee

On July 11, the second-place Dodgers swept a two-game series from the Braves in Milwaukee to stay within one game of the Giants. In the first game, Roger Craig came in from the bullpen in the third inning and pitched a remarkable 11 scoreless innings in relief, allowing three hits on only 88 pitches for his fourth victory without a defeat. After he retired from managing, Roger Craig would recall that night at County Stadium: "One game really stands out in my mind — when I pitched 11 innings in relief at Milwaukee. I don't think I had three balls on any hitter. I was in a zone, so focused and full of confidence. I can't remember anybody else pitching 11 innings in relief."[27] In the second game, Don Drysdale also came in from the bullpen to win the game for the Dodgers.

Craig Shuts Out Giants as Dodgers Sweep San Francisco

On July 22, in a ferocious pitcher's duel at Seals Stadium, Roger Craig shut out the Giants, 1–0, on three hits. Losing pitcher Sam Jones, who also pitched a complete-game three-hitter, gave up a ninth-inning run-scoring single to Gil Hodges for the only run of the game. The victory gave the Dodgers a sweep of the two-game series and brought the second-place Dodgers to within one-half game of the Giants. The Braves had slipped to fourth place, 3½ games off the pace.

Baseball Is Fully Integrated

Over in the American League, July 22, 1959, was a momentous date. At Comiskey Park in Chicago, the White Sox beat Ted Williams and the Boston Red Sox, 5–4, to take sole possession of first place. They would not relinquish the lead for the rest of the season. When Elijah "Pumpsie" Green started at second base that day for the Red Sox, he became the first Negro player in the team's history. Because Boston had held out for 12 years— since Jackie Robinson's debut in 1947—as the last remaining team to exclude black players, Major League Baseball was now fully integrated.[28]

Banned from the team's hotel in Scottsdale, Arizona, during spring training, Green was shunted to the Adams Hotel 17 miles away in Phoenix. In a daily humiliation, the Red Sox sent a car to Phoenix to pick him up and take him their training camp.[29] When Green was optioned to the minors at the end of spring training, Boston owner Tom Yawkey and General Manager Bucky Harris were called to appear before the Massachusetts Commission on Discrimination, where they were charged with racial discrimination by Herbert E. Tucker of the Boston branch of the National Association for the Advancement of Colored People. Tucker argued that the Red Sox were the only major league team without a Negro on the roster because they had pursued an anti–Negro policy for more than twelve years, turning down such outstanding black players as Jackie Robinson and Willie Mays. But Yawkey and Harris denied that the decision to option Green had been prompted by racial bias.[30] Richard O'Connell, Red Sox vice president and business manager, told the commission that he "wished" his club had a Negro player. "We have seven Negroes in our organization now," claimed O'Connell, "and we have absolutely no discrimination against race, color, or creed."[31]

The Dodgers Lose Hodges

July 23 was a bittersweet day for the Dodgers. Larry Sherry beat the Cubs, 5–3, at the Coliseum for his first major league victory. But in the sixth inning, Gil Hodges injured his right ankle when his spikes caught while sliding into second base, and had to be carried off the field on a stretcher. While x-rays showed no fracture, Hodges would be lost to the Dodgers for a full month. The Dodgers had to call on utilityman Norm Larker to play first base.

Craig Puts the Dodgers in First Place

On July 29, Roger Craig pitched a six-hit shutout over the Pirates at the Coliseum to propel the Dodgers into first place by a half-game over the Giants, and one game over the Braves. The Dodgers were alone in first place for the first time in more than three months, when Drysdale beat the Pirates at Forbes Field on April 27. Six weeks before, Craig was hopelessly stuck in Triple-A. Now with a 6–2 record, the resurrected Craig had reestablished himself as a key member of the Dodgers' starting staff.

1959 NL Rookie of the Year Willie McCovey. His dazzling debut on July 29, 1959, is still one of the greatest in baseball history: two triples and two singles — 4-for-4 — off future Hall-of-Fame Phillies pitcher Robin Roberts. (George Brace photograph)

"Stretch"

On July 29, after losing their fourth consecutive game, the San Francisco Giants relinquished first place to the Dodgers. But the next day in San Francisco marked an historic event: the stunning major league debut of Willie McCovey. In an attempt to shake up their slumping offense, the Giants brought up McCovey, who was causing a sensation in the Pacific Coast League with his .377 batting average. The 21-year-old didn't know until 11:30 P.M. the night before that he was to fly in from Phoenix to start the next day against Robin Roberts and the Philadelphia Phillies at Seals Stadium.[32] His teammates had no trouble finding a nickname for the lanky 6'4" first baseman: "Stretch."

Robin Roberts had been one of the National League's premier pitchers since 1950, when he started a run of six consecutive 20-win seasons. Though past his prime by 1959, he was still the ace of the Philadelphia staff. McCovey treated Roberts like a batting practice pitcher, torching him for two triples and two singles—each one a vicious line drive. In the fifth inning, he hit a ball so hard against the right-field wall that he had to stop at first base with a single.[33]

The perfect 4-for-4 performance of July 30, 1959, was no fluke. McCovey would murder National League pitching for the remainder of the year to finish with a .354 batting average and 13 home runs in only 192 at-bats. He would be the unanimous choice as National League Rookie of the Year.

The same day Willie McCovey made his major league debut, a fellow future Hall of Famer made his debut on the mound in Cincinnati as 23-year-old St. Louis Cardinal rookie right-hander Bob Gibson shut out the Redlegs, 1–0, at Crosley Field.[34]

Drysdale Strikes Out 14 Phillies to Close Out July

On July 31 at the Coliseum, Don Drysdale (14–6) struck out 14 Phillies in a complete game eight-hit win. Thanks to the recall of Larry Sherry and four wins by Roger Craig, the Dodgers played at a 15–12 clip for July and ended the month tied with the Braves for second place, one-half game behind the Giants.

	W	*L*	*Pct.*	*
San Francisco	57	45	.559	—
Milwaukee	55	44	.556	½
Los Angeles	58	47	.552	½
Chicago	50	51	.495	6½

*Games behind leader

August: Now Anything Is Possible

On August 2, after five starts, Larry Sherry received his second major league win in a new capacity: as a reliever. In a near-perfect five-inning performance—one hit, no runs, no walks—he gave the Dodgers a three-game sweep of the Phillies and leapfrogged them past Milwaukee into second place, one-half game behind the Giants.[35]

While Los Angeles Plays Host to the Second All-Star Game, Bavasi Acquires Chuck Essegian

On the afternoon of August 3, the second All-star Game was played at the Los Angeles Memorial Coliseum, where the American League defeated the National League, 5–3, before 55,105 sun-baked fans. Hometown hero Don Drysdale started the game for the Nationals, but was tagged for the loss after giving up two home runs. Boston's Frank Malzone rocked him for a game-tying solo homer in the second, and the Yogi Berra's 340 foot 2-run home run over the right field foul pole in the third put the American League ahead for good.[36]

While the Drysdale was struggling against the American League at the Coliseum, Buzzie Bavasi was on the phone arranging a deal to bolster the Dodgers' offense to compensate for the loss of Gil Hodges ten days before. Bavasi purchased the contract of Chuck Essegian from the Dodgers' Pacific Coast League farm team in Spokane. Essegian was a former Stanford Indian fullback-linebacker who had given USC fits on the Coliseum's football field in 1950-51-52. Now 27, the 5'11" Essegian had won two batting titles in the minors, and was tearing up the PCL with his current Indians in Spokane.[37]

Essegian, another graduate of Fairfax High in Los Angeles, made an inauspicious return the next day by going 0-for-4 against Cincinnati's Joe Nuxhall at the Coliseum. But the Dodgers had a valuable power source on the bench that would pay off in October.[38]

In a solemn ceremony at the White House the same day, President Eisenhower formally proclaimed Hawaii as the 50th state, and unfurled the nation's new 50-star flag.[39] He also announced that Soviet Premier Nikita Khrushchev had accepted Nixon's invitation to visit the United States in September.[40]

Rocky Road Trip

The Dodgers struggled on the road in the middle of August. After dropping a double-header at Forbes Field in Pittsburgh on August 23, the Dodgers had fallen to third place, 4½ games behind the Giants. Don Drysdale had the dubious distinction of losing both games, lasting only 2⅔ innings as the starter in the first game and pitching the last 2⅔ innings as a reliever in the second game.[41] The only good news was that Gil Hodges returned to the starting lineup after missing 26 games because of the ankle injury he sustained on July 23.

Fortunately for the Dodgers, the last two games of the road trip were scheduled at Philadelphia, the National League get-well station. In the first game on August 24, Sandy Koufax struck out 13 Phillies and Hodges drove in five runs as they buried Philadelphia, 8–2. In the second game on August 25, Larry Sherry relieved Johnny Podres in the eighth inning with the bases loaded and nobody out. Sherry proceeded to shut down the Phillies to preserve the 5–2 victory.[42]

Sherry's value as a reliever was becoming evident, allowing only nine hits and no runs in six relief appearances. Walter Alston would salt that information away for the future. Thanks to the two-game sweep at Connie Mack Stadium, the Dodgers ended the road trip with a more respectable 8–9 record to regain second place, 3½ games behind San Francisco.

Dodger pinch-hitter extraordinaire Chuck Essegian. The former Stanford fullback-linebacker was acquired by the Dodgers from St. Louis in the Summer of '59, a Bavasi deal that would pay huge dividends in October. (George Brace photograph)

Another Gift Arrives from Philadelphia

On August 27, their second consecutive day off after a grueling 17-game road trip in 15 days, the Dodgers received another gift from Philadelphia. The last-place Phillies swept a double-header from the Giants. The idle Dodgers were not only able to recharge, but managed to pick up a full game in the NL standings. They were now just two games behind San Francisco as they prepared to collide with the first-place Giants in a crucial three-game series at the Los Angeles Memorial Coliseum.[43]

The Giant-Dodger War to Close Out August

The Giants came into Los Angeles on August 27 with a two-game lead over the Dodgers. In the Friday night opener at the Coliseum, Sad Sam Jones shut out the Dodgers, 5–0, on eight hits before a crowd of 66,068. The Giants shelled Dodger starter Don Drysdale for five earned runs in 1⅓ innings with four San Francisco doubles and a home run by Willie Mays. Drysdale's fourth consecutive defeat dropped Los Angeles to three games back.

The Dodgers received a gift win in the second game. The second of two errors by rookie first baseman Willie McCovey cost the Giants dearly: a 7–6 loss and a full game in the standings. The Dodgers entered the bottom of the ninth trailing, 6–5. Charlie Neal got aboard on Jackie Brandt's error at third base. Wally Moon tripled him home to tie the game at 6–6. Moon eventually scored the winning run when McCovey fumbled Norm Larker's routine grounder with the bases loaded and two outs. Starter Larry Sherry left with a no-decision after completing 7⅓ innings and allowing five earned runs. Roger Craig earned his seventh win by pitching the last inning and two-thirds. It was a dramatic turnaround. Instead of falling to four games behind the Giants, the Dodgers went into the final game of the series on the last day of August only two games behind.

23-year-old Don Drysdale won 17 games for the 1959 Dodgers. The year before he hit seven home runs in the team's first season at the Coliseum. (George Brace photograph)

August 31, 1959: A Window to the Future

As the sun came up in Los Angeles on August 31, 1959, the Giants, who had been in first place all month, were still in the driver's seat, two games ahead of the second-place Dodgers and three games ahead of the third-place Braves. But as 82,794 fans packed the Los Angeles Memorial Coliseum that night to watch the Giants and Dodgers conclude their three-game series, the winds of change began to stir. The Giants started right-hander Jack Sanford (12–10). With the Dodgers' starting rotation taxed, manager Walter Alston was forced to call on Sandy Koufax, the 23-year-old left-hander who had been nursing a severe cold for days. The hard-throwing but inconsistent lefty had been used sparingly all season as a spot starter and had a record of 7–4.

Exactly one year before to the day, on August 31, 1958, Sandy Koufax lasted only two-thirds of an inning as the Giants destroyed him and the Dodgers, 14–2. But tonight Koufax would make history.

Wild Young Left-hander

Sanford Braun Koufax was an enigma. He could throw a baseball 100 miles per hour—just not always over the plate. Two years ahead of Oscar Robertson at the University of Cincinnati, Koufax, an 18-year-old freshman from Brooklyn, walked onto the basketball team in the winter of 1953-54 as a left-handed guard and was awarded a partial scholarship after the coach watched him practice.[44]

In 1959, 23-year-old Sandy Koufax was still an erratic young left-hander. After striking out a MLB-record 18 Giants on August 31, he virtually disappeared until Game 5 of the World Series, which he lost, 1–0, on a double-play ground ball. (George Brace photograph)

That spring, when the baseball team was having difficulty finding players, Koufax told basketball teammate Norman Lefkowitz, "I think I'll go out for it. I played a little in high school." During the basketball season, when he told his basketball coach, Ed Jucker (also the Bearcats' baseball coach), "I can pitch," Jucker replied, "Don't bother me now, kid. When the season's over, I'll come over and watch you throw."[45] The University of Cincinnati held baseball tryouts in an old gym that was so cramped there was barely enough room for a pitching rubber and home plate, with about two and a half feet to spare behind the pitcher and catcher. Anyone who tried to catch Koufax was punished by his wild lasers ricocheting off the wood paneling behind them. Don Nesbitt, also trying out for pitcher that day, witnessed the casualties in the shower. "Anyone who tried to catch him, they were just a mass of bruises ... from the ball hitting the floor and the tile wall and bouncing back." Koufax made the 1954 Cincinnati baseball team as a walk-on, his only season of intercollegiate baseball. He was 3–1 with a stunning fifty-one strikeouts in thirty-two innings to go along with his thirty walks. His catcher, Danny Gilbert, remembered the challenge of catching the young Koufax: "With other pitchers, I'd work inside, outside, up and down. With Sandy, we were working just to get it over the plate. When he got it over the plate, it was Katie bar the door."[46]

After his freshman year at the University of Cincinnati, he signed a lucrative Major League Baseball contract with the Brooklyn Dodgers. As a "bonus baby," the good news was that he received $20,000 ($6,000 for the first year's salary and a bonus of $14,000), then the cost of a four-year college education.[47] The bad news was that he had to sit on the Dodger bench for two years when he could have been learning how to pitch in the minor leagues. Forty-eight years later, Roger Craig recalled the 1959 version of Sandy Koufax: "He was still a young kid. Because of the bonus rule, he didn't have that much experience. He probably should have gone to the minors first."[48] Thus, by 1959, he was still raw, the typical "wild young left-hander," full of promise, but unreliable.

Dodger manager Walter Alston had little confidence in Koufax. Alston liked take-charge holler guys like Pee Wee Reese and Don Zimmer. As a soft-spoken Jewish kid from Brooklyn, he was quieter and more remote than most players— something Alston mistook as a "lack of desire."[49] Further, Alston liked steady, dependable pitchers who threw strikes. But with Koufax, Alston never knew what he was going to get: "He's either awfully good or awfully bad — just like the way I play pool."[50]

An Amadeus Sighting: 82,794 See Mozart on the Mound

August 31, 1959, turned out to be a historic performance and a turning point in the career of Sandy Koufax. Relying on only two pitches, a devastating fastball and an unhittable "12-to-6" curveball that started above the shoulders and then "dropped off the table" to below the strike zone, Koufax struck out 18 Giants to tie Bob Feller's major league record for most strikeouts in a nine-inning game. He struck out the side three times, and every Giants starter at least once for a clutch 5–2 victory over the league leaders.

Although the game was played before a deafening crowd of 82,794, ironically, it was the strange gaps of silence that the author still remembers to this day from listening to Vin Scully describe the game on the radio. Home plate umpire Tom Gorman had a delayed call, deliberating like Chief Justice Earl Warren before rendering a decision as to whether a pitch was a ball or a strike.

The noise reached a crescendo as Koufax wound up and released each pitch. This was followed by a seemingly interminable gap of dead silence until Gorman would either raise his right arm for a strike, or remain frozen behind the plate for a ball.

The game did not begin like a historic Koufax performance. He struck out only three Giants in the first three innings, and actually fell behind, 1–0, in the top of the first when Mays and Cepeda rocked him with back-to-back doubles. But in classic Koufax style, he seemed to get stronger as the game progressed. After one out in the fourth inning, he got 15 of his last 17 outs by strikeout. In an ominous sign that the Giant hitters were beginning to press as they headed into the September pennant stretch, Koufax observed, "They must have been anxious. I never saw so many bad pitches swung at in one game."[51]

Facing Giants relief pitcher Al Worthington in the bottom of the ninth inning of a 2–2 tie, after Koufax had struck out the side on only ten pitches, Dodger right fielder Wally Moon broke the deadlock with a dramatic three-run "Moon Shot" over the screen in left field. On the way up to home plate to deliver his walk-off homer, the supremely confident Moon had told on-deck batter Norm Larker to "relax, I'll take care of Worthington."[52]

* * *

As the dog days of August faded into September, not only had the Giants' lead been reduced to only one game over the Dodgers and 2½ games over the idle Braves, they were forced to come to grips with the fact that their arch rivals had a weapon of historic proportions in Sandy Koufax. On the Dodger team there was a feeling that, after August 31, anything was possible. Thanks to Buzzie Bavasi's "drastic actions," the summer of '59 was truly a transformational summer.

	W	*L*	*Pct.*	*
San Francisco	73	58	.557	—
Los Angeles	72	59	.550	1
Milwaukee	70	60	.538	2½
Pittsburgh	70	62	.530	3½

*Games behind leader

CHAPTER 17

September 1959: A Pennant Race for the Ages

ON SEPTEMBER 14, AFTER A FLIGHT of 35 hours, the Soviet spacecraft *Lunik II* hit the moon carrying a red flag with the hammer and sickle. The moon mission was strategically timed for Soviet Premier Nikita Khrushchev's two-week state visit to the U.S., which began the next day when he was greeted by President Eisenhower and 200,000 Americans at Andrews Air Force Base.

Given Khrushchev's bellicose behavior, Eisenhower had been opposed to inviting the premier. But after being blind-sided by Nixon's invitation to the Soviet chairman in Moscow, Eisenhower made the best of the situation. The first challenge the president was confronted with was Khrushchev's demand that he be received as a "head of state," when in fact he was not. Eisenhower, employing the skills he had developed during World War II to handle such prima donna generals as Montgomery and Patton, solved the problem by informing the American people that Khrushchev was visiting "in the capacity of a head of state."[1]

After receiving a 21 gun salute, Khrushchev gave the crowd hope for a thaw in the Cold War when he called for harmony between the two nations as "relations between good neighbors."[2]

* * *

If September would bring a thaw in the Cold War, it would bring an American hot war — the NL pennant race — to a boiling point. As the September stretch drive began, both the Dodgers and Braves got off to slow starts. The Dodgers won only one of their first four games to fall three games behind the Giants in second place. The Braves lost three of their first four, sinking to 4½ games off the lead in third place. Despite being soundly beaten, 11–5, by Robin Roberts and the last-place Phillies on September 2, Red Schoendienst provided some consolation as he made his first appearance of the season as a pinch-hitter. In San Francisco, the Giants recovered from their August 31 humiliation at the hands of Sandy Koufax and burst out of the gate to win three of their first four.

Is It Time to Stick a Fork in the Braves?

With the Braves 4½ games behind on September 5, murmurs began to be heard in Milwaukee that the team was finished. But on September 6, the Braves beat the Reds at Crosley Field in Cincinnati to began an heroic seven-game winning streak to climb back into the race. They returned home on September 7 to sweep a double-header from the Pirates. They swept a two-game series from the Cardinals, and won two out of three from the Reds at County Stadium. Suddenly, by September 12, the "finished" Milwaukee Braves were tied for second place with the Dodgers, only one game behind the Giants.

The Dodgers Ruin a Perfect Face

On September 7, the Dodgers started a five-game winning streak of their own as Johnny Podres struck out 14 Cubs to beat Chicago, 7–1, at the Coliseum. The Dodgers then feasted on the hapless Phillies as Don Drysdale shut them out, 1–0, on three hits, and Roger Craig followed suit, 5–0, also on three hits.

On September 11 the Pittsburgh Pirates came to Los Angeles for a twilight-night double-header. Wally Moon hit three home runs to lead the Dodgers to a 5–4 and 4–0 sweep before 48,526 at the Coliseum, thereby increasing the win streak to five. In the second game, Larry Sherry shut out the Pirates, 4–0, allowing just six hits while striking out 11. But it was the first game that created the headlines. Little Elroy Face, with a 17–0 record and 22 consecutive victories over two seasons, relieved Pirates starter Bob Friend in the eighth inning, and entered the ninth with a slim 4–3 lead. For the first time all season, Face's famous forkball failed him. The Dodgers handed him his first defeat as Charlie Neal singled home Junior Gilliam with the winning run after Gilliam had tripled home Maury Wills to tie the game. The loss would be Elroy Face's only defeat for 1959. He would finish the season at 18–1 with a winning percentage of .947, still the major league record.[3]

The Braves Make Their Last Trip to L.A.

First-Game Blues

On September 14, 1959, the Braves arrived in Los Angeles to open a brief two-game series— their last regularly scheduled games at the Coliseum for 1959. The day before at County Stadium, the Cincinnati Redlegs had snapped Milwaukee's seven-game winning streak by denying Warren Spahn his twentieth victory. The Braves and Dodgers entered their series tied for second, two games behind the Giants.

At 7:00 P.M., it was a typical Monday night on Seventh Street in Los Angeles. It was evident that the tattered men who inhabited the sidewalk were down on their luck. They had completed their foraging for dinner and were settling in for the evening. The author was a 10-year-old on his way to his first major league baseball game, but not before viewing the poor souls on skid row in order to better count our blessings.

At 7:30 P.M., it was nearly dark outside the Coliseum as we walked up the steps, through the tunnel, and into a dazzling emerald world where night was turned into day. Snap! Pop! Snap! The Dodgers— Junior Gilliam, Maury Wills, Charlie Neal, and Gil Hodges— were throwing the baseball around the infield with hand-numbing velocity. In opposite bullpens, 6'6" sidewinding Don Drysdale, with a record of 16–12, warmed up for the Dodgers, while Bob Buhl, with a record of 12–9, warmed up for the Braves. At 8:00 P.M., when the organist played the National Anthem, a glance into the Milwaukee dugout produced a shock to the senses. When Eddie Mathews and Warren Spahn took off their caps, they were as bald as que balls!

In the top of the second, with Frank Torre leading off first base, Braves catcher Del Crandall tied into a Drysdale fastball, sending it soaring toward the 42-foot screen in left field. As the ball disappeared into the crowd, the Braves had taken a 2–0 lead, and the author had witnessed his first home run. In the bottom of the fourth, Wally Moon made it 2–1 when he hit a Bob Buhl curveball over the chain-link fence in right-center field. The baseball cleared the 385-foot sign, took a few bounces, and came to rest at approximately the Los Angeles Rams' 50-yard line — a lonely white spheroid in stark isolation against a sea of green.

The Braves knocked Drysdale out of the game in the seventh when Bill Bruton touched him for a two-run single to make it 4–1 in favor of Milwaukee. After Danny McDevitt walked Ed Mathews to load the bases, Walter Alston brought in Larry Sherry to pitch to Hank Aaron, who came into the game hitting a cool .358 against the league and .378 with seven home runs against the Dodgers. But it was not Aaron's night as Sherry got him to hit into an inning-ending double play. Aaron came up again with the bases loaded with two out in the ninth, only to hit into a force play. He took a rare 0-for-5 collar, failed to add to his 115 runs batted in by leaving an army of men on base, and *slumped* to .355.

Bob Buhl took a one-hitter to the ninth inning before he showed any signs of stress. But the complexion of the game changed as Charlie Neal led off with a walk, Wally Moon bounced a single off ancient Milwaukee first baseman Mickey Vernon's glove, and Braves second baseman Felix Mantilla, who in two weeks was to play a pivotal role in the outcome of the pennant race, was unable to handle Duke Snider's slow roller. With the bases loaded and still nobody out, Fred Haney removed Buhl and brought in his ace reliever, Don McMahon. McMahon —from Brooklyn, of all places— put out the fire in no time. He first got Norm Larker to pop up to Mantilla. The crowd of 53,765 rose to its feet as Gil Hodges, with a then–NL record 14 career grand slam homers, came to the plate as the potential winning run. But their hopes were quickly deflated as Hodges watched a called third strike go by with the bat resting on his shoulder. When McMahon also coaxed Johnny Roseboro to stare at a third strike, it was over.

The Thing Giveth, the Thing Taketh Away

In a rare mid-week day game at the Coliseum the next afternoon, the Dodgers and Braves played the concluding contest of their two-game series. Bob Buhl's victory over Los Angeles the night before caused the Dodgers and Braves to switch places in the standings. The Dodgers fell to third place, two games behind the league-leading Giants, and the Braves replaced them in second, one game off the lead. But the Dodgers came from behind that afternoon to beat the Braves, 8–7, in 10 innings to regain a tie with Milwaukee for second place. After the Braves went ahead, 7–6, in the top of the tenth, the Dodgers rallied for two runs in the bottom half, with rookie Ron Fairly forcing in the winning run with a bases-loaded walk off the Braves' ace reliever, Don McMahon, who had shut them down less than 20 hours earlier. In a sign of things to come, the Dodgers got a perfect 5-for-5 performance from their hot-hitting rookie shortstop, Maury Wills. His triple and four singles gave him a string of 15 hits in his last 24 at-bats.[4] But it was an incident in the fifth inning involving the infamous left-field screen for which the game will be remembered.

After Braves slugging first baseman Joe Adcock gave them a 2–0 lead with a two-run home run in the top of the first inning, he led off the fifth with what appeared to be his second home run of the game. His towering drive off Dodger reliever Johnny Podres ricocheted off one of the supporting towers high atop the left-field screen (derisively referred to as "The Thing" during pre-game ground-rule discussions between the managers and the umpires at home plate), and became lodged in the mesh where the main screen and a connecting screen overlapped. Umpire Vinnie Smith made a circular motion with his right arm declaring it a home run. But after Adcock had rounded the bases and returned to the dugout with his putative second home run of the game to cut the Dodgers' lead to 5–3, the umpires huddled at the pitcher's mound like conferencing Supreme Court justices to consider this "case of first impression." Lead umpire Frank Dascoli announced the decision of the court: a ground-rule double. The court then imposed a harsh remedy: Adcock was ordered back to second base, and the run was erased from the scoreboard.

A rhubarb erupted as Braves manager Fred Haney argued that the tower was beyond The Thing; the ball, therefore, had sailed over it, and should be ruled a home run. Haney further argued that when the fans shook the ball loose, it fell out of the park and into the stands. But the umpires were unmoved, citing the ground rule that provided in pertinent part, "Ball going through screen or sticking in screen: two bases." Dascoli later commented, "Everybody knew they had a bad setup here, but they all agreed to play. Now they've got to take the consequences."[5]

The ruling turned out to be critical. Had it been called a home run, the Braves would have won the game, 7–6, in nine innings. Instead, Adcock was left stranded at second base, and the game went into extra innings where the Dodgers won in the bottom of the tenth, 8–7. Bob Buege, in his book *The Milwaukee Braves: A Baseball Eulogy*, captured the gravity of the ruling: "In a 154-game season that ended in a tie, Adcock's 'stolen' home run stands as a crucial event."[6]

After the game, the Braves filed an official protest with the league office. Under league rules, a call involving a judgment by the umpires is not subject to appeal; only a rule interpretation may be protested. Therefore, the Braves based their protest on the umpires' interpretation of the official definition of a home run: a fair ball that leaves the playing field. Because the ball cleared The Thing and did not return to the field, they argued that Adcock's ball should have been ruled a home run. Instead, in a misinterpretation of the rules, he was sent back to second base and did not score.[7]

In a blow to the Milwaukee Braves three days later, their protest was denied by National League President Warren Giles. Due to the importance of the game, Giles had visited the site to personally inspect The Thing. In a telegram to the Milwaukee Braves, he pontificated:

> After personal inspection of the left field screen at the Los Angeles Coliseum, and satisfying myself as to the place the ball hit the screen support, and the exact spot the ball lodged in the screen, and as a result of a verbal report from all our 16 umpires in the last two days, I have definitely concluded the call of the ground rules double on a hit by Adcock in your game of Sept. 15 was a correct decision.[8]

Unfortunately for Joe Adcock and the Braves, the league president—just like the Pope—was infallible. There would be no appeals. The book was thus closed on the game of September 15. It would prove to be a devastating result for the Braves.

* * *

On September 18, a United Nations audience sat in stunned silence as Nikita Khrushchev called for a "general and complete disarmament" by all nations over a four-year period, including the destruction of all atomic and nuclear bombs. Under Khrushchev's proposal, each state would be left with "only strictly limited contingents of police with small arms" for maintaining internal order.[9]

The Soviet premier's radical plan was met with immediate skepticism. "I think he must take us for morons," said an Asian delegate to the U.N.[10] After listening for over an hour to Khrushchev's plan that called for the withdrawal of U.S. forces from Western Europe and the liquidation of U.S. bases overseas, Secretary of State Christian Herter was more circumspect: "Obviously, the disarmament proposal made by Chairman Khrushchev is one which will require very careful examination."[11]

* * *

Showdown in San Francisco

The same day Khrushchev called for complete world disarmament—September 18, 1959—the San Francisco Giants seemed confidently entrenched in first place by two games, with Milwaukee and Los Angeles tied for second. The day before at Seals Stadium, they had sent the great Warren Spahn to the showers after only 18 pitches on their way to crushing the Braves, 13–6. That last Braves–Giants game of 1959 was a tour de force for Willie Mays, who went 4-for-4 (including his 31st home run), scored four runs, and drove in five. On this night, the Dodgers and Giants were scheduled to begin a crucial three-game series in San Francisco. It also marked the beginning of a perilous final stretch for the Dodgers, who had to play the last eight games of the season in hostile environments on the road. But a record two inches of rain deluged San Francisco to wash out the game, which was re-scheduled as part of a double-header the following day. Since the Braves had the night off, the standings remained unchanged.

	W	*L*	*Pct.*	*
San Francisco	82	64	.562	—
Milwaukee	80	66	.548	2
Los Angeles	80	66	.548	2

*Games behind leader

The September 18 deluge in San Francisco was only the calm before the storm in the National League pennant race. Over the next nine turbulent days, the lead would change hands seven times, including ties.[12]

* * *

Khrushchev Does Hollywood

On September 19, 1959, Khrushchev did Hollywood when he was invited for lunch at the Café de Paris at the Twentieth Century studios. Scores of the world's biggest movie stars listened in astonishment as he pounded the podium with his fist and shouted, "Live as you like under capitalism — may God help you. We still have a long way to go to catch up, but we'll do it and surpass America!" When Mrs. Khrushchev passed him a note informing him that they were not going to be driven to Disneyland as they had requested due to security concerns, the 65-year-old man-child erupted, "I was told I could not go to Disneyland!" Shaking his head and clenching his fists, he asked, "Why not? What is it? Do you have rocket-launching pads there? Have gangsters taken over the place that can destroy me? What am I to do now, commit suicide?"[13] Frank Sinatra and Shirley MacLaine tried to diffuse the crisis by escorting the Khrushchevs to a shooting of their musical, *Can-Can*.[14]

* * *

Nearly 400 miles north in San Francisco, the rain stopped and the Dodgers and Giants collided in a rare day-night double-header witnessed by two separate sell-out crowds at Seals Stadium.

In the afternoon game, Maury Wills and Roger Craig led the Dodgers to a 4–1 victory. Craig, now 9–5 since being recalled in June, beat the Giants for the third straight time.

The red hot Wills went 3-for-4 to extend his streak to 19 hits in his last 33 at-bats. The staggering Giants committed three errors. With some heads-up baserunning, Wills scored what turned out to be the winning run in the second inning. On third base with Craig at the plate, Wills dashed for home when Giants catcher Hobie Landrith lobbed the ball out of pitcher Johnny Antonelli's reach. Before shortstop Daryl Spencer could retrieve the ball, Wills had crossed home plate to give the Dodgers an insurmountable 2–0 lead.[15]

With a wicked slider, Craig went the distance, allowing the Giants only six hits. All four Dodger runs were cobbled together by the bottom of the batting order without the aid of a home run. The Dodgers chased Giants starter Johnny Antonelli in the fourth inning.

Don Drysdale and Giants rookie left-hander Mike McCormick squared off in the night game won by the Dodgers, 5–3. McCormick clung to a 1–0 lead for the first six innings, allowing just three hits. But the Dodgers reached him in the seventh, scoring all five of their runs, paced by a pair of two-run doubles by Junior Gilliam and Charlie Neal. Drysdale pitched a strong six innings, allowing the Giants only one unearned run and three hits. The Giants scored their final two runs in the bottom of the eighth off reliever Larry Sherry, knocking him out of the game. Danny McDevitt, usually a starting pitcher, had to come in from the bullpen to kill the San Francisco rally by striking out the dangerous Willie McCovey with the tying runs on base.

In Philadelphia, Braves moved to within a half-game of the lead with a 9–3 win over the Phillies at Connie Mack Stadium. Veteran catcher Del Crandall drove in five runs with a grand slam home run and a sacrifice fly, and young left fielder Lee Maye drove in the other four runs with a pair of clutch singles to account for all the Braves' scoring. Milwaukee right-hander Bob Buhl went all the way for his 14th win.

When the dust settled at the end of September 19, the Dodgers had moved into a first-place tie with the Giants by beating them twice. It was the first time the Dodgers had been in first since July 29. With eight days left in the season, the National League pennant race was thrown into a near three-way tie.

	W	*L*	*Pct.*	*
San Francisco	82	66	.554	—
Los Angeles	82	66	.554	—
Milwaukee	81	66	.551	½

*Games behind leader

On September 20, while Khrushchev sparred with U.S. labor leaders in downtown San Francisco, a few blocks away at Seals Stadium the Dodgers and Giants met in the final game of their three-game series, each team determined to break the first-place logjam in its own favor. With Candlestick Park nearly finished, it was the last game the Giants would play at Seals Stadium.

In a classic battle between the north and the south (Northern California versus Southern California and southpaw versus right-hander), left-hander Johnny Podres pitched Los Angeles to an 8–2 victory over San Francisco right-hander Sad Sam Jones. Duke Snider ignited the Dodger offense by ripping Sad Sam for a solo homer in the top of the second. In the fourth, in typical Dodgers style, they scratched together a run on two walks, plus singles by Wills and Podres. Down 2–0, and two games in the series, Giants manager Bill Rigney panicked and brought in one of his starters from the day before, Johnny Antonelli, who temporarily stopped the bleeding. But the Dodgers scratched together two more runs in the seventh with two walks, a single by Snider, and a sacrifice fly by Don Demeter to take a commanding 4–0 lead.

Podres, who shut out the Giants on four hits through the first seven innings, ran out of gas in the bottom of the eighth. After striking out the first two batters, he walked Hobie Landrith and gave up a single to Willie McCovey. Alston brought in Larry Sherry, and then held his breath while hoping the rookie had his good slider. But Sherry walked Willie Mays to load the bases, and gave up a two-run single to Orlando Cepeda. Sandy Koufax had to be rushed in from the bullpen to get Felipe Alou for the final out. After eight innings, the Dodger lead was cut in half, to 4–2.

The Giants, who had just clawed back into the game, were buried by the Dodgers' four-run outburst in the ninth. Koufax then tortured the Dodger fans watching on television back in L.A. by walking the bases loaded in the bottom of the ninth. The Dodgers brought in their old Brooklyn bullpen ace, Clem Labine, to pitch to the dangerous Leon Wagner. The Dodgers were trying to forget how Wagner had devastated them back on May 26 at the same Seals Stadium with a walk-off grand slam homer in the bottom of the ninth. But this time Labine struck him out, and then got Eddie Bressoud to ground into a game-ending double play.

For his clutch 7-for-13 performance, Maury Wills won the prize for the outstanding player in the series: an all-expense-paid trip for two to Japan.[16] In the clubhouse after the game, reporters asked Wills if he intended to take his wife to Japan after the season ended. "No," replied Wills, "after the *World Series*."[17] In 2007, Roger Craig said of Maury Wills, "He was such a leader on the field. When he got on base, he disrupted the whole game. Pitchers then had to worry about him in addition to the hitter. With his speed, if he hit it on the ground, he had a base hit. You had to be a good offensive player to get on base as often as he did. And you sure didn't want to walk him."[18]

The Giants, who entered the weekend in first place by two games, were stunned to find themselves in third place as they left for Chicago.

That same Sunday in Philadelphia, the Braves' 43-year-old pinch-hitter, Mickey Vernon, delivered a clutch two-run ninth-inning single to lead Milwaukee to an 8–5 victory over the Phillies at Connie Mack Stadium.

Rocked by another San Francisco earthquake, the National League standings were in turmoil at the end of September 20. The Dodgers' three-game sweep catapulted them into sole possession of first place, and dropped the Giants into third. The victorious Braves remained in second, a half-game behind.

	W	*L*	*Pct.*	*
Los Angeles	83	66	.557	—
Milwaukee	82	66	.554	½
San Francisco	82	67	.550	1

*Games behind leader

The Final Week: A Three-Team Death Struggle

From September 21–23, the Braves took two out of three from the Pirates at Forbes Field, the Dodgers, thanks to a three-hit shutout by Roger Craig, split a two-game series with the Cardinals in St. Louis, and the Giants continued their freefall, losing a pair to the Cubs at Wrigley Field. When play concluded on September 23, the Dodgers and Braves were again tied for first place with three games left in the season. The Giants, who had now lost five straight, were stuck in third, but still only two games behind the leaders.

	W	L	Pct.	*
Los Angeles	84	67	.556	—
Milwaukee	84	67	.556	—
San Francisco	82	69	.543	2

*Games behind leader

No games were scheduled for September 24, causing a brief lull in the storm. For once, the turbulent National League standings remained unchanged. The Dodgers traveled to Chicago to meet the Cubs, the Giants traveled to St. Louis to meet the Cardinals, and the Braves went home to Milwaukee to get ready for the last-place Phillies. The season would come down to the final weekend.

Friday, September 25

In the waning light at Wrigley Field, Gil Hodges hit a home run over the left-field fence to give the Dodgers a 5–4 victory in 11 innings over the stubborn Cubs. Hodges had been a doubtful starter due to a severely bruised arm caused by a Bob Miller pitch in St. Louis. It was the third RBI of the game for Hodges, who rocked the Cubs in the sixth with a 2-run double off the center-field ivy to break a 2–2 tie.

In the bottom of the 11th, with two out and the tying run on second base, reliever — and the winning pitcher — Larry Sherry struck out the dangerous Dale Long to end the game while the players could still see the ball. These were the days before lights were installed at Wrigley Field. Just before the final out, the four umpires huddled at the mound to discuss the fast-fading light. If the Cubs had tied the game, it probably would have been called on account of darkness, forcing the Dodgers to play a double-header on Saturday, thus putting added pressure on their weary pitching staff.[19]

Meanwhile, at County Stadium in Milwaukee, the cellar-dwelling Phillies stunned the Braves by knocking out 21-game winner Lew Burdette in the third inning on their way to a rain-soaked 6–3 victory. The Braves' best chance to avoid defeat came in the top of the fourth inning when rain stopped the game for 15 minutes with the Phillies ahead, 6–1. The County Stadium fans prayed for a rainout, but the rain stopped and play resumed. By the time the rain started again in the sixth, it was too late to help the Braves since the game could no longer be called incomplete.[20]

The weather front that was to wreak havoc on the contenders all weekend claimed its first casualty in St. Louis when the game between the Giants and Cardinals was washed out. The game would be made up as part of a double-header scheduled for the next day.

After the games of September 25, the National League standings showed the Dodgers had broken free of their deadlock with Braves to move a full game in front. The Giants, rendered helpless by the elements, slipped to 2½ games behind.

	W	*L*	*Pct.*	*
Los Angeles	85	67	.559	—
Milwaukee	84	68	.553	1
San Francisco	82	69	.543	2½

*Games behind leader

Saturday, September 26

With a win in Chicago, the Dodgers could have clinched no worse than a tie for the pennant. But it was not to be as the Cubs — sparked by two ghosts from their October 3, 1951, nightmare at the Polo Grounds — buried them, 12–2.

The players knew that the first order of business when they entered Wrigley Field was to look at the flags, not to demonstrate their patriotism, but to determine the direction of the wind. On this rainy day in the Windy City, the flag flying atop the left-field foul pole was stretched out as straight and stiff as a board, blowing OUT toward Lake Michigan. It was to portend disaster for the Dodgers, as a 12-run avalanche, set in motion by Alvin Dark's three-run homer in the second inning — nothing but a lazy fly that was caught by the wind and carried into the left-field bleachers — put the Dodgers behind for good. Dark, an old Dodger nemesis who was on base when Bobby Thomson hit his historic "shot heard 'round the world" home run off Ralph Branca on October 3, 1951, would go on to break the Dodgers' hearts again in 1962 as manager of the Giants. Now in a Cubs uniform, Bobby Thomson continued to haunt the Dodgers this day with four hits.

The Dodger pitching, which was largely responsible for putting them in a position to win on this last weekend of the season, chose an inopportune time to collapse against the seventh-place Cubs. Walter Alston's "money pitcher," Johnny Podres, went into the game with a 7–1 lifetime record against Chicago, but he was pummeled for six runs in less than three innings. None of the next five Dodger pitchers could stop the onslaught, and after four innings, the score was a grotesque 12–0.[21]

Two future Hall-of-Famers, Warren Spahn for the Braves and Robin Roberts for the Phillies, squared off in Milwaukee. Twice the Braves fell behind on solo home runs hit by the Phillies off Spahn. But with the scoreboard showing the Dodgers behind as much as 12–0, the Braves knew that if they could somehow pull the game out, they would probably go to the last day of the season tied with the Dodgers. Thus motivated, the Braves were able to come from behind twice with three runs off Roberts to win the game, 3–2. Spahn survived the home run balls to notch his 21st win of the season and his 267th career win, at that time the most in National League history for a left-hander.[22]

On a dark, threatening night in St. Louis, the Giants went into their twi-night double-header with the Cardinals knowing they had to win both games to have any chance on the last day of the season. In the first game, 20-game winner Sad Sam Jones took the mound for the Giants. Wilmer "Vinegar Bend" Mizel, the future congressman from Vinegar Bend, North Carolina, started for the Cardinals.

Jones, with the familiar toothpick protruding from his mouth, completely shut down the Cardinals, holding them hitless through the first seven innings. As he began the bottom of the eighth with a 4–0 lead, the tentacles of an enormous tornado-producing storm reached St. Louis. Jones had retired the first two Cardinal batters when the umpires suspended play as the sky fell in at Busch Stadium. Wind gusts shook the rooftop press box, torrents of rain flooded the field, and lightning flashes were accompanied by rumbling thunder as radios blared reports of tornadoes and warned listeners to hide in their basements.

After a rain delay of nearly two hours, the game was called off, and the Giants were credited with a 4–0 victory, thereby keeping them within 1½ games of the leaders and their pennant hopes alive. The Giants' runs were produced by Willie Mays' solo home run in the first, Orlando Cepeda's run-scoring double in the fifth, and rookie sensation Willie McCovey's two-run home run in the seventh. The washed-out second game was rescheduled for the final day of the season as part of an afternoon double-header. Sad Sam's 7⅔-inning gem was declared a "fractional" no-hitter, since only no-hitters of nine or more innings were considered bona fide for the record books.[23]

At the end of play on September 26, the Braves had moved into a tie for first with the Dodgers, and the Giants, thanks to Sad Sam's tornado-tainted no-hitter, advanced a full game to within 1½ games of the leaders going into the last day of the regular season.

	W	*L*	*Pct.*	*
Los Angeles	85	68	.556	—
Milwaukee	85	68	.556	—
San Francisco	83	69	.546	1½

*Games behind leader

Sunday, September 27

On the final day of the season, it was mathematically possible for the National League pennant race to end in a three-way tie if the Giants swept their double-header and the Dodgers and Braves both lost their single games.

At Wrigley Field, the Dodgers handed the ball to right-hander Roger Craig (10–5) and asked him for one more clutch effort. Nearly fifty years later, Craig recalled the confidence Walter Alston had in him that day: "We had to win the game, and Alston always had confidence in me. He started me in the 1955 World Series when I was a rookie."[24] The day before, after the Dodgers' 12–2 trouncing at the hands of the Cubs, a confident Craig tried to rally the team by promising to "pick them up" on the last day of the season. The resurrected Craig clearly wanted the baseball, and he came through. He gave the Dodgers a complete game, allowing only six hits and one run for a pennant-tying 7–1 victory. It was the fifth consecutive win for Craig down the stretch, and the Cubs' only run was just the second he had allowed in his last 30 innings. "I remember down the stretch I would tell my teammates to just get me one run," recalled Craig. "That's all I needed."[25] Craig's performance approached one-man-team proportions when he drove in the Dodgers' first two runs with a single in the top of the second inning.

The Dodgers got a break when Ernie Banks, on his way to his second consecutive National League MVP award, was injured and unable to start. With 45 home runs and 143 RBIs, Banks hobbled to the plate to pinch-hit with two out and two on in the seventh. A three-run homer by Banks would have cut the Dodgers' lead to 5–4, but Craig got him to pop up to Maury Wills. "I had more success against Banks than just about any other pitcher," recalled Roger Craig. "I would pitch him 'backwards'— with curves when he expected fastballs and with fastballs when he expected curves."[26]

When the last out was recorded, the Dodgers had clinched no worse than a tie for first place. The Braves–Phillies game, meanwhile, was only in the fourth inning at Milwaukee. The Dodgers had won six out of their last eight pressure-packed games on the road, but they could now only huddle around the radio in the clubhouse to sweat out the afternoon listening for word of their fate from Milwaukee.[27]

While the Dodgers battled the seventh-place Cubs in Wrigley, the Braves faced the eighth-place Phillies at County Stadium. If the "Banksless" Cubs seemed uninspired, the cellar-dwelling Phillies were simply inept, rolling over to give the Braves a 5–2 victory. The Phillies gave the Braves five unearned runs with four errors, a balk, a wild pitch, and a passed ball. "We handed the Braves the playoff on a silver platter," said Phillies shortstop Joe Koppe. And Philadelphia manger Eddie Sawyer lamented, "I never saw so many cheap runs in my life." When the circus ended, the Braves had kept pace with the Dodgers to end the season in a flat-footed tie for first.[28]

The Giants' hopes for a double-header sweep and a three-way tie were dashed in the first game when rookie left-hander Mike McCormick lost a 1–0 lead in the bottom of the eighth inning after shortstop Eddie Bressoud's first error in 41 games allowed the Cardinals to score their only two runs. The Cardinals held on to win, 2–1, thereby eliminating the Giants. The Cardinals, led by Stan Musial's 412th career home run, pounded San Francisco, 14–8, in the anti-climactic second game.[29]

* * *

At the end of the 154-game regular season, the Braves and Dodgers were tied for first heading into a three-game playoff for the National League pennant. A playoff seemed only fair, since Milwaukee and Los Angeles had been in a first-place tie for five of the last seven games of the season. After entering the final week of the season with a two-game lead over both the Dodgers and Braves, the Giants proceeded to lose seven of their last eight games—and eleven of their last sixteen—to finish in third place, three games off the pace.

	W	*L*	*Pct.*	*
Los Angeles	86	68	.558	—
Milwaukee	86	68	.558	—
San Francisco	83	71	.539	3

*Games behind leader

"Just Gimmie the Ball!"

Roger Craig would recall that after he won the last game of the season at Wrigley Field to force a playoff, "Alston came over to me and asked me if I could pitch on two days rest (if the playoff series went to a third game). I said, 'Just gimmie the ball!'"[30]

* * *

At 10:00 P.M. on the evening of September 27, Khrushchev departed Andrews Air Force Base after his second 21-gun salute, thus ending of his 13-day U.S. visit.[31] Khrushchev had spent the final three days at Camp David in private talks with President Eisenhower. Going into the talks, the superpowers were deadlocked over the issue of Berlin. The U.S. had insisted that the Soviet Union withdraw its threat — made the previous November — to oust allied troops from West Berlin. At a press conference the day after Khrushchev left for Moscow, it was evident that Eisenhower had achieved a breakthrough in U.S.–Soviet relations when he said he believed the Berlin impasse had been broken at Camp David. Eisenhower said that he was willing to take Khrushchev at his word when the Soviet premier told him, "No one is under any duress, no one is under any kind of threat, and no deadline will be imposed on the future status of Berlin."[32] Khrushchev had withdrawn the threat.

Chapter 18

We Go to Chicago!

On the evening of September 27, after agreeing with President Eisenhower to keep talking about their differences, Nikita Khrushchev ended his turbulent 13-day tour of the U.S. Before boarding the plane for his return flight to Moscow, his last words to his American hosts were, "Until we meet again."[1] As the baseball season headed into a rare post-season playoff, Americans breathed easier.

* * *

The same evening in Chicago, after their pennant-tying victory at Wrigley Field, the Dodgers won a flip of the coin and chose to play the first game of the best two-out-of-three-game series at County Stadium in Milwaukee, and the remaining game(s) at the Coliseum in Los Angeles.[2] There would be no time to celebrate, no time to reflect. The Dodgers immediately boarded a train to Milwaukee for the showdown with the Braves, due to start in less than 24 hours.

Playoffs and the Dodgers

The word "playoff" struck fear into the hearts of Dodger fans, and elicited bitter memories for 14-year Dodger veteran Carl Furillo. There had been only two playoffs in National League history — the Dodgers and Furillo were involved in both — and the results were disastrous.

In 1946, a torrid pennant race between the Dodgers and Cardinals ended in a tie as both teams lost on the final day of the season. The Cardinals, led by Stan Musial and Enos "Country" Slaughter, swept the first two games of the playoff series, and went on to a World Series triumph over Ted Williams and the Boston Red Sox.

But it was 1951 that proved to be the most disastrous end of the season ever for the Brooklyn Dodgers. On the last day of the campaign, the New York Giants caught the Dodgers, who had led by 13½ games in August, and forced a three-game playoff series that ended in bitter defeat for the Dodgers with Bobby Thompson's "shot heard 'round the world."

As the only 1959 Dodger player who was a regular in 1946 and 1951, Carl Furillo remembered those traumatic events well. With only nine games left in his career, he was destined to reverse the Dodgers' playoff fortunes.

Monday, September 28

After such a grueling finish to the regular season, both teams had to improvise to find a starting pitcher for the opening game of the playoff series. At the last minute, Braves manager Fred Haney scratched 21-game winner Lew Burdette and went with his young right-hander, Carlton Willey (5–9). Dodger manager Walter Alston was forced to name little left-hander Danny McDevitt (10–8) as his "surprise starter." Alston had intended to start Sandy Koufax, but he reconsidered, since in his mind the erratic left-hander had been largely "ineffective" with two losses and two no-decisions in his four starts since striking out 18 Giants on August 31. Neither starting pitcher would be around at the finish.

The game, scheduled to start at 1:00 P.M., began with dark and ominous signs for the Braves. The first pitch was delayed for 47 minutes by rain showers, and due to the darkness caused by the overcast, had to be played entirely under the lights. Although the Braves were trying for their third consecutive World Series appearance, only 18,297 fans turned out — a sign of the deteriorating support that would cause them to abandon Milwaukee for Atlanta six years later.

A less-than-sharp McDevitt survived the first inning but could retire only one Braves batter in the second. After the Braves tied the game at 1–1, the Dodgers brought in their 24-year-old rookie right-hander Larry Sherry to inherit a 2–0 count with one out and runners at first and third. The Braves promptly loaded the bases on an error by Maury Wills. Sherry got Bobby Avila on a ground out to Wills that should have gotten the Dodgers out of the inning. Instead, the extra out enabled Del Crandall to score an unearned run — charged to McDevitt — and the Braves took a 2–1 lead. Sherry shut down the rally as he got the eventual 1959 NL home run champion, Eddie Mathews, to ground out to Charlie Neal at second base.

Gil Hodges tied the game, 2–2, in the top of the third inning as he knocked in Wally Moon with a single to left field. In the top of the sixth inning,

Dodger catcher John Roseboro put the Dodgers ahead for good, 3–2, as Hank Aaron watched his home run sail over the right-field fence.

Meanwhile, Larry Sherry was getting stronger inning by inning. He had only two crises, pitching through one and relying upon luck to survive the other. In the bottom of the fifth inning, he got behind in the count to shortstop Johnny Logan with two out and runners at first and third, but he steadied himself and got Logan to ground out to preserve the 2–2 tie. Within one out of victory in the bottom of the ninth inning, he hung a curveball to Braves center fielder Billy Bruton, who nearly tied the game. Dodger center fielder Don Demeter hauled in Bruton's drive with his back against the center field fence — the deepest part of the park — to save the win for Sherry and the Dodgers. The come-from-behind win sent the Dodgers back to Los Angeles with a one-game lead in the series.

All told, Sherry pitched 7⅔ scoreless innings in relief, giving up only four hits. Though he came into the game in a pressure situation — with a one-run lead, two runners on, and inheriting a 2–0 count — he downplayed the pressure after the game: "I guess I was concentrating so much on getting outs that I didn't have time to feel the pressure."[3] Sherry prevailed despite not having command of the slider, the pitch that had transformed him from a journeyman minor leaguer to a major league sensation. "My slider wasn't sharp, so I had to rely on my fastball,"[4] said Sherry. Ironically, Walter Alston maintained that he might have named Sherry, the rookie, as the starter had it not been for his outstanding relief work in Chicago the last weekend of the regular season.

It was the seventh straight win for Larry Sherry (7–2) and his fifth in relief since his call up from Triple-A St. Paul in July. He had now given up only three runs in 36⅓ innings of relief (winning five games and saving three), lowering his ERA to a remarkable 0.74.

A Tragic Irony

While Larry Sherry was shutting down the Braves, John "Red" Corriden died of a heart attack in Indianapolis while watching the game on television. Corriden, a former major league infielder and manager of the Chicago White Sox in 1950, scouted Sherry as a prep prospect in Los Angeles and had recommended to the Brooklyn Dodgers that they sign him.[5]

No Rest for the Weary

After the last out, the players showered, dressed, and immediately embarked on the 1,700-mile flight to Los Angeles, where Game 2 was scheduled for the next afternoon at the Coliseum.[6]

Tuesday, September 29

For Game 2, both teams sent their star right-handers to the mound: Don Drysdale (17–13) for the Dodgers, and Lew Burdette (21–15) for the Braves. Neither ace pitcher would be around for the climax — Drysdale was gone in the fifth inning, and Burdette would last until the ninth.

Seventh Inning — Colliding Fates

Burdette took a 4–2 lead to the bottom of the seventh and got an inning-ending double play to shut out the Dodgers for the third straight inning. But the play resulted in a cruel twist of fate for the Braves. Norm Larker took out veteran shortstop Johnny Logan with a bone-crushing slide at second base. Though Logan somehow completed the double play, he had to be carried off the field on a stretcher after the collision. The loss of Johnny Logan would reverberate for the remainder of the game.

Twenty-two-year-old Felix Mantilla was moved from second base to replace Logan at shortstop, a position he was not comfortable with. This proved to be a crucial change, as Mantilla would commit two errors — the last one would cost the Braves the pennant. Red Schoendienst came off the bench to play second base despite having played in only four games at the end of the season and batting just twice since returning from his struggle with tuberculosis.

Johnny Logan was hitting nearly .500 for the season against the Dodgers, and was 2-for-3 in the game. He was due to lead off the eighth inning. Instead, Schoendienst, batting in his slot, made the first out. Had he gotten on base, he would have scored on Del Crandall's triple.[7]

Ninth Inning — Hodges and Furillo Act One: Survival

In the top of the ninth, the Dodgers survived a showdown between two grizzled veterans. The Braves loaded the bases with two out. Again, the scheduled hitter was Schoendienst, batting in Logan's spot. But Fred Haney sent in the 41-year-old Mickey Vernon to pinch-hit for Schoendienst against Clem Labine, whose best days were behind him as the ace of the Brooklyn bullpen. Labine struck out Vernon — looking — to prevent the Braves from adding to their 5–2 lead and putting the game out of reach.

With a three-run lead, Burdette, MVP of the 1957 World Series, appeared to have the Dodgers hopelessly beaten as he took the mound in the bottom of the ninth. He was seeking a league-leading 22nd win of the season and his third straight over the Dodgers. Cruising through the first eight innings, Burdette had held the Dodgers to five hits with no walks, and was virtually unhittable after the fourth inning when the Dodgers scored their last run as Charlie Neal lobbed a lazy fly ball over the left-field screen for a solo homer. But Burdette's command suddenly deserted him, and he was unable to get anyone out.

Taking dead aim at Burdette, Wally Moon and Duke Snider shot sharp singles past him into center field, and Gil Hodges loaded the bases with a single to left. With no one out, the Braves pulled Burdette and brought in their top reliever, Don McMahon. Left-handed-hitting left fielder Norm Larker (nicknamed "Dumbo" for his prodigious ears), with 15 hits in his last 32 at-bats during the stretch run, greeted McMahon with two-run single off the left-field screen to pull the Dodgers to within one run at 5–4.

With runners on first and third and none out, the Braves turned to their great left-handed starter and future Hall of Famer, Warren Spahn, to pitch to the Dodgers' left-handed-hitting catcher, John Roseboro. For the season Spahn had been 21–12 as a starter but 0–3 in relief to give him an undistinguished career relief record of 2–13. The chess match continued between Dodger manager Walter Alston and Braves manager Fred Haney, as Alston countered by sending the right-handed-hitting Carl Furillo up to pinch-hit. Furillo promptly sliced a fly ball to right field. Hank Aaron made a fine play on the ball, but it turned into a sacrifice fly as Gil Hodges scored from third base to tie the game at 5–5. After Maury Wills singled to put Larker on second base as the potential winning run, Fred Haney pulled Spahn and brought in Joey Jay to get the final two outs. Jay, the first Little Leaguer to play in the major leagues, had to face former USC star Ron Fairly, pinch-hitting for former Stanford star Chuck Essegian. Jay got the rookie Fairly to hit into a force play. With two out and runners at first and third, lead-off batter Jim Gilliam connected with a Jay fastball for what looked like the dispositive blow. Henry Aaron describes the play he made to send the game into extra innings and prolong the season for the Braves: "Gilliam hit a ball toward the right-field corner and deep. I got there just before it hit the fence and managed to hang onto the ball as I bumped the wall at a pretty good clip."[8] Thanks to a sensational defensive play by the 1959 NL batting champion, the game moved to the tenth inning tied, 5–5.

Stan Williams—The Forgotten Man

With their bullpen nearly depleted after using five pitchers and with their ace reliever, Larry Sherry, recharging on the bench after pitching 7⅔ brilliant shut-out innings the day before, the Dodgers were forced to bring in Stan Williams, their 23-year-old fire-balling right-hander, for the tenth inning. At the age of 76, Roger Craig would recall, "Stan Williams was a big strong right-hander with a good fastball."[9] But Williams was clearly the forgotten man. Principally a starter, he had not won a game since August 17. Since then, he had made only two "mop-up" relief appearances in games that were already hopelessly lost.

Alston took a big risk with Williams, and it paid off. Williams rose to the occasion, pitching three scoreless, hitless innings in the tenth, eleventh, and twelfth. It was a great clutch performance, but not without tension. He gave 36,528 Dodger fans a fright by walking the bases loaded with two out in the eleventh prior to getting the power-hitting Joe Adcock to ground into an inning-ending force play.

12th Inning—Hodges and Furillo, Act Two: One Ball, Two Crazy Bounces, and "We Go to Chicago!"

After retiring Wally Moon and Stan Williams to start the bottom of the twelfth inning, the Braves' fifth pitcher, Bob Rush, gave the Dodgers an opening by walking Gil Hodges. Next, Rush gave up a single to the Dodgers' .237-hitting second-string catcher Joe "Piggy" Pignatano, with Hodges playing it safe and stopping at second. With two out, two runners on, and the score tied, 5–5, 37-year-old Carl Furillo came to the plate for the third time in the game. Rush got ahead in the count one ball and two strikes before Furillo hit Rush's next pitch sharply on the ground, bounding over the pitcher's head, and heading for center field. Shortstop Felix Mantilla initially thought he could catch the ball and step on second base for a force play to end the inning and extend the game to the thirteenth. But again, fate intervened for the Dodgers as described by Mantilla: "The ball took a crazy bounce and pulled me across the bag before I got it."[10] After making a fine play on the wayward baseball to prevent it from going into center field, he had no realistic chance to get Furillo at first. But Mantilla showed how pressure can do strange things to a young player's judgment. Off-balance, he made a desperate throw that never reached first base, exploding instead into the dirt in front of Braves first baseman Frank Torre. Fate then intervened a final, fatal time for the Dodgers as witnessed by Torre (older brother of current Dodger manager Joe): "If the ball had taken a normal bounce, I could have dug it out. But the ball hit a ridge or a stone and bounced over my head. It hit Mulleavy (Dodger first-base coach) and bounced off his shoulder."[11] In fact, Torre never actually touched the ball, which ended its erratic journey in the stands. Gil Hodges, who had taken off from second base with the crack of the bat, was waved home by third-base coach Pee Wee Reese. As a leaping, arm-rotating Gil Hodges landed on home plate with the winning run, thousands of the 36,528 hysterical Dodger fans listening to their transistor radios in the stands heard Vin Scully lead the celebration as he yelled into his microphone, "We go to Chicago!"

Thanks to the heroics of two old "Boys of Summer," the Dodgers now had a date with the White Sox for the World Series.

In the Braves clubhouse, an inconsolable Mantilla sobbed, "It was my only play. It was my only play. I had to throw to first."[12] But in retrospect, young Mantilla's lapse of judgment was clear. After making a fine stop, had he held on to the ball, Gil Hodges would have stopped at third base, and Bob Rush could have had another chance to retire the side and prolong the Braves' season.

No Game 3

There would be no Game 3. Roger Craig, who promised Walter Alston that he would pitch the next day if necessary on two days rest, would get to rest an additional day before taking the ball for Game 1 of the 1959 World Series.

Roger Craig recalled the Dodgers' two-game sweep cost him the ERA title: "I had pitched 152⅔ innings, and back then, you had to pitch 154 to qualify for the ERA championship. My ERA was 2.06 and Sam Jones was at 2.89. In 1959, the playoff counted in the regular season statistics. I probably could have given up 13 earned runs and still won the ERA title. But I'd rather win the National League pennant, anyway."[13]

Though his team lost, Eddie Mathews benefited personally from the playoffs. Tied with Ernie Banks with 45 home runs at the end of the regular season, he won the NL home run title with number 46 — a solo shot off Don Drysdale in the fifth inning of Game 2.

"It Was Unbelievable!"

Asked how he felt when Gil Hodges touched home plate when a mere 100 days before he was in the minor leagues and now was scheduled to start Game 1 of the World Series, Roger Craig observed nearly fifty years later, "It was unbelievable! We were not supposed to win. Milwaukee had the better ball club."[14]

* * *

After being written off before the season started, the Dodgers had done the impossible by rising like Lazarus from seventh place to first in one year. In stark contrast to the six pennants won by the 1947–1956 all-star-packed teams in Brooklyn, this flag was earned by a collection of underdogs and misfits. Including their two playoff series victories, the 1959 Los Angeles Dodgers won only 88 games—the fewest for a pennant winner in National League history. But again, there was no time to celebrate. Immediately after their four-hour pennant-clinching marathon with the Braves, the Dodgers had to board a plane to Chicago and prepare to meet the White Sox in 36 hours.

Chapter 19

The Go-Go Sox

El Señor

Former St. Louis Cardinal shortstop Marty Marion was hired to manage the White Sox for the 1955 season, Luis Aparicio's rookie year. Though it had become evident that Marion and Sox co-owner Chuck Comiskey did not get along, Chicago fans blamed Dick Donovan's emergency appendectomy for the team's disappointing third-place finish, and Marion was retained.

After a promising start in 1956, culminating in a four-game sweep of the mighty Yankees at Comiskey Park, a dismal 9–21 July condemned the Sox to another third-place finish. When the Chicago front office learned that Al Lopez was about to be let go by the Indians, they dumped Marty Marion and signed Lopez to a contract on October 29, 1956. "El Señor" Lopez led the White Sox to consecutive second-place finishes in 1957 and 1958.

But even the brilliant Al Lopez was not given much of a chance for 1959 by the sportswriters gathering in Tampa, Florida, for spring training. The consensus was that the Sox were aging and had no long ball threat. Thwarted in his attempt to get Washington Senators slugger Roy Sievers during the off-season, Lopez was the only one who thought the White Sox had enough firepower to go all the way in 1959. After finishing a distant 10 games behind the New York Yankees in 1958, Lopez sounded like an extreme minority voice. Chicago sportswriter William Barry Furlong wrote that the White Sox would not finish in the money. If the team proved him wrong, he promised to roll a peanut down State Street — with his nose.[1]

History shows that if not for Al Lopez, the American League would have been a joke as a competitive organization. But for his pennant-winning clubs in Cleveland in 1954 and Chicago in 1959, the Yankees would have won every AL pennant from 1949 through 1964 — 16 straight years.[2]

The Go-Go Sox

Go-Go Sox manager Al Lopez. In leading the 1954 Indians and 1959 White Sox to the World Series, El Señor prevented 16 straight Yankee AL pennants from 1949 to 1964. (National Baseball Hall of Fame Library, Cooperstown, N.Y.)

Chicago was known as the "Go-Go Sox" because of their relentless hustle and spirit.[3] Their 5'9" 160-pound shortstop and lead-off man, Luis Aparicio, led the major leagues with 56 stolen bases in 1959, an unusually high number for the 1950s. Boston's Jackie Jensen led the AL with just 22 in 1954—two years before Aparicio arrived from Venezuela. For 1959, the White Sox team led the American League with 113 stolen bases, 45 more than runner-up Boston.

The White Sox liked to run and put pressure on the opposing defense. Once Aparicio got on base, the fans at Comiskey Park would begin chanting, "Go-Go-Go!" It soon became their trademark.

In perfect Stengelese, Casey Stengel described the effect that the Go-Go Sox had on the opposition. "When I (the batter) get on first base and you're the pitcher, and everybody's yelling Go! Go! Go!, you forget that the man who is going to do the damage is the man up at the plate with the big bat. He is the man we put the pitcher out there to fool.[4]

The Annoyance Factor

Casey Stengel reduced the Go-Go Sox to a single word: annoying. From bitter experience as manager of the Yankees, he observed, "When the (Sox) baserunner annoys you, you think about him instead of the hitter. You forget about the weakness of the hitter. If you give them any kind of opportunity, they'll be all over you, in your hair, snapping at your heels, and annoying you in a number of ways. They force the other team to beat themselves just like they did to us and the other American League clubs all season."[5]

White Sox Hitting (or Lack Thereof)

In his tenth season, the 5'7" bald tobacco-chewing second baseman, Jacob Nelson "Nellie" Fox, was the heart and soul of the 1959 Go-Go Sox. With a .306 average, he was the only Sox .300 hitter, and was eventually named Chicago's first American League Most Valuable Player. As one of the best bunters in baseball, Fox was the perfect number-two man in the batting order behind Aparicio.[6] White Sox fans sensed they were in store for a special season on Opening Day in Detroit, when Fox — who hit zero home runs in 1958 — beat the Tigers with a 14th-inning home run on a frigid 37-degree day at Briggs Stadium. He had a total of five hits and seven runs batted in, one-seventh of his 1958 total.[7]

Since Al Lopez was thwarted in his efforts to trade for Washington's Roy Sievers (42 homers in 1957 and 39 in 1958), catcher Sherman Lollar was the only legitimate power threat with a modest 22 home runs. In Jim Landis, the Sox had one of the best defensive center fielders, but he hit only five home runs and batted .272. Chicago's lack of offense was apparent from a survey of the balance of the starting lineup: right-fielder Al Smith .237; first baseman Earl Torgeson, .220; third baseman Bubba Phillips .264; and Aparicio .257.

Fleet center fielder Jim Landis contributed 20 stolen bases and seven triples to the Go-Go Sox offense. (National Baseball Hall of Fame Library, Cooperstown, N.Y.)

The 1959 White Sox hit Major League Baseball's lowest number of home runs (97). But they also had the lowest earned run average (3.29), and the highest fielding percentage (.979) in the American League.[8] Clearly, Chicago had to rely on pitching, speed, and defense.

White Sox Pitching

The ace of the White Sox pitching staff was Early Wynn. "Burly Early" was one of Al Lopez's "Big Four" starters from the 1954

Cleveland Indians, along with Bob Lemon, Mike Garcia, and Bob Feller. In the winter of 1957, Lopez brought him to Chicago in exchange for Minnie Minoso. After a so-so 14–16 record in 1958, the 39-year-old right-hander produced his last great season in 1959 with a 22–10 record and the Cy Young Award. Wynn's reputation for toughness was illustrated by the variations on the question of whether he would knock down his son, his mother, or his grandmother. On various instances, he responded, "It would depend on how well he was hitting," "Only if she was digging in," and "If she crowds the plate."[9]

Early Wynn won 22 games for the 1959 White Sox to capture the Cy Young Award. He (and reliever Gerry Staley) shut out the Dodgers, 11–0, in Game 1 of the World Series, then lost the Game 6 finale while pitching on only two days rest. (George Brace photograph)

Complementing Early Wynn with an 18–6 record, young right-hander Bob Shaw gave the Sox an effective one-two punch. But as the 1948 Boston Braves learned with their "Spahn and Sain and Pray for Rain" strategy, the White Sox suffered from their over-reliance on two stars. After Wynn and Shaw, there was a large drop-off in the starting staff, with Dick Donovan (9–10) and left-hander Billy Pierce (14–15) rounding out the rotation.

The White Sox relied heavily on their strong bullpen tandem of Gerry Staley and Omar "Turk" Lown. Together they made 127 appearances, winning 17 games and saving 29.[10]

White Sox Defense — Strong Up the Middle

The experts called Chicago's up-the-middle defense the best in baseball, consisting of Nelson Fox at second base, Luis Aparicio at shortstop, Jim Landis in center field, and Sherman Lollar behind the plate. By giving the team the ability to hold a lead, it was the main reason the White Sox were so dominating in one-run games. At 35–15, Chicago had the best record in baseball in that category.[11]

The 1959 Al Pennant Race

By May 20, the Yankees had fallen to last place, and they stayed there until the end of the month. It took an 18–12 June recovery to get them back into contention.

With the Yankees having a rare off-year, the race was between the Indians and the White Sox. On paper, the powerful Indians, managed by Joe Gordon, looked like the superior team. Outfielder Rocky Colavito had 42 home runs and 111 runs batted in. On June 10 in Baltimore, he joined Lou Gehrig as only the second player in American League history to hit four consecutive home runs in one game.[12] Shortstop Woody Held had 29 home runs. Outfielder Minnie Minoso had 21 home runs and batted .302. Outfielder Tito Francona (father of current Red Sox manager Terry) hit .363 with 20 home runs, but with only 399 at-bats (and 443 plate appearances), he failed to qualify for the batting title.

Known as "Buster" to his teammates, Calvin Coolidge Julius Caesar Tuskahoma (Cal) McLish was the ace of the Cleveland pitching staff with a record of 19–8. Rounding out the Indians' starting staff were Gary Bell (16–11), Jim Perry (12–10), and Jim "Mudcat" Grant (10–7). Left-hander Herb Score, trying to make a comeback after being struck in the face by a Gil McDougald line drive in 1957, continued to struggle at 9–11.

The Indians sat atop the American League standings for most of the first half of the season, with the White Sox staying within striking distance until they took over the lead for good on July 22.[13] The race eventually came down to a critical four-game series between the White Sox and the Indians at the end of August before the largest crowds of the year in Cleveland Municipal Stadium. With eight straight wins going into the series, the Indians had clawed to within 1½ games of Chicago's lead. But with a crushing double-header sweep on August 30, the visiting Sox swept the four-game series, escaped Cleveland with a commanding 5½-game lead, and never looked back. The next day, the *Cleveland Plain Dealer* captured the mood of the devastated Indians fans when they declared "Go-Go Home White Sox!"[14]

The White Sox added insult to injury when they returned to Cleveland to clinch the American League pennant on September 22. The Sox entered the bottom of the ninth inning with 4–2 lead with right-hander Bob Shaw (17–6) pitching in relief of their ace, Early Wynn, who was seeking his 21st victory. The Indians loaded the bases, and with one out, Al Lopez pulled Shaw and brought in his top reliever, Gerry Staley, to face the dangerous Vic Power. On the first pitch, Power hit a sharp grounder up the middle for an apparent game-tying hit, but Aparicio grabbed it and turned a scintillating double play.[15] In the steamy, jam-packed, and beer-spattered dressing room, Aparicio called it "the best double play I ever made."[16] The pennant-clinching game also marked the end of the Indians–White Sox season series, which Chicago dominated, 15 games to seven.

It was bedlam in the Windy City after the White Sox won their first pennant in forty years. There were so many wailing sirens that those who did not follow baseball were terrified that the Russians were attacking. Mayor Richard Daley and fire commissioner Robert Quinn — both White Sox fans— were forced to issue a public apology.[17] As he promised, sportswriter William Barry Furlong rolled a peanut down State Street with his nose. When the Sox arrived at Midway Airport in Chicago at 2:05 A.M. the next morning, a crowd estimated at 100,000 was there to greet them. Some delirious fans risked life and limb to get a better view of their heroes by climbing telephone poles and standing on top of buses, cars, and trucks.[18]

The Old-Old Sox

By 1959, age was becoming a factor for the White Sox. Although Bob Shaw, Jim Landis, and Luis Aparicio were in their mid-twenties, most of the team's best players were over 30. Early Wynn and Gerry Staley were 39, "Jungle Jim" Rivera was 37, Turk Lown, Sherman Lollar, Earl Torgeson, and Ted Kluszewski were all 35, Dick Donovan and Billy Pierce were 32, and Al Smith and Nellie Fox were both 31.

With aging players and a rare New York Yankee off-year, AL Lopez knew that if the Sox were ever going to win the American League pennant again, this was their best chance.

A Yankee Off-Year

Crippled with injuries and consumed by salary holdouts, the Yankees were never a legitimate contender in 1959.[19] After winning the last four AL pennants, the New York Yankees finished an embarrassing third, 15 games behind the White Sox. One of the reasons was the loss of first baseman Bill "Moose" Skowron for the second half of the season due to a broken wrist. Another was the ineffectiveness of right-handers Bob Turley (8–11) and Don Larsen (6–7).

Also having an off-year was superstar Mickey Mantle, who plunged to a .285 batting average (80 points below his 1957 average of .365). Mantle had only 75 runs batted in, an unusually low number in relation to his 31 home runs.

Little second baseman Bobby Richardson was New York's only .300 hitter, at .301. The Yankees scored only 687 runs— their fewest since 1946.[20]

Left to right, manager Al Lopez in the Comiskey Park dugout with his Go-Go Sox starting lineup for Game 1 of the 1959 World Series: Luis Aparicio SS, Nellie Fox 2B, Jim Landis CF, Ted Kluszewski 1B, Sherman Lollar C, Billy Goodman 3B, Al Smith LF, Jim Rivera RF, Early Wynn P. They pounded the Dodgers, 11–0, in a very un–Go-Go-like display of power. (National Baseball Hall of Fame Library, Cooperstown, N.Y.)

By a margin of 13 games to nine, the White Sox won the season series with the Yankees for the first time since 1925.

Third place was clearly unacceptable by New York standards. The Yankees were determined to take the necessary measures to rectify the situation in the off-season. On December 11, 1959, they sent Hank Bauer, Don Larsen, Norm Sieburn, and Marv Throneberry to Kansas City for a promising young outfielder named Roger Maris.

Bill Veeck Takes Over

Events off the field captured Sox fans' attention in the early months of 1959. The "battling Comiskeys" fought for control of the team in probate court, which allowed Bill Veeck (as in wreck) to take over ownership. Original owner Charles A. Comiskey owned the White Sox from 1901 until his death in 1931, when the controlling shares passed to son, J. Louis. J. Louis' son, Charles "Chuck" Comiskey, thought the team was his by birthright. Since childhood, the family had prepared him for the day he would take over active management of the club. But with the death of his mother, Grace, in 1956, internecine feuding between Chuck and his sister Dorothy Rigney ruined the family plan.

Grace Comiskey's will left daughter Dorothy 500 more shares than son Chuck, thereby assuring Dorothy voting control of the team with 54 percent. For months, Chuck had tried to buy Dorothy's share but she refused to sell, blaming him — as a Sox vice president —for the team's poor earnings performance.[21] With the siblings unable to agree on a fair price, the courtroom drama lasted until March 10, 1959, before a judge made it possible for Veeck and his partners, including Hank Greenberg, to take over the club.

Comiskey Park

Located on the South Side of Chicago at the corner of West 35th Street and South Shields Avenue, the original Comiskey Park had been the home of the White Sox since July 1, 1910. The dimensions reflected Charles A. Comiskey's love of symmetry: 352 feet down both foul lines made of flattened garden hoses painted white, 365 feet to the power alleys, and 410 feet to center field, with 10-foot-high brick walls. The double-decked park held 52,934 fans in 1959.

Barnum Bill Veeck, master promoter, promptly turned Comiskey Park into a circus. He staged cow milking contests, a "martian invasion" (led by midget Eddie Gaedel), and "Al Smith Night," in which every Schmidt, Smith, Smyth, and Smithe was admitted free in order to encourage the slumping Sox left fielder. Unfortunately, the real Al Smith dropped a fly ball that gave the other Sox (the Red variety) a 7–6 victory in front of all his namesakes.[22] Southsiders would be spared the shock of Veeck's new screeching, screaming, exploding scoreboard until Opening Day 1960.[23] Old Comiskey Park would remain the home of the White Sox through September 30, 1990.

Chapter 20

The Underdog Series

On September 30, 1959, a nationwide steel strike reached its 78th day. The strike had shut down the furnaces of two dozen steel companies that employed 500,000 workers and produced 85 percent of the nation's steel. At the White House, President Eisenhower urged representatives of the steel industry and the United Steelworkers Union to resume negotiations, which had collapsed the week before.[1] Eisenhower was reluctant to invoke the Taft-Hartley Act to end the strike, preferring instead to let market decide the outcome. "I believe that we have to thoroughly test out and use the method of free bargaining," he said, and when the government starts pressuring, "then I believe it's not free."[2]

* * *

That day the Dodgers arrived in Chicago exhausted at 5:30 A.M. after completing a whirlwind trip — Chicago to Milwaukee to Los Angeles to Chicago— and playing two pressure-packed playoff games with the Milwaukee Braves, all in less than 48 hours. The Dodgers cancelled a scheduled workout at Comiskey Park, and most of the players hung "do not disturb" signs on their doors and slept until noon. They were expected to be ready to face Early Wynn the next day in the opening game of the Series. With a 22–10 record, Wynn was the winningest pitcher in baseball. The Dodgers would go with their new meal ticket, Roger Craig, on his normal three days rest. When asked how he felt after the Dodgers' brutal travel schedule delivered them to Chicago exhausted, Roger Craig would observe in hindsight, "When you're in the World Series, you don't think of how tired you are."[3]

Before the season, both teams expected to spend October in front of their black and white television sets watching the Milwaukee Braves and the New York Yankees play their third consecutive World Series. But here they were, two underdogs, about to play the first Dodgers–White Sox World Series in baseball history.

Game One

Thursday afternoon October 1, 1959— The 56th World Series opened in Chicago before 48,013 fans at Comiskey Park, scene of their last World Series triumph of 1917.

Thanks to a third-inning defensive collapse and a career performance by Ted Kluszewski, the travel-weary Dodgers fell behind, 11–0, after four innings and never recovered. Kluszewski tied a World Series record by driving in five runs on two home runs and a single, and American League Cy Young Award winner Early Wynn breezed through seven shutout innings for the win. There was now talk of a four-game Chicago sweep.

The Official 1959 World Series Program of the Chicago White Sox. The Go-Go Sox took advantage of a rare Yankee off-year to play in their first Fall Classic since the infamous 1919 Black Sox. (National Baseball Hall of Fame Library, Cooperstown, N.Y.)

Return of the Black Sox

The day was crisp and bright, with a touch of autumn, as 71-year-old Red Faber took the mound and 67-year-old Ray Schalk settled in behind the plate. This was the Chicago battery of the infamous 1919 "Black Sox" World Series of 1919, the last time the White Sox were in the Fall Classic. Red loaded up and threw his signature "spitter" to officially open the Series.[4]

Early Wynn: Meanness Personified

Al Lopez called on ace right-hander Early Wynn to start Game 1. The 39-year-old Wynn, who would win the Cy Young Award, had been the Sox workhorse all season with 37 starts and 256 innings pitched in a 154-game schedule.

Yankee manager Casey Stengel said of the hard-nosed Wynn, "He's a great asset to start a Series because of his meanness. He's got a mean stare. I had him in several All-Star games and nothing fazes him. He's a cardshark who dares you to take a certain pitch and he throws it on a dime."[5]

Abandoned Brooklyn Dodger fans outside Ebbets Field listening to the 1959 World Series on the radio. (National Baseball Hall of Fame Library, Cooperstown, N.Y.)

Big Klu

The Dodger scouts traveling with the Sox during the month of September did not pay much attention to National League cast-off Ted Kluszewski, the 35-year-old first baseman the White Sox picked up on waivers for $20,000 from the Pittsburgh Pirates at the end of August.[6]

Although he hit well for the Sox during their pennant drive, he produced only two home runs.[7] The 6' 4" 250-pound "Big Klu" had to cut off the sleeves of his jersey to accommodate his huge blacksmith arms. The former Indiana University football player had been one of the most dominant sluggers in the National League, averaging 43 home runs, 116 RBIs, and only 35 strikeouts with Cincinnati from 1953 to 1956. Perhaps Los Angeles chose to forget how he had been a Dodger-killer in his heyday: in 1955 he hit seven home runs off the Brooklyn Dodgers, including one off rookie Roger Craig, and in 1956 had another three home runs off the Dodgers, again all off Craig. Asked whether he was conscious that day of Kluszewski's past success against him,

Ted Kluszewski, "Big Klu," was picked up by the White Sox as an afterthought from the Pirates in August 1959. He destroyed the Dodgers in Game 1 of the 1959 World Series with two home runs and five RBIs. (George Brace photograph)

Roger Craig would later recall, "Allan Roth, the Dodgers' statistician, would tell me all that, but I had to get him out *now*!"[8]

After suffering a back injury in 1957 that forced him to wear a corset, he was traded to the Pirates, where his production precipitously declined to four home runs per season in 1958 and 1959.[9] Scheduled to start at first base, and supported by a large contingent of fans from his home town of Argo, Illinois, this would be the greatest game of his career.

The Sox Abandon Small Ball

It soon became apparent that the "Go-Go" Sox did not show up to play small ball. They jumped on Roger Craig for two runs in the first on an RBI-single by Ted Kluszewski and a sacrifice fly by Sherman Lollar.

Then the roof caved in on Craig in the third as 11 White Sox batters came to the plate in an offensive orgy. The inning started quietly as Aparicio flied out, but Craig would face only three more batters. Fox doubled and was singled home by Landis. Big Klu unloaded on a Craig slider, launching a towering fly to right. The ball had just enough carry to clear the wall and sail into the lower right-field stands—just out of the leaping Norm Larker's reach for a two-run homer to make it 5–0. It was a crushing blow that sent Craig to the showers after only 2⅓ innings. "He was a first baseman, not an outfielder," Roger Craig recalled of Norm Larker. "An average outfielder might have caught it. But Larker was a bulldog who gave 150 percent, and he had a tough 'don't bother me' attitude."[10]

Journeyman reliever Clarence Nottingham Churn, called Chuck, took the mound as the Dodger defense turned into a three-ring circus. Catcher Sherman Lollar ended up on second base as his pop fly was misplayed by Duke Snider for a two-base error. Sox third baseman Billy Goodman singled him home to make it 6–0. Al Smith doubled off the wall in deep left-center, sending Goodman to third, and Goodman scored on Snider's second error — a wild throw — to make it 7–0. Right fielder "Jungle Jim" Rivera hit a routine grounder to Charlie Neal, who inexplicably threw the ball home, past catcher John Roseboro, for a Series record-tying third Dodger error of the inning, as Smith scored Chicago's eighth run. In the final insult of the inning, White Sox pitcher Early Wynn humiliated Churn with a double to right field to score "Jungle Jim" to make the score 9–0 after three innings.

But Big Klu was not finished. In the fourth inning, after Landis singled, he hammered a hanging Churn curveball deep into the upper deck in right field for his second two-run homer — what Klu would characterize after the game as "a real Cadillac job."[11] Kluszewski thus finished another Dodger pitcher as Clarence Nottingham Churn's first and only World Series appearance was brought to an end.[12] Both Landis and Klu were now 3-for-3. The shell-shocked Dodgers were down, 11–0, after four innings and facing the American League Cy Young Award winner.

After cruising for seven scoreless innings, Early Wynn came out in the eighth to a deafening ovation when the cold weather caused his right elbow to tighten. The ace of the Sox bullpen, Gerry Staley, continued to shut out the Dodgers over the last two innings to save the game for Wynn, who squared his World Series record at 1–1. Pitching for the Cleveland Indians, he lost to the New York Giants on their way to a four-game sweep of the rare Yankee-less World Series of 1954. The 11–0 final score equaled the record shutout pitched by the St. Louis Cardinals' Dizzy Dean against Detroit in the last game of the 1934 Series.[13]

Ol' Case Knew the Curse of the Go-Go Sox

Up in the press box, Casey Stengel, who as manager of the Yankees had been victimized by the Go-Go Sox during the regular season, described their style of play: "Al Lopez is a depositor in my bank in Glendale ... and he puts on a running and bunting attack like they used to in the days of the dead ball era. They take everything and give nothing — stingy as hell. They harassed me all through the season, and they started right in harassing Los Angeles in the first game."[14]

Moved by empathy for the plight of the Dodgers, the Ol' Perfesser continued, "That's why so many balls went safe the first day when the Los Angeles pitchers looked bad, and the infielders developed five thumbs, and the outfielders were bumping into each other."[15]

"My Biggest Thrill"

"It was my biggest thrill I ever had," said Ted Kluszewski in the chaotic White Sox dressing room after hitting two home runs in front of his hometown friends and family.[16] With five RBIs in the game, Kluszewski tied a World Series record shared by Yankee immortals Tony Lazzeri and Bill Dickey.[17]

"I Was Completely Out of Sync"

After his clutch pitching down the stretch got the Dodgers to the World Series, Craig recalled that day in Chicago, "I was completely out of sync that day. I left too many balls in the middle of the plate. I was a low-ball pitcher, and Kluszewski was a good low fastball hitter — not a good matchup from my point of view."[18]

"Don't Count Us Out"

After their humiliating 11–0 defeat at the hands of Chicago's "hitless wonders," who uncharacteristically stole no bases and made no great defensive plays, the Dodgers' World Series record sunk to 20–37. It was the worst defeat ever suffered by the Dodgers in a World Series game.[19] Down a game, they faced the challenge of having to even the Series the next day against Bob Shaw — 18–6 for the season — in front of another hostile crowd at Comiskey Park.

In the jubilant White Sox clubhouse, manager Al Lopez cautiously commented on the Dodgers' performance, saying, "They didn't win that pennant over there by playing like that."[20]

In a subdued Dodger clubhouse, Gil Hodges remained philosophical: "You can't lose a World Series on the first game. Remember, we dropped the first two games of the 1955 World Series to the Yankees and ended up winning the whole thing. Don't count us out."[21]

Strange Days Have Found Us

October 1, 1959, was the sight of some strange things in Chicago. An unlucky man, who had stood in line for two days to buy a $2 bleacher seat, sold it to the first passerby for $10. Unfortunately, the passerby was a cop on the "scalper detail."

To handle the traffic situation, the streets around the ballpark were all changed to one-way. The natives were so confused that traffic jammed up for miles.

Roses hung from lampposts all over Chicago, but there wasn't a scrap of traditional bunting inside Comiskey Park.

The American flag in Comiskey Park was stuck at half-mast all day.

A kid in the right-field stands, playing hooky from school, caught the first home run ball off the bat of Ted Kluszewski. The next day, to his horror, he found his beaming face plastered on every newspaper in Chicago.

But the strangest thing happened on the field. The White Sox, whose entire offense was supposed to be built around a walk, a stolen base, an infield single, and a sacrifice fly, looked more like the 1927 Yankees. White Sox owner Bill Veeck quipped, "In the third inning, when we scored seven runs, I almost left. I thought I'd come to the wrong park."[22]

Game Two

Friday afternoon, October 2, 1959— A crowd of 47,368 fans squeezed into Comiskey Park in Chicago to witness the second game of the Series. The Dodgers sent left-hander Johnny Podres to the mound against White Sox right-hander Bob Shaw.

The Dodgers rebounded from their 11–0 thrashing in Game 1 to beat the White Sox, 4–3, in a gutsy come-from-behind win to tie the Series at one game apiece. The Dodgers scored all their runs with two outs on three homers off Bob Shaw: two by 156-pound second baseman Charlie Neal and one by pinch-hitter Chuck Essegian. Due to a baserunning blunder, the "Go-Go Sox" blew a golden opportunity to tie the game in the bottom of the eighth inning. In a clutch relief performance, Larry Sherry pitched the last three innings to save the game for Podres.

The White Sox looked more like the White Sox. They had eight hits and no home runs. The Dodgers looked more like the Dodgers. They scratched and clawed back to win.[23]

Endless Shutout

The White Sox shutout continued as they scored two runs in the bottom of the first inning to take a 2–0 lead. Sox lead-off batter Luis Aparicio doubled and took third on a fly ball by Nellie Fox. Landis walked to put runners on first and third for the dangerous Kluszewski. Podres got Klu to hit a perfect double-play grounder to Charlie Neal, but Neal bobbled the ball and could only get Kluszewski at first base, allowing Aparicio to score. Sherman Lollar then singled home Landis to make it 2–0 in favor of the Sox. Instead of an inning-ending double play and a scoreless tie, the Dodgers were down, 2–0. After the game, Neal recalled, "The ball Klu hit to me in the first inning was a cinch double play ball, only it took a sharp jump at the last second and landed against my stomach."[24]

"Too Thin to Hit with Power"

Casey Stengel observed of Charlie Neal, "They got a second baseman named Neal who looks too thin to hit with power. He is fast and shifty around the bag, the last one you'd expect to go knocking them out of the park."[25]

After his defensive lapse cost the Dodgers two runs in the first, Neal hit a high slider from Shaw into the left-field stands for a solo homer with two outs in the fifth to cut the Sox lead to 2–1. Finally, the 13⅔-inning shutout was over.

White Sox starter Bob Shaw was consistently up in the strike zone, and the Dodgers finished him in the seventh inning. Shaw retired the first two batters. Running out of opportunities to tie the game, Walter Alston pulled Podres for a pinch-hitter. It was a tough decision for Alston. Although the White Sox had managed only five hits against Podres, the Dodgers were down to their last seven outs. "We were a run behind, there were two out, and it was getting late," said Alston. "I wanted somebody who could hit the ball out of the park."[26]

The pinch-hitter was Chuck Essegian, the 200-pound former Stanford fullback-linebacker who once belonged to the Phillies and the Cardinals after drifting in the minors. On a three-and-one count, Essegian hit another high Shaw slider into the upper deck in left field to tie the game at 2–2. After the game, when asked whether it was the best he hit all year, Essegian replied, "It had to be the best ball I *ever* hit!"[27] The blow rattled Shaw, who promptly walked Junior Gilliam. Then the 156-pound Neal finished him by sending a high fastball 415 feet into the Sox bullpen, where Billy Pierce nonchalantly caught it on the fly and gave it to a policeman. The gamble paid off for Alston. Just like that, the Dodgers had a 4–2 lead. Larry Sherry came in from the bullpen to hold the Sox scoreless in the bottom of the seventh.

A Baserunning Blunder by the Go-Go Sox

Ironically, the "Go-Go Sox" blew a golden opportunity to tie the game in the bottom of the eighth inning by committing a baserunning blunder. Kluszewski led off with a single against Sherry. Sherman Lollar followed with a vicious line-drive single off third basemen Gilliam. It looked like the White Sox would tie the game when Al Smith rocked Sherry's 3–2 pitch for a long double off the left-center-field wall between Moon and Snider. Earl Torgeson (running for Kluszewski) scored easily. But Wally Moon craftily faked making a catch on a ball he knew he could not reach. This completely fooled Lollar, who slowed up as he approached second, and caused him to be thrown out at the plate by ten feet on a perfect relay from Wally Moon to Maury Wills to John Roseboro. Lollar was so surprised when the ball arrived ahead of him that he never attempted to slide. Walter Alston made a trip to the mound with some calming words for his rookie right-hander: "Just settle down and keep on pitching the way you have been."[28] With Smith, the potential tying run on third base and only one out, Sherry gathered himself to strike out Billy Goodman and retire "Jungle Jim" Rivera on a pop foul behind the plate.

This turned out to be the turning point of the Series. If Lollar had scored, the game would have been tied, 4–4, with the go-ahead run on third base and no one out. A blown save by Sherry would have put the White Sox up two games to none and changed the complexion of the Series.

White Sox fans were left to ponder what made third base coach Tony Cuccinello wave home the plodding Lollar after Sherman hesitated. The answer was related to the very essence of the 1959 White Sox. While Sherman Lollar was clearly not Aparicio or Landis, when in doubt, the Sox GO. After the game, Cuccinello admitted he made a mistake. "Lollar was the tying run," he said. "I thought it would take a perfect play to beat him." The Dodgers, who had been kicking the ball around for two days, made the perfect play when it counted.[29]

After many years as a major league coach and manager, Roger Craig, who was in the Dodger bullpen that day, would observe, "The third base coach should not have sent that guy. Lollar was a slow runner."[30]

The Moon Bluff: An Analysis by Perfesser Stengel

After the game, Casey Stengel described what he considered the key play of the Series in the bottom of the eighth inning:

> At that time Chicago is behind 4–2, but they get a rally going with the help of the Los Angeles infield. Big Klu, who must be taking dancing lessons, bloops a single over the second baseman and Lollar, the next man up, hits into a double play, only the Los Angeles infield is unable to make the play, and both runners are safe.
>
> Now the tying runs are at first and second and the Chicago manager has a decision. Both men are slow. Should he take them out for pinch runners? He decides to send in a runner (Torgeson) for Kluwszewski at second base, but he leaves Lollar, the other slow man, at first. "I may want him to hit later," says Al Lopez.
>
> So then Al Smith gets up there and tries to bunt and fails and now this is very fortunate for him because he hits a very sharp ball to left center between Moon and Demeter. Moon is closest to the ball, but I see he has no more chance of catching it than I do sitting up in the stands. But he pulls off the greatest bluff anyone has seen in years. Up goes the glove like he has the ball in his pocket. It fooled the Chicago base runners, and you don't fool them often. It could be the greatest play of the 1959 World Series.
>
> It confused and frightened the runner at second base (Torgeson), who says, "I will wait to see that the man don't make a sensational catch." He knew he could score anyhow. But this makes Lollar, the runner on first, hesitate before rounding second. When the ball goes past Moon and rolls to the wall, the man on second scores, and Lollar rounds third and he gets the wave to keep on going for home plate. If he scores,

the game is all tied up and there are no outs, and the winning run is at third base.

Now they have a very shrewd man coaching at third in Cuccinello. He used to play for me in Brooklyn and Boston.... Well, you might say Cuccinello made an error sending the runner, because he was thrown out by 10 feet. But it took a great throw, and that's where we get back to Mr. Moon. Having slowed the runners down with a bluff, he got the ball to the catcher in time to finish the job.

What made the play so outstanding was the fact that Los Angeles lost the first game and could have lost the second. Then they would have been two games behind.... It's not a very good feeling.[31]

Catcher Sherman Lollar led the 1959 White Sox in home runs with 22. (National Baseball Hall of Fame Library, Cooperstown, N.Y.)

Sherry Saves the Game, the Dodgers Tie the Series

Larry Sherry returned to the mound in the bottom of the ninth with the Dodgers clinging to a 4–3 lead. With renewed confidence after surviving his eighth-inning crisis, he retired the White Sox in order without allowing a ball out of the infield. "I never was worried a bit, I had my stuff," the brash rookie told reporters in the clubhouse.[32] It was a clutch performance, featuring three innings of three-hit baseball to save the win for starter Johnny Podres.

Casey Stengel recognized that, in Sherry, the Dodgers had a special pitcher who would turn in an historic four-game World Series performance. "They brought out a young fellow named Sherry that I never seen before who has great ability out there. He rears back and throws bullets. If they got a lead they could call the bullpen and say, 'Hey boy! Come in here and throw a few.'"[33]

"Go-Go Sox My Ass!"

Roger Craig would recall a post-game comment by the fiery Don Zimmer, who was by then relegated to a back-up role to Maury Wills, "In the bus after the game, Zimmer said 'Go-Go Sox my ass— we're going to beat 'em in six games!'"[34]

* * *

Twenty-four hours after their humiliating 11–0 defeat at the hands of the White Sox, the Dodgers got off the mat to tie the Series at one game apiece. Suddenly people who had been talking about a four-game Chicago sweep remembered that the team winning the first game in the last four years had lost the Series.[35] In the clubhouse, baseball philosopher Gil Hodges summed up the Dodgers' Series after two games: "We weren't down yesterday, and we weren't up today. We just play 'em as they come along."[36]

Game Three

Sunday afternoon, October 4, 1959— A record crowd of 92,294 packed the Los Angeles Memorial Coliseum on a scorching Sunday afternoon for the third game of the 1959 World Series— the first Series game ever played in Los Angeles. The first ball was thrown out by the newest Brooklyn Dodger Hall of Famer, Zach Wheat. Just eight months after his induction ceremony, the 71-year-old Wheat made it to home plate on only one bounce.[37]

The Dodgers continued to build on their Game 2 momentum as 37-year-old veteran Carl Furillo drove in two runs in the seventh inning with a bases-loaded, pinch-hit single to break a tense scoreless tie. That proved to be all the Dodgers needed for a 3–1 win that put them up two games to one over the White Sox. Rookie reliever Larry Sherry pitched brilliantly for the last two innings to save the game for starter Don Drysdale. It was Sherry's second save in 27 hours.

Pitcher's Duel in the Sun

Like the first game, this was another battle of right-handers: Don Drysdale for the Dodgers against Dick Donovan for the White Sox. Neither team put a run on the scoreboard through the first six innings. Donovan shut out the Dodgers on one hit. Drysdale, forced to pitch without his best stuff and behind on almost every batter, gave up 11 singles, but continually pitched out of trouble to keep the Sox off the scoreboard.

Played in scorching 90-degree heat, on the floor of the Coliseum it felt like the hottest World Series game in history. After toiling for six innings in a concrete bowl where the sun blazed down without mercy, both pitchers were nearing the breaking point.[38]

Old Man Furillo Comes Through Again

In the bottom of the seventh, Charlie Neal opened with the Dodgers' second hit off Donovan — a fluke pop-fly double off the 250-foot left-field screen. Though it would have been a routine out in any other ballpark, it precipitated Donovan's downfall as he suddenly lost his control and walked the next two batters on nine pitches to load the bases.[39]

A managerial chess match ensued, as Sox manager Al Lopez took the ball from Donovan and handed it to the 39-year-old Gerry Staley. Walter Alston countered by sending up 37-year-old Carl Furillo to hit for Don Demeter. Furillo, a veteran of six World Series, starting in 1947, and hero of the second and decisive playoff game against the Braves five days earlier, rifled Staley's second pitch up the middle, heading for center field. "It felt like a good hit — then I saw Aparicio close in on it and guessed I was a goner," explained Furillo.[40] But the agile Sox shortstop lost the high-bouncing ball momentarily in the blinding background created by a sea of white shirts, and it barely evaded his glove for a two-run single to break the scoreless tie.[41]

Sherry Saves Drysdale and the Dodgers

Given a 2–0 lead to protect, Drysdale hit a wall in the eighth inning. Kluszewski opened with a sharp single to left. Sherman Lollar's fly ball to left dropped in for Chicago's eleventh single after Wally Moon lost the ball in the white shirts. "I never saw it leave the bat," admitted Moon.[42] Alston had seen enough struggling by Drysdale, and he brought in Sherry, who promptly drilled Billy Goodman in the ribs with a fastball to load the bases with nobody out. The White Sox scored their only run as Sherry got Al Smith to ground into a double play, allowing the runner to score from third. On only his sixth pitch of the inning, Sherry got "Jungle Jim" Rivera on a pop fly in front of the plate to end the inning and preserve the Dodgers' 2–1 lead.

After the Dodgers scored an insurance run on Neal's RBI double in the bottom of the eighth, Sherry took the mound for the ninth inning with a slightly more comfortable 3–1 lead. He put on a brilliant exhibition by striking out the side to hold the White Sox scoreless and save the victory for Don Drysdale.

The Shocked Sox

The White Sox left the field in a state of shock. They had runners on base in every inning with twelve hits and four walks and only one run to show for it — leaving eleven runners stranded. It was maddening how the Dodgers had squeezed three runs out of only five hits.[43] The White Sox tried to steal four times, and three times Dodger catcher John Roseboro gunned them down.[44]

After the game, Alston explained how he won the eighth inning chess match with Al Lopez and the third game of the World Series. "In the second game I used Essegian because I needed a home run," said Alston. "Today I needed a single, so I used Furillo."[45]

Pronounced dead-on-arrival in Chicago three days earlier, the Dodgers now had a two games-to-one lead over the White Sox with the next two games scheduled for the Los Angeles Coliseum and 92,000+ rabid Dodger fans.

Record Crowd

The crowd of 92,294 smashed the pervious single-game record of 86,288 established at Cleveland Municipal Stadium for the fifth game of the Indians–Boston Braves World Series of 1948. Fans armed with binoculars in the most remote section of the Coliseum — the 79th row at the peristyle end — were a whopping 700 feet from home plate.[46] But later they could say, "I was there."

Game Four

Monday afternoon, October 5, 1959— Gil Hodges hit a solo home run in the bottom of the eighth inning to break a 4–4 tie and give the Dodgers a 5–4 victory over the White Sox and a three games-to-one lead in the Series. Larry Sherry, making his third appearance in four games, got the win by throwing the last two hitless innings in relief of Roger Craig. The Dodgers set another World Series attendance record as 92,550 fans packed the Coliseum.

Craig vs. Wynn Redux

In a rematch of Game 1, Early Wynn and Roger Craig squared off again. Wynn started where he left off in Chicago, shutting out the Dodgers for the first two innings. But after retiring the first two batters in the third, he was tagged for five consecutive singles. The Sox defense provided no help as it yielded two errors and a passed ball. When the dust cleared, the Dodgers had a 4–0 lead, and Wynn was gone after only 2⅔ innings of work.

Although Roger Craig shut out the White Sox for the first six innings, he was not that sharp, walking four and allowing several batters to work him to a 3-and-2 count before he could put them away. By the seventh, he was showing signs of fatigue as the White Sox put three singles together to score their first run, thereby reducing the Dodger lead to 4–1. With two outs and runners on first and third, a nervous Alston trotted out to the mound to talk to Craig, who convinced the manager that he could handle Sherman Lollar. "I never wanted to come out of any game,"[47] recalled Craig nearly 50 years later. "You had to *take* me out. Alston wanted to take me out, but I probably talked him out of it."[48] As soon as Alston settled back down on the Dodger bench, Craig left a slow slider hanging over the plate for Lollar to loft over the left-field screen to tie the game at 4–4.[49]

Hodges Provides the Winning Blow

Through the first seven innings of the fourth game, the Dodgers had scored all of their runs in the Series with two out. That would change in the bottom of the eighth inning when lead-off hitter Gil Hodges jumped on a Gerry Staley sinkerball and launched a towering fly over the left-center-field screen to put the Dodgers ahead for good, 5–4. This was no cheap "screeno" home run, but a blast that probably would have landed in the upper deck at Ebbets Field.[50] It was the fifth home run in seven Fall Classics for Hodges.[51]

Sherry Gets the Win

In his third consecutive relief appearance, Larry Sherry took over for Roger Craig to start the eighth inning. He again dazzled the White Sox with a glittering repertoire that included a blazing fastball, curve, and slider.[52] Sherry pitched the last two innings without allowing a hit and was declared the winning pitcher. "After Gil came through with that homer, nothing was going to make me blow that lead," said Sherry in the Dodger clubhouse.[53] Thanks to Sherry's one win and two saves, the Dodgers now had a three games-to-one lead in the Series and a chance to end it the next day in Los Angeles.

A Sox Character Change

All season the White Sox built their hopes on slickness and quickness, on poise and determination, on pitching and speed. By the time Game 4 was over, it was clear that the Dodgers were better in all these departments.

Already down a game, the White Sox were nervous and tight. It was obvious in their faces and the way they played. The Dodgers' aggressiveness seemed to force Chicago into mistakes. They committed three errors, and catcher Sherman Lollar was charged with a passed ball. Although Luis Aparicio stole a base, they still had to rely on a three-run home run by Lollar to get back into the game.

Four days after the 11–0 laugher in Chicago, there was now a different tone. In the Dodgers' dressing room after the game, someone wrote on the blackboard, "One to Go-Go-Go!" In the White Sox dressing room, a sober Al Lopez only said, "We still have a chance."[54]

Game Five

Tuesday afternoon, October 6, 1959— Wearing their lucky black socks, the White Sox staved off elimination in Game 5 with a 1–0 win before a third straight record crowd of 92,706 at the Los Angeles Memorial Coliseum. Sox right-hander Bob Shaw, who lost Game 2 in Chicago, gave up nine hits in 7⅓ innings, but repeatedly escaped with runners on base for the win. Shaw collaborated with Billy Pierce and Dick Donovan for the only three-man shutout in World Series history. The Dodgers went with their 23-year-old left-hander, Sandy Koufax. Asked in 2007 whether he was surprised at the time that Alston named Koufax after scratching him at the last minute from the first playoff game in Milwaukee, Roger Craig said, "No. He was unhittable if he could get the ball over the plate."[55] But the fates would be unkind to Koufax, who gave up the only run of the game in the fourth inning when he got Sherman Lollar to ground into a double play, with Nellie Fox scoring the game's only run on the play.

The Dodgers squandered one opportunity after another, leaving eleven men on base. Gil Hodges had three hits but could not score, even after hitting a triple with one out in the fourth. Junior Gilliam had four hits, but was left stranded on the bases.[56]

Superstitious White Sox Revert to Black

When the Series began, Chicago broke out their white socks for the first time in more than 20 years in an attempt to help fans forget the "Black Sox" scandal of 1919.[57] But after losing their third game in a row, superstition got the better of them. Sox trainer Ed Froelich outfitted them with their traditional black socks with red and white stripes for Game 5 — and it worked.[58]

The Sox Double-Play "Rally"

Sandy Koufax cruised through the first three innings, shutting out the White Sox with overpowering stuff. Then in the top of the fourth, Nellie Fox led off with a single, and Jim Landis followed by singling Fox to third. Koufax bore down and got Sherman Lollar to ground into a double play, but Fox scored on the play. It would be the only run of the game.[59]

An aerial view of the largest crowd in World Series history: 92,706 at Los Angeles Memorial Coliseum for Game 5 of the 1959 World Series. (National Baseball Hall of Fame Library, Cooperstown, N.Y.)

"The Thing" Turns on the Dodgers

Trailing, 1–0, in the sixth inning, the left-field screen — so useful to the Dodgers during the regular season — turned against them. Gil Hodges connected with a line drive that was just taking off when it was caught by the top cross bar of the mesh netting. Instead of what would have been a game-tying home run in Comiskey Park, Hodges had to settle for a single.[60] Saved by "The Thing," Bob Shaw recovered to leave Hodges stranded on first.

"Jungle Jim" in Right Field

Al Lopez made a brilliant move in the bottom of the seventh when he sent "Jungle Jim" Rivera in to play right field in place of rookie starter Jim McAnany with two Dodgers on base, two outs, and Charlie Neal at the plate.[61] After Bob Shaw uncorked a wild pitch to move the runners up to second and third, Neal connected on a towering drive to deep right-center field between Landis and Rivera. The fleet Rivera ran the ball down and hauled it in with a sensational over-the-shoulder catch in front of the 400-foot sign. Rivera's catch saved two runs and robbed the speedy Neal of a sure triple. "I ran like hell and stretched out as far as I could go, and the ball stuck. I knew if I didn't get it, the game was over," said Rivera after the game.[62]

The Great Alston-Lopez Chess Game

The Dodgers made their last serious scoring threat in the bottom of the eighth inning. In what turned into a chess match between managers Alfonso Ramon Lopez and Walter Emmons Alston, the eighth saw two Sox pitchers, a substitute outfielder, and three pinch-hitters.[63] Wally Moon opened with a high fly to dead center field off Shaw. Sox center fielder Jim Landis was directly under it, but at the last instant lost the ball in the glaring sun, and it dropped for a single. Norm Larker flied out to Rivera. Gil Hodges, who already had a triple and a single, brought the crowd to its feet with a scorching drive into the left-field seats ... FOUL! He then singled again to center. Moon slid into third base a split-second ahead of Landis' throw, the play allowing Hodges to slide safely into second.[64]

Jungle Jim Rivera patrolled right field for the 1959 White Sox. His sensational over-the-shoulder catch robbed Charlie Neal of a sure two-run triple and saved Chicago's 1–0 victory in Game 5 of the World Series. (National Baseball Hall of Fame Library, Cooperstown, N.Y.)

With runners on second and third and one out, left-handed-hitting rookie Ron Fairly was announced as a pinch-hitter for Don Demeter. Al Lopez removed Bob Shaw and brought in left-hander Billy Pierce, but Alston countered by sending up another right-handed hitter, Rip Repulski. Lopez neutralized that move by ordering Pierce to walk Repulski intentionally to load the bases. The crowd of 92,706 erupted when Alston countered by sending up Carl Furillo to bat for Roseboro. But Lopez wasn't about to let "Skoonj" hit against the southpaw Pierce, so he brought in right-hander Dick Donovan. That set off the alarm on brain wave meter, and proved to be the deciding move. All the Dodgers needed was a fly ball to tie the score. But Donovan, the starter and losing pitcher of Game 3 (which Furillo won), exacted revenge by inducing Furillo to pop up to third base for the second out. He then disposed of the feisty—but rusty—Don Zimmer, hitting for the first time in more than a month, on an easy fly to Al Smith in short left field to extinguish the Dodgers' last scoring opportunity.[65]

It's Back to Chicago

With the Dodgers out of pinch-hitters, the omnipresent Larry Sherry, who hit two home runs during the regular season, batted for Stan Williams in the bottom of the ninth. He was the sixth pinch-hitter used by the Dodgers, a new Series record for a nine-inning game. But Sherry couldn't work any more magic in front of the home fans as Donovan got him, Gilliam, and Neal to ground out to end the game and send the Series back to Chicago for Game 6.

Game 5 was a blow to the Dodgers. They had many chances to win the game and clinch the World Series at home. The Dodgers were worn out, having traveled to San Francisco, St. Louis, Chicago, Milwaukee, Los Angeles, Chicago, and back to Los Angeles—all since September 18. Now they had to fly back to Chicago to face a resurgent White Sox team in their "big barn." The oddsmakers now favored the Sox to win the sixth game and square the Series at 3–3.[66]

Sandy Koufax—What Might Have Been

It was another devastating loss for Sandy Koufax. But for a run-scoring double play by the White Sox in the fourth inning, he had Chicago shut out through seven innings on five hits with six strikeouts. Had the Dodgers only managed to score a run, he was one double play away from winning the final game of the 1959 World Series in front of a record crowd of 92,706 and a national television audience. Just as Johnny Podres would always be remembered for shutting out the Yankees in Game 7 of the 1955 World Series, a shutout to win the final game of the 1959 Series would have done the same thing for Koufax. Combined with his record 18-strikeout performance of August 31, this would have put him "on the map" two years before he blossomed into one of the greatest pitchers of all time.

Instead, an inconsistent Sandy Koufax would continue to drift through the next season with confidence and control problems, posting an 8–13 record with 100 walks.

Game Six

Thursday afternoon, October 8, 1959— The Los Angeles Dodgers won the second World Series in their history by defeating the White Sox, 9–3, with three home runs on an overcast afternoon at Comiskey Park. The game was essentially over after four innings. By the time the Dodgers scored six runs in the top of the fourth to go ahead, 8–0, the game was out of reach. The desperate White Sox clawed back in the bottom of the fourth as Ted Kluszewski finished Dodger starter Johnny Podres with a mammoth three-run homer. But Larry Sherry, in his fourth relief appearance of the Series, came in to shut out the Sox for the last 5⅔ innings to get credit for the victory. Of the Dodgers' four wins, the 24-year-old rookie right-hander won two and saved the other two, and was named the Most Valuable Player of the Series.

Mr. Excitement

Even the imperturbable Walter Alston was excited before Game 6. While undressing in the clubhouse, he discovered that his socks did not match.[67]

Sox Call on Wynn for Survival Start

With their backs to the wall, the White Sox called on 39-year-old ace right-hander Early Wynn to help them survive Game 6 and send the Series into a sudden-death seventh game. It was the third start of the Series for Wynn — this time on only two days rest. The Dodgers went with Johnny Podres, the hero of their only World Series championship of 1955. Neither pitcher would survive the fourth inning.[68]

From the press box, Casey Stengel observed, "Early Wynn looks as mean as ever, but his arm is tired after all the overwork he's had all season and they got to Early early."[69]

The Duke Calls His Shot

Duke Snider, who was limited to pinch-hitting duty during the games in Los Angeles due a bad knee, asked Walter Alston to start him in center field. "I want to play against Wynn. I feel in my own heart that I am going to get a hit that will help us win," Snider presciently told him the day before.[70]

In the top of the third inning of a scoreless tie, Snider came to the plate against Wynn with two outs and a runner on first. The weary Wynn grooved a 1-and-1 pitch that Snider connected with, sending it over 400 feet into the left-center-field stands to give the Dodgers a 2–0 lead.

It was evident to everyone that Wynn was tired. But inexplicably Al Lopez let him bat for himself in the bottom of the third, then allowed him to resume pitching in the next inning.[71]

The Dodgers Break It Open in the Fourth

In the top of the fourth, the Dodgers sent ten batters to the plate to work on Wynn, Dick Donovan, and Turk Lown. When the dust settled, Los Angeles had an insurmountable 8–0 lead. It was the bottom of the Dodger batting order that finished Early Wynn. Wills singled home Demeter, and Dodger starter Johnny Podres doubled him home to make it 4–0 and send the overworked Wynn to the showers. Dick Donovan came in from the Sox bullpen to walk Gilliam. Charlie Neal followed with a two-run double, and Wally Moon made it 8–0 with a two-run homer into the right-field seats—both off Donovan, who exited without retiring a batter. Turk Lown had to come in to get the last two outs.

Big Klu with the Team on His Back

In the bottom of the fourth with an 8–0 lead, Podres appeared to be cruising as he retired lead-off batter Nellie Fox. But then he lost control of a high fastball that struck Jim Landis in the head. Thanks to his batting helmet, Landis was not injured and stayed in the game, taking first base. But the beaning unnerved Podres, who immediately walked Sherman Lollar to put runners on first and second. Ted Kluzsewski exploited the situation by smashing his third home run of the Series into the upper deck in right field to make it 8–3. When Podres walked the next batter, Al Smith, on five pitches, Walter Alston had seen enough. This set the stage for Larry Sherry who was brought in for his fourth relief appearance of the Series.

Sherry walked Bubba Phillips, but struck out Billy Goodman for the second out. He then gave up a single to Earl Torgeson to load the bases. With Aparicio coming to the plate with a .333 average in the Series, the White Sox now had an opportunity to get back into the game. Sherry calmly got Aparicio to pop up to Wills to end what would be the last Chicago threat.

Essegian Ties a Series Record

In the top of the ninth, Chuck Essegian, pinch-hitting for Snider, lined Ray Moore's first pitch into the left-field stands to make the score 9–3. Essegian's second pinch-hit homer tied a World Series record held by Lawrence Peter "Yogi" Berra.

Local television newsman Bill Welsh at Los Angeles International Airport as delirious fans welcome home their 1959 world champion Los Angeles Dodgers on the night of October 9, 1959. (National Baseball Hall of Fame Library, Cooperstown, N.Y.)

Larry Sherry's Moment in the Sun

Larry Sherry went on to shut out the White Sox for the last 5⅔ innings and was the winning pitcher. He retired the White Sox in order in the bottom of the ninth to give the Dodgers a 9–3 victory and their second world championship.

After the game, the Ol' Perfesser, Casey Stengel, held forth on the futility of the White Sox's attempt to mount a comeback against Sherry, "The score is 8–0 Los Angeles before the Sox get a rally going. Then all Los Angeles does is signal down to the bullpen for 'Mr. 51,' and that's it, brother. He rears back and fires the ball right at that home plate, and the Sox batters just do not seem to be able to do anything."[72]

Bedlam in Darrtown, PA

Walter Alston's father called after the game to tell him, "Walt, they just shot off every damn shotgun shell in Darrtown!"[73]

"I Was Almost Ready to Go Back Home and Get Another Job"

Asked how he felt when Wally Moon squeezed Luis Aparicio's fly ball for the final out to make the Dodgers world champions, Roger Craig recalled, "It felt great. In 1958, after I hurt my arm, I was almost ready to back home to get another job. I had to beg my manager in St. Paul to let me pitch one game of a double-header."[74]

* * *

On October 9, 1959, the day after the World Series ended in Chicago, President Eisenhower invoked the Taft-Hartley Act to end the longest nationwide steel strike in U.S. history. Before invoking the act's provision calling for an 80-day back-to-work period when a strike "threatens to imperil the national health or safety," Eisenhower told a press conference, "I am getting sick and tired of the impasse, and so are the American people."[75]

That evening, 5,000 baseball-crazed Southern Californians, including civic officials and Hollywood stars such as master of ceremonies Desi Arnaz, greeted the world champion Dodgers at Los Angeles International Airport. The crowd mobbed Larry Sherry for autographs and sang "Happy Birthday" to Walter O'Malley on his 56th birthday. Walter Alston received an official scroll signed by Los Angeles Mayor Norris Poulson certifying October 9, 1959, as "Baseball Champions of the World Day." The rooters brought hundreds of signs, including "The Greatest World Champions of All," and "Our Dodgers, Bless 'Em."[76]

These were the days before all-day civic orgies for World Series victors. There would be no parade. The ceremonies broke up in twenty minutes, and the Dodgers went home to enjoy a long weekend before starting their winter jobs.

Chapter 21

An Analysis of the 1959 World Series

The Go-Go Sox Fall Flat-Flat

The Go-Go Sox, highly touted for their speed, defense, and pitching, proved to be inferior to the Dodgers in all three categories.

For all the talk about the Go-Go Sox and their speed, only Aparicio and Landis had exceptional wheels, and they stole one base each to account for Chicago's modest total of two, compared to five for the Dodgers. Los Angeles catcher John Roseboro stopped the Sox running attack dead with his strong and accurate arm by throwing out five baserunners. Covering the Series for *Life*, Casey Stengel observed in Stengelese, "By handicapping the Sox base runners and putting restraint on them, Roseboro took the Go-Go out of the White Sox and changed it to Stop-Stop. Now this is an outstanding thing because it hurt their style of play, and what's more, disrupted their spirit."[1]

Roger Craig, who would later play for Stengel on the Amazin' Mets of 1962-63, evaluated Roseboro's contribution in hindsight: "He was a big key to the Series. The Sox could run, and you had to keep them out of scoring position. And Roseboro did that. He could get rid of the ball real quick."[2]

The Dodgers had superior speed with Wills, Neal, Gilliam, Moon, and Roseboro. They outperformed the White Sox on the bases—stealing, taking the extra base, advancing on fly outs, and forcing the Chicago defense into hurried throws and errors. The Dodgers essentially out–Go-Go'ed the Sox. Whereas Roseboro neutralized Chicago's running attack, Casey Stengel raised the question of whether there was a physical problem with Sox catcher Sherman Lollar: "The Los Angeles runners, who go pretty fast too, stole plenty of bases before the Sox stole one, and nobody expected that. But they (Dodgers) were stealing on a catcher (Lollar) with a bad hand. I asked the Sox how is their catcher and they give me a wink. But Los Angeles must have known something because they can't wait to get on base and start stealing."[3]

The famed Sox middle of Aparicio and Fox was a disappointment, executing only two double plays, compared to seven that the Wills-Neal duo turned in for the Dodgers. Aparicio failed to come up with a couple of ground balls in key situations that no one expected him to miss.

The Dodgers' pitching staff, led by Larry Sherry's 0.71 ERA in 12⅔ innings, bested the White Sox in team ERA, 3.23 to 3.46. This was despite the 11–0 blowout of Game 1, and the 27.00 contribution of Clarence Nottingham "Chuck" Churn. Chicago yielded seven home runs compared to the four given up by Los Angeles.

Pressure

Since the middle four games were decided by a total of five runs, both teams' ability to handle pressure was critical. All season, the White Sox had applied constant pressure on the other team until the opponent cracked. This approach did not work against the Dodgers, who had been living with pressure all season, culminated by surviving a tense three-team September pennant stretch and playoff series. In the end, it was the White Sox who succumbed to pressure.[4]

Clutch Dodger Hitting

The Dodgers scored 19 of their 21 runs with two outs.[5] The Dodger pinch-hitters produced, while Chicago's failed. Chuck Essegian tied a World Series record with two pinch-hit home runs, and Carl Furillo won Game 3 with a clutch bases-loaded pinch-single.

Dodger Aggression

The Dodgers' aggressive style of play threw the Sox off-balance. Perfesser Stengel "clarified" the difference in baseball philosophy between the Chicago School and the Dodger School: "The White Sox are thinkers rather than yellers, and they look like little gentlemen next to Los Angeles, which is very aggressive."

On the Dodgers' aggressive baserunning, Ol' Case observed from the press box, "...it is noticeable that Chicago is playing a nice clean game. But Los Angeles has got so aggressive that they're attacking those men when sliding into second and they bodily went into several men in which the infielders dropped the ball."[6]

To Shave Or Not to Shave, That Is the Question

Aggressiveness — or lack thereof — was also a factor in the pitching styles. The Dodger pitchers were provocative in their use of the "shave" to defend the inside part of home plate. As Perfesser Stengel defined the art form, "That's when you pitch in close to a man and we call it 'shaving him.'" Stengel paid tribute to the Dodger barbers: "Every time I look around, I see Chicago hitters leaning back or hitting the dirt ... Drysdale, Koufax, and Mr. 51 threw very close to their necks."[7] It was evident to Ol' Case that the White Sox were deficient in the art of shaving: "Any aggressive manager wants that style of play. But except for Wynn, I don't see Chicago pitchers shaving anybody, so the Los Angeles hitters are leaning into the plate...."[8]

Roger Craig would recall, "We were taught as Dodger pitchers to pitch inside. Larry Sherry, Don Drysdale, Stan Williams, and me — we all pitched inside against the power hitters so they couldn't extend their arms."[9] Reduced to its essence: the Dodgers shaved, the Sox didn't.

Fox vs. Neal

Chicago's Nellie Fox, later named American League Most Valuable Player, played well during the Series, with nine hits and a .375 batting average. But he was outplayed by Charlie Neal, who displayed more speed, more range, and more power. Neal had 10 hits, including two home runs in Game 2 that helped the Dodgers get off the mat to tie the Series after being blown out 11–0 in Game 1.

Sherry Was the Key

Within days after he was called up from St. Paul in early July, Walter Alston was referring to brash, confident rookie reliever Larry Sherry as the best pitcher on his staff. Minutes after winning the World Series, Alston would be moved to say, "I hate to single out any one player because it was teamwork every step of the way from spring training. But how about that kid Larry Sherry! He gave us tremendous pitching the last part of the season and he carried us through this Series. I just have to say something special about him."[10]

On paper, the Dodgers' starting rotation of Drysdale, Craig, Koufax, and Podres was not as impressive as Chicago's Wynn, Shaw, Pierce, and Donovan. But the White Sox did not have a Larry Sherry waiting in the bullpen to bail them out.

Game 2 was critical for Larry Sherry and the Dodgers. Leading 4–2 in the eighth inning at Comiskey Park, he began by giving up three straight hits, including a ringing double off the left-field wall by Al Smith that should have scored Sherman Lollar to tie the game. But Sherry was the beneficiary of the brilliant bluff by Moon and the perfect Moon-Wills-Roseboro relay to nail Lollar at the plate. After some comforting words from Walter Alston, Sherry retired the next five batters to save the game and gain a split for the Dodgers in Chicago.

Casey Stengel recognized the contribution of Larry Sherry. "The minute Mr. 51 comes in and starts pitching, the White Sox let up in their work at bat," commented Stengel. "He appeared on the scene four times and he was tremendous."[11] With Shakespearean eloquence, Ol' Case wrote a King Sherry soliloquy: "Boy," he says, "that plate looks very small to the hitters, but it looks very big to me."[12]

The heroic performance of Larry Sherry inspired the Dodgers and demoralized the White Sox. Perfesser Stengel captured the essence of the Sherry effect: "...It's amazing that he can come in and instill a club so that the infielders perk up and the outfielders stop fretting, and something happens to the other side which has got up momentum with an attack. Now the hitters are so nervous and get so ruffled they can't even watch the signs, and then is the time when they say, 'Oh, my goodness, what's going to happen to me?' and the first thing you know, it does."[13]

Larry Sherry appeared in relief in four games, winning two and saving two. He had an ERA of 0.71 in 12⅔ innings. The Dodgers won the Series four game to two, winning whenever Sherry appeared, and losing when he did not.[14] He was named the Most Valuable Player of the 1959 World Series.

Recalling Larry Sherry's performance, Roger Craig in his seventies would observe, "Sherry was the big key. Larry was my roommate. He had a mean streak in him. Most relievers would walk in from the bullpen in those days, but Larry would jog in and kick the rosin bag toward second base. He was phenomenal during the Series—in a groove. He had total command of his three pitches: fastball, curve, and slider."[15]

Record Attendance

The 1959 World Series drew record crowds to the three games played in Los Angeles. Throngs of 92,394, 92,650, and 92,796 swarmed into the Memorial Coliseum for Games Three, Four, and Five, each crowd breaking the previous single-game record of 86,288, established at Cleveland Municipal Stadium for the fifth game of the Indians–Boston Braves World Series of 1948.[16] The six-game total of 420,784 even broke the record for a *seven-game* series, as did the total receipts of $5,626,973.44.[17]

Record Winners' Share

The net receipts for the Series were a record $5,628,809, including $3 million in TV-radio revenue.[18] Each Dodger player received a paycheck in the then-unheard-of amount of $11,231. The runner-up White Sox received $7,275 each.[19]

As Roger Craig would recall nearly fifty years later, "That was like $100,000 today. They had a players' meeting to vote on who would get a full share. Carl Furillo told me, 'You aren't allowed to go to the meeting if you weren't there all year,' and slammed the door on me. If you didn't help the club, they wouldn't give it to you. But I got a full share. It was a real compliment."[20]

Vindication for O'Malley

It was only the second world championship in Dodger franchise history. What had taken 75 years to accomplish in Brooklyn (1880 to 1955) had taken only two years in Los Angeles. After winning the final game in Chicago on his 56th birthday, Walter O'Malley threw a gala party of champagne and caviar to celebrate his team's Cinderella victory as well as his own ultimate vindication.[21]

"This Team Never Quit"

In the jubilant visitors clubhouse at Comiskey Park after Game 6, Walter Alston reflected on what his team had just accomplished. "This is the greatest team I ever was connected with," shouted Alston, "or any manager ever was connected with. This team never quit. It came from behind all the way. It won against big odds."[22]

A Belated Gift from the U.S. Supreme Court

On October 19, 1959, ten days after his team won the world championship, the U.S. Supreme Court gave Walter O'Malley a belated victory celebration gift by dismissing the appeals of Louis Kirschbaum and Julius Reuben, thereby ending the legal challenges to the Chavez Ravine contract.

O'Malley could now proceed with his construction of Dodger Stadium without risk of further interference.[23]

CHAPTER 22

1959: A Year of Transition

THE YEAR 1959 WAS A transitional season for baseball. As the country entered the turbulent sixties, the national pastime entered a period of profound change.

A New Weapon: The Stolen Base

With his daring baserunning, Maury Wills changed the way the game was played. Until 1959, when Luis Aparicio led the American League with 56 stolen bases, stealing had become a lost art. In 1950, Dominic DiMaggio of the Red Sox led the American League with 15 steals, and both league leaders stole a mere 25 bases in 1955. The scoring philosophy of 1950s baseball was conservative: be patient and wait for the three-run home run. Aparicio was the catalyst, but Wills accelerated baseball's transformation to a greater reliance on speed and baserunning, leading to his record 104 stolen bases in 1962.

In the first seven years of the previous decade, no *team* had stolen 100 bases. In the last weeks of 1962, Wills made the head-first slide a common practice — out of necessity. He had to resort to the technique to save his legs, which were a mass of "strawberries" caused by sliding on the new Dodger Stadium crushed-brick infield.

Baseball's concept of speed was forever changed. Speed was now not only a weapon to gain an extra base, it was used as a disruptive force. With Wills dancing off first base, pitchers tended to lose their concentration. In 2007, Roger Craig would observe of Maury Wills, "He changed the whole game of baseball."[1] Lou Brock accelerated the baserunning trend from the mid–1960s and into the 1970s.

Integration Is Complete

When Boston's Elijah "Pumpsie" Green first donned a Red Sox uniform on July 22, 1959, in Chicago, the 12-year process of integrating Major League Baseball was complete. All 16 teams now had black players on their rosters. The domination by the black superstars of the game would be clearly evident by 1959. In the National League, Ernie Banks was named the MVP for the second consecutive year, the eighth time in the decade a black player had won the award. Banks led the league in runs batted in; Hank Aaron had the highest batting average, the highest slugging percentage, and the most total bases; Willie McCovey was named the Rookie of the Year, despite having played only 52 games over the last two months; Charlie Neal had the most triples; Vada Pinson hit the most doubles and scored the most runs; Willie Mays stole the most bases; and Sam Jones was the ERA champion while tying for the most wins and shutouts.

The percentage of black players in Major League Baseball would continue to grow before reaching a peak of 27 percent in 1975 — the year Frank Robinson became the first black manager. Whereas in 1959 Vic Power and Minnie Minoso were the only black players on the American League All-Star team, by 1975 there were 10, representing 40 percent of the squad.

Expansion Looms on the Horizon

In December 1957, in the wake of losing both the Dodgers and Giants to the West Coast, New York Mayor Robert Wagner appointed a three-member committee to investigate the possibilities of securing a new National League team for New York. Brooklyn-born attorney William Shea became the driving force behind the committee. After Shea failed to persuade the Phillies, Reds, or Pirates to move to the Big Apple, and he failed to persuade the NL owners to expand the league to ten teams, he decided to try going outside of the existing structure. If the owners were opposed to expansion, perhaps as successful businessmen they would be motivated by a concept they understood: competition. On July 27, 1959, Shea and 77-year-old Branch Rickey announced the formation of a new eight-team Continental League to begin play in 1961, with Rickey soon to be named league president.

The major league owners were aghast at the prospect of a third league. In 1914-15, the opening years of World War I, they had fought the baseball equivalent of the Great War with the upstart Federal League, which stole their players, sent salaries through the roof, and brought unwanted attention to baseball's exemption from the federal antitrust laws. With the inaugural season set for 1961 with teams in New York, Houston, Denver, Toronto, Minneapolis-

St. Paul, Atlanta, Dallas, and Buffalo, the Continental League plans moved forward until June 28, 1960. On that day, Senate Bill 3483 (the Kefauver bill), which would have ended baseball's antitrust exemption, failed to pass by only four votes. This near legislative catastrophe, combined with the imminent threat of competition from the Continental League, moved the major league owners to schedule meetings between their own expansion committee and the Continental League to seek a compromise.

On October 17, 1960, four days after Pittsburgh's shocking David and Goliath triumph over the Yankees in the World Series, the National League owners unanimously voted to expand from eight to 10 teams by Opening Day 1962. Two Continental League teams, New York and Houston, would be brought in, and the new league would be dissolved before it could get off the ground. Nine days later, the American League owners also voted to add two teams, but they would start one year earlier than the NL — by Opening Day 1961. Washington Senators owner Calvin Griffith was granted the right to move his team to Minneapolis-St. Paul, where it would be renamed the Minnesota Twins. Two new teams would be formed: a "new" Washington Senators and a second Los Angeles franchise, the Angels. To stock the four new teams, an expansion draft would be held allowing the newcomers to buy players at $75,000 apiece from a pool of major league and minor league players populated by the existing 16 major league clubs.[2]

Expansion of the two leagues required an enlargement of the schedules, from 154 games to 162. The first year of expansion, 1961, the new American League schedule ignited a controversy, thanks to Roger Maris. When Maris broke Babe Ruth's single-season home run record by hitting his 61st homer on October 1, 1961— in the Yankees' 163nd game — baseball commissioner Ford Frick ordered that an asterisk be attached to his name in the record book. In 1962, the National League had its own expansion-year record book controversy. In the Dodgers' 156th game, Maury Wills broke Ty Cobb's single-season stolen base record of 96, established in 1915.

In 1969, each league expanded to twelve teams, split into two divisions, and instituted a League Championship Series to determine the pennant winners.

The End of Train Travel

In the 1942 film, *Pride of the Yankees*, Babe Ruth played himself as the Yankees celebrated on the train after winning the 1928 World Series in St. Louis. By the late fifties, the days of leisurely train travel between major league cities were numbered. On January 4, 1957, the Dodgers became the first team to obtain their own plane when they purchased a forty-four passenger, twin-engine airliner for $775,000.

Don Zimmer recalled his days on the train with the Brooklyn Dodgers, saying, "On trains we were together. On the plane, you're only talking to one guy — the guy next to you. There isn't the closeness now that there was then. We'd eat in the same dining car, and we were always together. That was the biggest difference from today."[3]

By 1958, with two teams on the West Coast, air travel had become a necessity for National League teams. As the major airlines began to offer jet passenger service for both domestic and international flights at the end of 1958, players across the major leagues began to spend more time in the air the following season. Not everyone was pleased. Two months after he was named the AL Most Valuable Player for 1958, Red Sox star Jackie Jensen retired from baseball due to a fear of flying. In 1961, after missing two years, he would come back to Boston for one last attempt to overcome his fear. For the 1959 season, nine teams traveled exclusively by air on their road trips, while others still did some of their travel by train. The marriage of baseball and the train was rapidly becoming an anachronism.

An Explosion of New Ball Parks

By the middle of the sixties, some sports commentators were proclaiming that professional football had overtaken baseball as the national pastime.[4] The decade, meanwhile, saw an explosive growth of new baseball parks, located in San Francisco (1960), Minneapolis (1961), Los Angeles (1962), Washington, D.C. (1962), New York (1964), Houston (1965), Atlanta (1966), and St. Louis (1966).

In 1960, the San Francisco Giants opened the season in a desolate wind tunnel on Candlestick Point. A national television audience was first introduced to Candlestick Park on July 11, 1961, when San Francisco hosted the first of the two 1961 All-Star Games. In the ninth inning, aided by a balk caused by a gust of wind that blew Giants reliever Stu Miller off the mound in mid-delivery, the American League scored two runs to tie the game.[5]

From 1962 to 1964, the Houston Colt 45's played in Colts Stadium, known as "Mosquito Heaven." Though the Colt 45's instituted the first Sunday night games during the oppressive summer heat months, the players were still eaten alive by the largest and most aggressive mosquitoes in major league history, despite between-innings spraying by the grounds crew.[6]

In 1965, the Houston team, renamed the Astros, inaugurated the first domed, air-conditioned stadium in an attempt to escape the heat and the mosquitoes. Costing a then-astronomical $31.6 million, the Astrodome was proclaimed by Texans as the "Eighth Wonder of the World." While it had the brightest lighting in the majors, the first closed-circuit television system, the first cushioned seating, and the first skyboxes, it was not perfect.[7] When the plan to grow indoor grass failed because of insufficient sunlight, the Astros merely dyed the dead grass green. In Texas, the home of NASA, there was no problem that could not be solved by technology. For the 1966 season, the Astros covered the field with AstroTurf, an artificial surface developed by the Monsanto Company. Who needed grass? Baseball could now be played on a bright green plastic carpet.

Change Begins at the Players Association

The Major League Baseball Players Association (MLBPA) was formed in 1953 to protect the players' interests, but was largely ineffective for its first dozen years.

1959 Rumblings

Changes began to stir in 1959. On March 24, 1959, the organization fired its lawyer, J. Norman Lewis, who had been hired in 1953 by Allie Reynolds, the then AL players' representative, and Ralph Kiner, at the time the NL players' representative. The players were unhappy with the way Lewis represented their interests at the July 1958 Senate subcommittee investigation into the antitrust aspects of organized baseball.[8] After the departure of Lewis, the association went without a permanent counsel for almost nine months until it replaced him with Robert C. Cannon, son of Wisconsin Congressman Raymond J. Cannon, who had attempted to unionize the players in 1920.[9]

Marvin Miller and the Transformation of the MLBPA

Despite affecting a change in counsel in its seventh year, the MLBPA continued to be impotent until 1966, when it named Marvin Miller, the highly respected economist for the United Steelworkers of America, as its first permanent executive director. Miller immediately transformed the MLBPA into a bona fide labor union. Thus began a new era of baseball wars between the players and the owners over collective bargaining, the reserve clause, and salary arbitration.[10] In 1968, Miller negotiated the MLBPA's first collective bargaining agreement between the players and the owners that increased the minimum salary 67 percent, from $6,000 to $10,000, the first increase in two decades. In 1959, Ted Williams was the highest-paid player in Major League Baseball with a salary of $125,000. By 2006, the major league *minimum* was $380,000, thanks to Miller's greatest gift to the players: emancipation from the reserve clause.

Before the start of the 1972 season, when the owners refused to increase their contribution to the players' pension fund, Miller advised the MLBPA to act. By a vote of 663–10, the players decided to begin the first general walk-out in modern baseball history. When the strike forced spring training to end early and delayed Opening Day, the *Sporting News* called it "the darkest day in sports history." When the players went back to work in mid–April, it was obvious they had wrung concessions out of the owners reflected in a new agreement that strengthened the pension fund, increased the minimum salary, and created a new right to salary arbitration.[11]

For a century, owners had exploited the reserve clause in the standard player's contract to unilaterally renew the contract — at the same salary — in perpetuity. A player was effectively bound to one club for life, or until that club decided to get rid of him. Dodger pitcher Andy Messersmith successfully challenged this practice on December 23, 1975, when a three-member arbitration panel decided, 2–1, that owners could only control a player for one year. After that, a player would become a *free agent*—free to sign with another club. Recognizing the negative impact on their profits, the owners attempted to have the arbitration panel's decision overturned in the federal courts, but lost. The decision was binding on the owners, the reserve clause was dead, and the free agency era was born.

Marvin Miller was not done. He next negotiated a key provision in the contract between the owners and the players: the players would have to play six years in the majors before they would be eligible for free agency. The owners were initially pleased that they could at least control their best players for six years. But on further examination, this proved to be costly for management. As an economist, Miller understood that if every player became a free agent every year, the market value of the players would be constrained. But by allowing a small number of free agents to enter the market each year, the owners would bid up their price. When the average player salary doubled in 1976, it was clear that baseball economics had been irrevocably changed.[12]

Winners and Losers—The Players Gain at the Expense of the Fans

The gains by the players came at a cost to the fans. Baseball fans had traditionally formed allegiances to their "home team," composed of a stable group of players, loyal to the city, in the same lineup year after year. After the Dodgers and Giants left New York after 1957, this concept began to crumble. But free agency destroyed it. To the fans, players had transformed themselves into mercenaries armed with bats, in an evil conspiracy with agents, willing to jump from team to team each winter based on the highest bidder.

The Changing Role of the Relief Pitcher

It would be a quarter century before *closer* and *setup man* became terms of art in the baseball lexicon. A complete game by the starting pitcher, who pitched every fourth day, was the standard in the fifties, with relief pitchers—with such notable exceptions as Hoyt Wilhelm and Elroy Face — relegated to the ignominy of the bullpen. By 1959, Face was a legitimate star in Pittsburgh with an 18–1 record — all decisions in relief. In the sixties, the relief pitcher began to play an increasingly prominent role. In the American League, the record for most games pitched was broken and re-broken five times by relief pitchers. The "save" would be adopted as the yardstick for the relief pitcher's performance in 1969, when it was deemed an officially recognized statistic by Major League Baseball.

Thanks to workhorses like Robin Roberts and Warren Spahn pitching every fourth day, on three days rest, the National League complete game leaders averaged 26 games from 1950 to 1959. By the 1980s, the average had plummeted to 15 complete games. By the 1990s, starting pitchers were pitching every fifth day — on four days rest. The starter's role was reduced to one of getting past the middle innings before handing the ball to the setup man, who would hand it off to the closer.

The Beginning of the End of the Post-War Era

The 1959 season was the beginning of the end of the post–World War II era. For the first time, Ted Williams and Stan Musial, the period's two gods of hitting, showed signs of mortality. Casey Stengel, who had led the Yankees to the World Series nine times since 1949, turned 69. Critics said his age was a factor in New York's third-place finish.

Teddy Ballgame

After winning two consecutive AL batting crowns, by hitting .388 at the age of 39 in 1957 and .328 at the age of 40 in 1958, Ted Williams— plagued by a pinched nerve in his neck —fell to a mere mortal .254 in 1959, his only season below .300. At 41, Williams returned for one more season in 1960, batting .318 with 29 home runs. On September 28, 1960, in Fenway Park, he hit a home run in the last at-bat of his 22-year career, all with the Boston Red Sox.

Stan the Man

The 1959 campaign also saw 39-year-old Stan Musial slump to .255 after 18 straight seasons above .300. He would play four more years for the Cardinals, hitting above .300 only once (.330 in 1962), before ending his 22-year career after the 1963 season. Before his last game in which he had two hits to bring his career total to 3,630, Musial told his adoring fans at Busch Stadium, "Baseball has taught me the opportunity that America offers to any young men who want to get to the top in anything."[13]

The Ol' Perfesser

By finishing a shocking third in 1959, 69-year-old Casey Stengel's Yankees failed to win the American League pennant for only the second time in the previous 11 seasons. Stengel led the Bronx Bombers back to the World Series in 1960, but the upstart Pittsburgh Pirates beat them in seven games despite being crushed, 16–3, in Game 2, 10–0, in Game 3, and, 12–0, in Game 6.

Five days after Bill Mazeroski's series-winning, ninth-inning home run in Game 7 at Forbes Field, the 70-year-old Stengel was "retired" at the expiration of his two-year contract. Asked by reporters at a press conference at the Savoy Hilton Hotel on Fifth Avenue in New York whether he had been fired, the visibly angry Ol' Perfesser barked, "No, I wasn't fired. I was paid up in full. Write anything you want — quit, fired, whatever you please. I don't care!" Later, waxing philosophical at the bar, Stengel told reporters, "I'll never make the mistake of being seventy again."[14]

The Stengel era was over. It was a public relations disaster for the New York Yankees, who were deluged with telegrams, letters, and phone calls protesting the way they treated him.[15]

Baseball Prepares to Pass the Torch

In his inauguration address of January 20, 1961, little more than three months after the final out was recorded in the 1960 World Series, President John F. Kennedy told the country, "The torch has been passed to a new generation of Americans." As baseball's post–World War II era was drawing to a close, it became increasingly evident that its heroes were preparing to pass the torch.

The Decline of the Baseball Hero

The Black Sox Scandal of 1919, in which eight players were banned from the major leagues for life for fixing the World Series, tarnished the image of the baseball player as American hero. The public's trust was eventually restored, mainly due to four decades of Yankee heroes: Babe Ruth in the 1920s, Lou

Gehrig in the 1930s, Joe DiMaggio in the 1940s, and Mickey Mantle in the 1950s. By the beginning of the 1960 season, the apotheosis of Mickey Mantle was complete. Even the boo-birds who had ridden him mercilessly the year before when he struck out joined the adoration army, mercurially turning their wrath on the surly upstart Roger Maris, who dared to steal the attention away from their beloved "Mick." But later that year, the baseball player as hero clashed with the baseball player as iconoclast author. In July, Jim Brosnan published *The Long Season*, his diary of the 1959 season as a member of the Cincinnati Reds. Brosnan was not the typical tobacco-chewing, crotch-scratching, expectorating ballplayer. He wore horn-rimmed glasses and a beret, smoked a pipe, read books on literature and philosophy, and played classical piano. Joe Garagiola called him "a kooky beatnik."[16] But his book became a best-seller and shocked the baseball world.

In *The Long Season*, Brosnan challenged the idea of the baseball player as larger-than-life American hero. It was a realistic — often cynical — insider's look at players, coaches, and managers. While the renowned sportswriter Jimmy Cannon called it "the greatest baseball book ever written," the baseball establishment took a different view. By undermining the players' mythical stature, many of Brosnan's colleagues accused him of betraying the baseball fraternity. As a result of the waves caused by *The Long Season*, the owners began to crack down on what their players could write for publication. And they were determined to make an example of Jim Brosnan.

In 1962, Brosnan published another best-seller, *The Pennant Race*, a diary of his 1961 pennant-winning season in Cincinnati. Before the 1963 season, after he refused the Reds' demand that he submit his writings to owner Bill DeWitt for "review" before publication, he was traded to the Chicago White Sox. In January 1964, after he refused to sign a contract with a clause prohibiting him from publishing during the season, the White Sox put him on waivers. When he was released after no team offered the $1 to claim him, the question of collusion reared its ugly head. Had the owners conspired to blacklist a troublemaker?[17]

In 1968, when the Tet Offensive showed that the Vietnam War was unwinnable, the world was shocked by the assassinations of Martin Luther King Jr. and Robert Kennedy, and America was questioning its values, songwriter Paul Simon pondered what had become of his boyhood hero, Joe DiMaggio, in his hit recording, "Mrs. Robinson." It was as if Americans were yearning for the spring-after-spring certainty of baseball and the inspiration provided by its past heroes. Two years later, Jim Bouton, a journeyman relief pitcher for the Houston Astros, published *Ball Four*. Ten years after Brosnan's *The Long Season*, Bouton again exposed the human frailties of America's heroes.

The baseball establishment's reaction to *Ball Four* was predictable: shock and outrage. In defending his candid description of the ballplayer's life on the road — women, alcohol, racial friction, profanity, pep pills, and spit balls— Bouton maintained that he was merely revealing the tawdry side of baseball that was as old as Abner Doubleday. Further, he was now letting the ordinary fan in on baseball's closely guarded secret. True, but the powers-that-be took the position that to reveal it was "bad for baseball." Translated, this meant bad for owners' profits and bad for players' reputations.

In the off-season, after *Ball Four* had sold more copies faster than any sports book in history, baseball commissioner Bowie Kuhn called Jim Bouton into his office for a *talk*. Kuhn, who had publicly declared the book "a disservice to baseball," told Bouton he was going to do him a big favor. All he would have to do was to sign a statement prepared by Kuhn that, in essence, said the book was a pack of lies, and blamed everything on his editor, Leonard Shechter. Bouton refused to sign. *Ball Four* stood on its own.[18]

Let's Play Two! Avarice and the All-Star Game

After the Dodgers had to turn away 15,000 fans to seat more than 93,000 for the May 7, 1959, Roy Campanella Night exhibition game with the Yankees, Walter O'Malley — with dollar signs in his eyes— was inspired to recommend to the Major League Baseball Executive Council that there be a second All-Star Game to be played at the Los Angeles Memorial Coliseum. The motion was passed by a unanimous vote of the seven-member Executive Council:

Chairman Ford Frick, Commissioner
Warren Giles, NL President
Joe Cronin, AL President
Walter O'Malley, NL Owner (Dodgers)
Bob Carpenter, NL Owner (Phillies)
George Weiss, AL Owner (Yankees)
Chuck Comiskey, AL Owner (White Sox)

Motivated by the prospect of 60 percent of the proceeds going to the Players Pension Fund, the major league players voted heavily in favor of the proposal. But the players refused to broaden the base of the pension fund to include umpires and old-timers (retired players). After the 16 major league owners, who stood to receive 40 percent of the proceeds, voted unanimously for it, the second All-Star Game was set for August 3, 1959, at the Coliseum.

There would be no regular season inter-league play until 1997. From 1933 to 1958, the chief appeal of the All-Star Game was the novelty of a clash between the leagues. But the players and owners were willing to dilute the original product to get their hands on the expected net proceeds of $700,000.

While the second 1959 All-Star Game drew only 55,105 at the 93,000-seat Coliseum, Major League Baseball continued to play two games through the 1962 season.

* * *

The post-war era was fast coming to a close. The baggy grey flannel uniforms would soon give way to tight, brightly colored double-knit suits worn by players with mustaches, beards, and long hair protruding from mandatory batting helmets with ear flaps. America would change, and baseball would change along with it.

Chapter 23

Turning the Page to the Sixties

The 1959 season saw one of the great pennant races, a rare Yankeeless "underdog" World Series, and the beginning of the changes that would transform baseball in the 1960s. The baseball teams that dominated the game that year would undergo significant changes in the post–1959 baseball world.

The Los Angeles Dodgers

After the Pittsburgh Pirates worked their "Miracle in Pittsburgh"[1] in 1960, and the Cincinnati Reds won the 1961 NL pennant — only to run into a Mantle & Maris Yankee meat grinder — the Dodgers entered one of their most successful periods in franchise history, from 1962 to 1966.

1962—Another Year That Would Live in Infamy

The Los Angeles Dodgers, managed by Walter Alston, had one of their best teams in 1962, drawing a major league record 2,755,184 fans to their new Dodger Stadium. With a career-best 25 wins, Don Drysdale won the Cy Young Award. Sandy Koufax, who ended his first six years of drift with an 18-win season in 1961, entered his otherworldly period. Now, while warming up before each game, the question was not, "Can Koufax find home plate?" but "Does Koufax have no-hit stuff tonight?" Maury Wills broke the record for most stolen bases in a season with 104 and won the MVP award. Outfielder Tommy Davis was the NL batting champion with a .346 average, 230 hits, and 153 runs batted in. Behemoth outfielder Frank Howard contributed 31 home runs and 119 runs batted in.

The *Taj O'Malley*, aka Dodger Stadium, opened on April 10, 1962, before a sellout crowd of 52,564. But the NL champion Cincinnati Reds spoiled the party when Wally Post stung Dodger starter Johnny Podres with a seventh-inning, three-run homer, turning the celebration into a 6–3 defeat.[2] The Dodgers otherwise got off to a fine start, and by the end of June, the race for the National League pennant was reduced to another classic dogfight between the Dodgers and Giants, with San Francisco clinging to a microscopic .008 lead at the end of play on June 30.

When the Dodgers arrived in Cincinnati on July 17, they were playing .660 baseball, had a two-game lead over the Giants, and had the advantage of sending Sandy Koufax to the mound with a 14–4 record—17 days after his first no-hitter (against Casey Stengel's expansion team, the Amazin' Mets). But that night in Crosley Field, the Reds hung a fifth loss on Koufax, who was removed after one shaky inning with numbness in his left index finger. Taking no chances, the Dodgers immediately flew him back to Los Angeles for treatment. Koufax would miss the next 58 games of the season.

By the time the Dodgers arrived in San Francisco for a three-game series on August 10, they had a comfortable 5½-game lead over the Giants. But Alvin Dark had a trick up his sleeve to stop Maury Wills, who was stealing bases and scoring runs in bunches. He ordered the grounds crew, armed with garden hoses, to flood the base path between the first and second bases, thereby creating a quagmire for any player — especially those with the initials MW — who attempted to steal second. The tactic worked, as Wills was held to one run scored, with no stolen bases, and the Giants beat the Dodgers three straight to move to with 2½ games of the lead.

The Dodgers entered September with a 2½-game lead over the Giants. And by September 21, on the road in St. Louis, things were looking even better for the Dodgers. They had a four-game lead over the Giants with nine games left, and Sandy Koufax was finally ready to make his first appearance since July 17. But the Dodgers got a rude shock as Koufax was routed in the first inning on the way to an 11–2 Cardinal blowout. He retired only two batters, walked four, and after walking the bases loaded, gave up a grand slam home run to Charlie James. The Giants, in turn, blew out the Colt .45s in Houston, 11–5, to cut the Dodger lead to three games with eight to play. The next day the Dodgers restored their lead to four with seven games left, thanks to Johnny Podres' 4–1 win over the Cardinals and the Giants' loss in Houston.

On September 23, in the Dodgers' final game on the road, Maury Wills stole his 96th and 97th bases to tie and break Ty Cobb's record — established in 1915 —for stolen bases in a season. Wills had his record, but the Dodgers appeared too distracted to take care of business. The Cardinals thwarted Don Drysdale's attempt for his 26th win by pounding Los Angeles, 12–2. Combined with the Giants' win at Houston, the lead was now three. But why worry? There were only six games left to play, and the Dodgers were going back home to play them: three with the eighth-place Colt .45s and three with the sixth-place Cardinals.

After the Dodgers lost two out of three to the Colt .45s at Dodger Stadium, and the Giants won two out of three from the Cardinals at Candlestick Park, the Dodgers' lead had shrunk to two as both clubs exchanged partners for the final weekend: the Cardinals flew down to Los Angeles and the Colt .45s flew up to San Francisco. Now all the Dodgers needed was to win two out of three over the sixth-place Cardinals to clinch the National League pennant. Though Dodger fans were accustomed to suffering from their Brooklyn days, what they were about to go through was almost too much to bear.

Friday night, September 28, the Dodgers had to face their old Cardinal nemesis, Larry Jackson. It was futile to hope for any help from Jackson, who pitched a 10-inning complete game for a 3–2 St. Louis upset. Charlie James, who ruined Koufax's return the week before in St. Louis, singled home the winning run in the top of the tenth. After the Giants and Colt .45s were rained out in San Francisco, the Dodgers' lead was cut to a game and a half. A day later, the expansion team from Houston would give the Dodgers yet another opening.

Saturday afternoon, September 29, the Giants and Colt .45s made up their rainout with a double-header at Candlestick Park. While the Giants had dominated the expansion Mets 14 games to four that year, the Colt .45s were more problematical. While the Giants would go into the double-header with Jack Sanford (23–7) and Juan Marichal (18–10), they had only a nine games-to-six advantage over Houston. Sanford and the Giants crushed them, 11–5, in the opener. But Norm Larker, whom the Colt .45s "stole" from the Dodgers for $75,000 in the expansion draft, hit a two-run home run off Marichal to beat the Giants, 4–2, in the second game.

The split in San Francisco meant that going into their game with the Cardinals that evening at Dodger Stadium, the Dodgers' lead was still 1½. All they needed was one more victory from their ace right-hander, Don Drysdale (25–8), to clinch the National League pennant. But it was not to be. Drysdale should have been out of the inning in the second when, with two outs and a runner on first, weak-hitting shortstop Dal Maxvill hit a lazy fly ball down the right-field line. But lumbering Frank Howard dropped the ball, barely in fair territory, for a three-base, run-scoring error. Cardinals pitcher Ernie Broglio singled home Maxvill for the second, and last, run of the game. The Dodgers committed two more errors and managed only two hits against Broglio, who went on to shut them out, 2–0. Though Drysdale gave up just five hits and no earned runs, he failed in his third try for his 26th victory. With a crowd of 49,012, the Dodgers broke the major league single-season attendance record set by the 1948 Cleveland Indians—small consolation for blowing a chance to clinch the pennant.[3]

On Sunday, September 30, 1962, the Dodgers limped to the last day of the season with a miniscule .006 lead over the Giants (.627 to .621). Again, they were in control of their own fate, merely needing to salvage the last game of their series with the Cardinals to win the pennant, regardless of what the Giants did in San Francisco. Walter Alston asked his "money" pitcher, Johnny Podres, to carry the Dodgers over the finish line on the left-hander's 30th birthday, the way he had saved them in Game 3 of the 1955 World Series on his 23rd birthday. But they had to face the Cardinals' veteran left-hander, Curt Simmons, who had beaten them with a five-hitter in St. Louis on September 21. In a tense pitcher's duel, the game was scoreless through the first seven innings. With one out in the top of the eighth, Cardinal journeyman catcher Gene Oliver made Podres pay for his only mistake: a hanging curve. Behind in the count 1–2, Oliver drove the errant pitch deep into the seats between the left-field foul pole and the Dodger bullpen. Oliver's solo home run was all the Cardinals needed, as Simmons shut them out, 1–0, with another five-hitter in only one hour and 50 minutes. Meanwhile at Candlestick, Willie Mays hit a solo homer—his 47th home run of the year—in the bottom of the eighth inning to break a 1–1 tie with Houston and force the first playoff with the Dodgers since 1951.[4]

In the Dodger clubhouse, there was an ominous silence. After being in undisputed first place since July 8, the Dodgers had lost 10 of the last 13 games, six of the last seven, and had been shut out for the last 21 innings. Asked by reporters how he felt about playing in the third playoff of his career, Duke Snider said, "That's why I have all these gray hairs. But the one that caused the most gray hairs was in 1951 when Bobby Thomson hit 'that homer'—I'd say we have a score to settle with the Giants."[5] If the Dodgers were dazed, the Dodger fans were in denial. This couldn't be happening! Besides, the *TV Guide* said the World Series between the Dodgers and Yankees would begin on October 3.

The parallels to the 1951 Giants-Dodgers playoff series were eerie. The 1951 Giants caught the Dodgers on the last game of the season. Leo Durocher, manager of the 1951 Giants, was now in the third-base coaching box for the Dodgers. Alvin Dark, the captain of the 1951 Giants, was leading them as manager from the dugout. Willie Mays, a rookie in 1951, was still in center field for the Giants, but now the game's premier player.

On Monday, October 1, in the opening game of the best two-out-of-three game playoff series at Candlestick Park, the Dodgers, still dazed by their failure to wrap up the pennant at home, were shell-shocked, 8–0, by Willie Mays' two home runs (numbers 48 and 49) and yet another shutout—this time a three-hitter by former White Sox left-hander Billy Pierce. Coming into the game, there was already bad blood between the Dodgers and Pierce. It was Pierce who had combined with Bob Shaw and Dick Donovan to shut out the Dodgers, 1–0, at the Coliseum in Game 5 of the 1959 World Series, preventing them from clinching the Series at home.

The next day in Los Angeles, the Dodgers overcame a five-run deficit to pull out the second playoff game at Los Angeles, 8–7, thereby staving off elimination. Down 5–0 in the bottom of the sixth inning, and after being shut out for 35 straight innings, they finally broke out with seven runs to take a 7–5 lead. The Giants battled back to tie the game, 7–7, with two runs in the top of the eighth. Dodger first baseman Ron Fairly came to the plate with one out in the bottom of the ninth and Maury Wills—who stole his 101st base in the sixth—on third base. After taking two strikes from Giants reliever Bob Bolin, Fairly hit a line drive to medium-deep center field. Willie Mays fielded the ball and threw it high to the plate, enabling Wills, celebrating his 30th birthday, to slide under Tom Haller's tag and the Dodgers to win the game, 8–7. After a 4-hour and 18-minute free-for-all, in which an NL-record 42 players were used, the Dodgers had survived to play Game 3 of the playoff series.

The showdown game of the playoff series was played at Dodger Stadium on Wednesday, October 3, the day Dodger fans had expected to see the start of the eighth Yankees-Dodgers World Series in baseball history. As he did in the last game of the regular season, Alston called on Johnny Podres (15–13) to pitch for the Dodgers. Alvin Dark named Juan Marichal (18–11) to take the mound. The game was scoreless after two innings, but then turned into a seesaw death struggle. Aided by three Dodger errors, the Giants scored two runs in the third to take a 2–0 lead. The Dodgers got one back in the fourth, and took a 3–2 lead in the sixth when Tommy Davis rocked Marichal with a two-run homer—his 152nd and 153rd RBIs. Los Angeles added an insurance run in the bottom of the seventh when Maury Wills hit his fourth straight single, stole second and third—giving him 104 stolen bases for the season—and scored on a Giant throwing error. When Podres, who was pitching on two days rest, hit a wall after completing five innings, Alston brought in Ed Roebuck, who shut out the Giants for two innings.

Roebuck brought the Dodgers to the top of the ninth inning with a 4–2 lead. Just three more outs to go. But the ninth inning turned into a nightmare as Roebuck, making his seventh relief appearance in the last nine days, ran out of gas. Dodger fans gasped as the Giants loaded the bases for Willie Mays with one out. Mays lined a vicious drive off Roebuck's glove to score Harvey Kuenn, thus making the score 4–3, and leaving the bases loaded. Alston pulled the exhausted Roebuck and brought in Stan Williams to pitch to Orlando Cepeda, who hit another line drive—this one was caught by Ron Fairly in right field. The Dodgers got the second out, but pinch-runner Ernie Bowman scored from third on the play to tie the game at 4–4. After being three outs away from the World Series, the Dodgers were now in survival mode.

With first base open, Williams walked Ed Bailey to load the bases again. But after Williams walked Jim Davenport on five pitches to force in a run and give the Giants a 5–4 lead, Alston brought in Ron Perranoski with the bases still loaded. In what should have been the third out, Perranoski got Jose Pagan to hit a routine ground ball to second baseman Larry Burright, who fumbled the ball, allowing Mays to score on the error. Perranoski struck out Bob Nieman to end the inning, but the damage was done. The Giants had turned a 4–2 deficit into a 6–4 lead.

Taking no chances, Alvin Dark brought in Billy Pierce, who had just pitched a complete-game shutout two days before, to pitch the bottom of the ninth inning. After Pierce retired the Dodgers in order, they and their 45,693 fans suffered the indignity of watching the Giants mob him as they celebrated in the middle of their new field.[6]

* * *

The next season, 1963, the Dodgers coasted to the pennant before sweeping the Yankees four straight in the World Series. After a disappointing sixth-place finish in 1964, mainly due to losing Tommy Davis in June and Sandy Koufax in August, Los Angeles won the next two National League pennants (1965-1966) and their fourth world championship in 1965. After Sandy Koufax abruptly retired following the 1966 season, the Dodgers entered a period of decline that lasted until 1974.

Larry Sherry

Had it not been for Larry Sherry's outstanding relief work in the NL playoff series and the World Series, the Los Angeles Dodgers could not have won the 1959 world championship. After his July 1959 recall from Triple-A St. Paul, he began as a starting pitcher before evolving into the Dodgers' principal reliever. With Sherry's 7–2 record and 2.19 ERA, 1959 would be his best season. He was the unanimous choice as the Most Valuable Player of the World Series, and finished second to Willie McCovey as the National League's Rookie of the Year.

Sherry would pitch for the Dodgers, primarily as a reliever, for four more years, from 1960–1963. He never regained his 1959 level of play, and was sold to the Detroit Tigers after the 1963 season. He was a mediocre reliever for four seasons at Detroit, then was traded to the Houston Astros after posting a 6.43 ERA in 1967. In 1968, he was dealt to the California Angels where, after three rocky relief appearances, he was released on July 7, 1968. Sherry returned to baseball as a pitching coach for the 1977-1978 Pittsburgh Pirates and the 1979-1980 California Angels.

Overall, Larry Sherry's 11-year career in the major leagues was unremarkable: 53 wins and 44 losses with an earned run average of 3.67. But he will always be remembered for his stirring performance in the 1959 World Series. It would be his shining — but fleeting — moment in the sun.

Carl Furillo

After his clutch hitting won both the pennant-clinching playoff games with the Milwaukee Braves and Game 3 of the 1959 World Series, Carl Furillo's 15-year career with the Dodgers came to sudden and unhappy end. In the spring of 1960, after appearing in only eight games, and hobbled by a calf injury, the Dodgers fired him.

At 38, Furillo knew he was nearing the end of his career, but it was the way the Dodgers handled the situation that destroyed their relationship. Furillo played his last game on May 7, 1960. Two days later, he had a meeting with Buzzie Bavasi in which the Dodger general manager not-so-subtly asked him, "What do you think of Frank Howard, Carl?"[7]

On May 12, as the team prepared to fly to San Francisco for a big three-game series with the Giants, a representative from the front office called to tell him, "Carl, don't bother to pack."[8] Furillo naively thought the Dodgers were giving him more time to rest his leg. But when Bavasi called on May 16 and coldly stated like a federal bureaucrat pronouncing a new regulation, "I'm sorry to inform you that you've been given an unconditional release," Furillo became enraged.[9]

Not only were the Dodgers unceremoniously terminating his career — there would be no "Carl Furillo Night" at the Coliseum — they were attempting to avoid paying him for the remainder of the season. He signed a $33,000 contract for 1960 and had drawn $12,000. A clause in his contract provided:

> Disability directly resulting from injury ... shall not impair the right of the player to receive his full salary for the period of such disability or for the season in which the injury was sustained.[10]

In his mind, he was due the balance of $21,000. Furillo would sue the Dodgers for breach of contract, arguing that since his calf injury precipitated his release, his "disability" should not have prevented him from receiving his full 1960 salary. The legal fight did not end until May 1961, when Furillo met with Major League Baseball Commissioner Ford Frick, who awarded him the $21,000 due him for 1960.[11]

Furillo's resort to the legal system enabled him to achieve financial justice, but it had a darker side: he was blacklisted by Major League Baseball. At 39, Furillo wanted to coach and pinch-hit, but no owner would touch him. He moved back to Queens in 1963, and bought a small delicatessen restaurant on Thirty-second Avenue. After seven years in the restaurant business, he returned to his birth state of Pennsylvania and took a construction job with Otis.[12]

Carl Furillo died in 1989 at the age of 66. He and the Dodgers never reconciled.

Gil Hodges

The 1959 season was Gil Hodges' last year as an everyday player. He spent two more years (1960-1961) with the Los Angeles Dodgers, primarily as a pinch-hitter and backup to the new regular first baseman, Norm Larker. In the NL expansion year of 1962, he joined the New York Mets, where he hit the last nine of his 370 career home runs. He spent the final two years of his career (1962-1963) playing for the "Amazin' Mets" under septuagenarian manager Casey Stengel.

Gil Hodges played his last game on May 5, 1963, in the old Polo Grounds. Two weeks later he was installed as the manager of the tenth-place Washington Senators. By 1967, their last year under Hodges, the Senators had improved to sixth place in the American League.

In 1968, Hodges took over as manager of the New York Mets. He suffered a heart attack on September 19, 1968, 10 days before the Mets finished in ninth place. The following year Hodges led the "Miracle Mets" to the world championship. Thus Hodges managed the biggest one-year turnaround in baseball history after playing for the team (the 1959 Dodgers) that had accomplished the biggest one-year turnaround in the pre-expansion era.

After guiding the Mets to two third-place finishes, in 1970 and 1971, he retired, turning the team over to his old World Series rival, Yogi Berra. Gil Hodges died on April 2, 1972, two days shy of his 48th birthday.

Roger Craig

Roger Craig would play only two more seasons with the Los Angeles Dodgers—1960 and 1961—primarily as their fifth starting pitcher. On October 10, 1961, he was drafted by the New York Mets in the National League's first expansion draft. The Amazin' Mets of 1962, losers of 120 games, provided little support for a starting staff that included Craig. He was 10–24 that first season in the Polo Grounds. With one of the best pick-off moves in baseball, he had several memorable battles with Maury Wills, his old Dodger teammate who was on his way to a new single-season record for stolen bases. Unfortunately, the Mets of 1963 were again hopelessly inept at scoring runs for Craig, who won just five games and lost 22, including a stretch of 18 decisions in a row, during which the Mets were shut out eight times. But his 27 complete games for 1962–1963 suggest that the quality of his pitching could not be judged solely by the number of his losses.

Mercifully, Roger Craig moved on to the St. Louis Cardinals in 1964, where he won Game 4 of the World Series against the Yankees by pitching 4⅔ scoreless innings in relief of Ray Sadecki to tie the Series at two games apiece. When the Cardinals won the Series in seven games, Craig had his third World Series ring as a player.

Two months after Craig helped the Cardinals win the 1964 World Series, they traded him to the Cincinnati Reds for Bob Purkey. After Craig pitched 40 games in relief for the Reds in 1965, they released him before the start of the 1966 season. The same day, he went to Philadelphia as a free agent and pitched the last 14 games of his career for the Phillies.

After his playing days concluded, Roger Craig became a successful coach and manager. He was a scout for the Los Angeles Dodgers in 1967, then manager of their Triple-A Albuquerque farm team in 1968. He was a coach with the San Diego Padres expansion team from 1969 to 1972. From 1973 through 1977, he was a pitching coach for the Dodgers, Astros, and Padres.

Craig received his first chance to manage at the major league level with the San Diego Padres in 1978 and led them to their first winning season. After two years of managing in San Diego, he was the Detroit Tigers' pitching coach from 1980 to 1984. When Sparky Anderson's Tigers beat his old team, the Padres, to win the 1984 World Series, Craig had his fourth World Series ring. In September of 1985, he took over as manager of a San Francisco Giants team that lost 100 games to finish in sixth place. For the next seven seasons (1986–1992), he managed the Giants to two division titles (1987, 1989) and one National League pennant (1989). His Giants lost the 1989 "Earthquake World Series" to their archrival Oakland Athletics, managed by Tony La Russa.

Roger Craig retired after managing the 1992 Giants. He lives in Hilton Head, South Carolina.

Sandy Koufax

Plagued by inconsistency and wildness, Sanford Braun Koufax drifted through another lackluster season in 1960, but his potential was clearly evident. He struck out 197 batters in only 175 innings, and on May 23 in Pittsburgh, he nearly pitched his first no-hitter. He had to settle for a one-hitter when opposing pitcher Bennie Daniels hit a grounder through his legs for Pittsburgh's only hit.

After backup catcher Norm Sherry advised him to ease up on his velocity to achieve control, Sandy Koufax achieved a breakthrough in 1961—his first year as a regular member of the starting rotation. But while he won 18 games and struck out a NL-record 269 batters, his ERA was a mediocre 3.52, and he still walked nearly 100 batters.

In the next five years, the baseball world would witness the apotheosis of a baseball pitcher. If he changed the trajectory of his career in 1961, in 1962 he appeared to be a completely different pitcher. He was already 14–5 on July 17 when a mysterious circulatory ailment that caused his pitching hand to go numb — later diagnosed as Raynaud's Phenomenon — sidelined him until late September. This has caused endless speculation among Dodger fans about whether the Giants would have been able to catch the Dodgers on the last day of the 1962 season, and beat them in a pennant playoff, if Sandy Koufax had played the entire year. In 1963, his 25–5 record earned him both the Most Valuable Player and Cy Young awards. On August 16, 1964, he shut out the Cardinals, 3–0, to improve his record to 19–5 and lower his ERA to 1.74. But he missed the rest of the season, at least a dozen starts, due to another arm injury that would eventually develop into an arthritic pitching elbow.

In his last two years, Sandy Koufax was arguably the most dominating pitcher in baseball history. In 1965 he broke his own major league record with 382 strikeouts, pitched a perfect game, and led the NL in wins (26), ERA (2.04), complete games (27), and innings pitched (335⅔). He won the Cy Young Award by a unanimous vote. In his last season, 1966, he led the NL in wins (27), ERA (1.73), complete games (27), and strikeouts (317). For the second consecutive year, he won the Cy Young Award by a unanimous vote, and became the first three-time winner of the award.

On November 18, 1966, Sandy Koufax announced his retirement at the age of 30 due to his arthritic left elbow. In 1972, at the age of 36, he became the youngest member of Baseball Hall of Fame when he was elected on the first ballot.

The Milwaukee Braves

Dreams of a Milwaukee Braves dynasty died on September 29, 1959, at 5:06 P.M. when Gil Hodges crossed home plate at the Coliseum and the Dodgers thwarted the Braves' attempt to win their third consecutive National League pennant. The Braves promptly fired manager Fred Haney. They would never again finish higher than second in Milwaukee, averaging fifth and 11 games out in their last five years before moving to Atlanta.

The Milwaukee fans lacked a key attribute: loyalty. For the first six years (1953–1958), the Braves averaged more than two million per year in attendance. By 1959, the novelty of County Stadium and Braves baseball had begun to wear off, as only 1,749,112 Milwaukee fans turned out — even in the thick of one of the great pennant races. By 1965, their last year in Milwaukee, the

Braves' attendance had plunged to a shocking 555,584. By then, the Green Bay Packers were clearly the center of attention. The Braves moved to Atlanta for the 1966 season and nearly tripled their prior year attendance.

Hank Aaron

The 1959 season was one of Hank Aaron's finest years. He won his second NL batting title with a career-best .355 average. His rare feat of 400 total bases has been equaled only nine times in NL history. The 1959 season was also the beginning of a five-year span in which he averaged 40 home runs, 125 runs batted in, and a .323 batting average.

In 1974, Aaron broke Babe Ruth's record of 714 career home runs, and retired after the 1976 season with 755. Henry Aaron was elected to the Baseball Hall of Fame in 1982, nine votes shy of becoming the first unanimous selection.

Warren Spahn

With a record of 21–15, 1959 was Warren Spahn's tenth 20-win season. He would go on to record three more 20-win seasons: 1960, 1961, and 1963.

The 1963 season was arguably his most remarkable campaign. At age 42, he tied his career-best record of 23–7. On July 2 of that year at Candlestick Park, he battled Juan Marichal in one of the greatest pitching duels of all time. Spahn shut out the Giants and Marichal shut out the Braves for the first 15 innings. The scoreless tie moved to the bottom of the 16th when, with one out, Willie Mays hit a solo home run off Spahn to win the game, 1–0, at 12:31 A.M. Marichal was the winner of a 16-inning shutout, while Spahn pitched 15⅓ scoreless innings

Warren Spahn, the left side of the Milwaukee Braves' great left-right combination, also won 21 games in 1959. It would be the 10th of his 13 20-win seasons. (National Baseball Hall of Fame Library, Cooperstown, N.Y.)

before Mays beat him. It has been argued that Spahn's Herculean effort of July 2–3, 1963, actually shortened his 24-year career.

Warren Spahn retired after the 1965 season with the San Francisco Giants. He had 363 career wins, and was elected to the Baseball Hall of Fame in 1973 on the first ballot.

The Chicago White Sox

The 1959 World Series failure convinced White Sox owner Bill Veeck that he needed to wheel and deal over the winter. This proved to be the undoing of the Go-Go Sox as he gutted the farm system that Chuck Comiskey built in the fifties. Ignoring the long range welfare of the club, he added aging veterans Roy Sievers, Gene Freese, and Saturnino Orestes Armas "Minnie" Minoso, from Havana, Cuba, for the 1960 season. But they came at a great cost, as a veritable sixties all-star team was sacrificed by Veeck, including Norm Cash, Johnny Callison, Earl Battey, and Don Mincher. Though Veeck sold the team in June 1961, it would take the Sox years to recover from his dealings.

After their 1959 World Series appearance, the White Sox sunk to third, fourth, and fifth place behind the pennant-winning Yankees for the three-year period 1960–1962. After their third straight second-place finish in 1965, manager Al Lopez quit after eight years in Chicago. By then, Nellie Fox, Luis Aparicio, Billy Pierce, Al Smith, and Early Wynn were all gone.

Early Wynn

In Kansas City on July 13, 1963, after struggling for five innings as the starter in the second game of a double-header with the seventh-place Athletics, Early Wynn won his 300th game. Now back in a Cleveland Indians uniform as a rotund 43-year-old, it was his eighth try to reach the coveted milestone. Wynn left the game with a 5–4 lead after completing his five innings—the minimum number required for a starter to be credited with a win. His roommate, Jerry Walker, had to come in from the bullpen to pitch the last four scoreless innings. By walking three batters, Wynn also broke Bob Feller's record for most career bases on balls.

The 1959 Cy Young Award winner had been released by the White Sox after the 1962 season at the age of 42, one win short of 300. After he won number 299 in Chicago on September 8, 1962, the Sox front office removed him from the starting rotation during a 10-day road trip so he could win number 300 in his final start at Comiskey Park. But after he failed in that attempt and in two subsequent starts on the road, his career with the White

Sox was over. On November 15, 1962, the Sox gave him his unconditional release so he could pursue a front office job with the Washington Senators. The job, however, fell through. The White Sox then gave him a chance to work out with the team in spring training, but he was not offered a contract for the 1963 season.

A man without a team for eight months, Wynn looked as if he would never get another chance to pitch in the major leagues. He was a mere shadow of the pitcher he had been in his glory days in Cleveland, but on May 31, 1963, he finally convinced the Indians to take him back as a free agent.[13] After he won number 300 in his fifth start with Cleveland, Early Wynn spent the remainder of 1963 in the bullpen, and retired at the end of the season after 23 years in the majors. He was inducted into the Baseball Hall of Fame in 1972.

Nellie Fox

Nellie Fox, the 1959 American League Most Valuable Player, would play four more seasons as the White Sox second baseman, but never hit .300 again. He played his last two years in Houston—1964 with the Colt .45s, and 1965 for the Astros under the dome.

Though he led the American League in hits four times and never struck out more than 18 times in any of his 19 seasons, Nellie Fox missed election to the Baseball Hall of Fame by just two votes in 1985, the final year of his eligibility.

Luis Aparicio

After Luis Aparicio led the American League in stolen bases for the seventh straight year in 1962, the White Sox traded him to the Baltimore Orioles. With the Orioles, the Venezuelan shortstop extended his streak to nine straight years before relinquishing the league's top base stealer role to Bert Campaneris of the Kansas City Athletics. In 1968, slower of foot but still a hero in Chicago, he returned to the White Sox for three more years. After a fine 1970 season in Chicago in which he batted a career-high .313, the White Sox traded him to the Boston Red Sox, where he retired after the 1973 season.

With nine Gold Gloves to go with his nine stolen base titles over 18 seasons, Luis Aparicio was inducted into the Baseball Hall of Fame in 1984.

The San Francisco Giants

After blowing the pennant in the last eight games of the 1959 season, the Giants disappeared into the baseball wilderness for two years. They finished

1959 Go-Go Sox keystone combination of shortstop Luis Aparicio (left) and second baseman Nellie Fox. Aparicio led the majors with 56 stolen bases. Fox led the team with a .306 batting average and won the American League MVP award. (National Baseball Hall of Fame Library, Cooperstown, N.Y.)

fifth in 1960 after Tom Sheehan replaced Bill Rigney as manager early in the season. In a rare bright moment, rookie right-hander Juan Marichal threw a one-hitter against the Phillies in his first major league start. In their new Candlestick Park, the Giants set a franchise attendance record that would survive for 27 years, as 1,795,356 hearty souls risked exposure on Candlestick Point. When Alvin Dark took over the managerial reins in 1961, the Giants climbed into third place, 16 games above .500, as Orlando Cepeda turned in a career year with 46 home runs and 142 runs batted in, and Willie Mays hit four home runs in a single game in Milwaukee.

1962—Out of the Wilderness and into the World Series

While it took the global catastrophe of World War II for Winston Churchill to escape 25 years in the political wilderness after his Dardanelles catastrophe of 1915, it took a baseball catastrophe — a late September collapse — by the 1962 Dodgers for the Giants to emerge from the baseball wilderness. Down two runs in the ninth inning of the third playoff game with the Dodgers, the Giants came back to win both the game and the National League pennant. The Giants had dared to defy the *TV Guide*, which said the 1962 World Series between the Dodgers and Yankees would begin on October 3 at Dodger Stadium. Correction: the Giants would host the Yankees on October 4 at Candlestick Park.

Willie Mays wreaked havoc on Dodger pitching in 1958 (.483 AVG, 12 HR, 32 RBI), then helped to keep the San Francisco Giants in first place until the last week of the 1959 season. (National Baseball Hall of Fame Library, Cooperstown, N.Y.)

On October 16, 1962, a seesaw World Series moved to a sudden-death seventh game in San Francisco. The Series had to be postponed four times due to violent storms on the West Coast, perhaps foreshadowing the crisis that would soon consume the nation. Ralph Terry, who served the Series-ending home run ball to Bill Mazeroski in the seventh game of the 1960 Fall Classic, was again on the mound for the Yankees. Alvin Dark named Jack Sanford to pitch for the Giants. Back on October 10, Terry had beaten Sanford in Game 5 at Yankee Stadium. On this day, Terry took a 1–0 lead to the bottom of the ninth inning. Pinch-hitter Matty Alou led off with a bunt single. When Terry struck out Matty's older brother, Felipe, and Chuck Hiller, he had one out to go. Only it would be Willie Mays—with 49 home runs and 141 runs batted in during the regular season — whom Terry would have to retire. Mays promptly ripped a double down the right-field line. Roger Maris made a fine play to cut the ball off and prevent Alou from scoring the tying run. Now with two out and the potential tying and winning runs on second and third, Yankee manager Ralph Houk decided to pitch to Willie McCovey, with Orlando Cepeda next in the batting order. McCovey already had a single, triple, and home run off Terry in the Series. After hitting a long, loud foul down the right-field line, the 6' 4", 225-pound future Hall-of-Famer hit a screaming line drive toward right field that was certain to score both runners for another Series-ending blow off Ralph Terry. But Yankee second baseman Bobby Richardson made a desperate leap and came down with the baseball. Ralph Terry was lucky to survive with a 1–0 shutout and redemption. The Yankees were lucky to get out of town with their 20th world championship. The Giants, blessed by the baseball gods all fall, had run out of luck.

* * *

The day before the 1962 World Series ended, U-2 reconnaissance photographs revealed the construction of launching sites for intermediate-range missiles in Cuba. Over the next 13 days, heart-broken Dodger fans, now joined by heart-broken Giant fans, would have something bigger than baseball to worry about: the Cuban Missile Crisis. On October 24, 1962, a U.S. "quarantine" of Cuba went into effect. The next day, while the world held its breath, Soviet ships heading for Cuba turned back. Secretary of Sate Dean Rusk observed, "We're eyeball to eyeball, and I think the other fellow just blinked."[14] On October 27, Soviet Premier Khrushchev announced that he had agreed to remove the missiles from Cuba. With the world still in one piece, baseball fans in Los Angeles and San Francisco could go back to arguing about the Dodgers and the Giants.

Epilogue: 50 Years On

ON JANUARY 1, 2008, as Vin Scully waved to the crowd — not from the broadcast booth at Dodger Stadium, but from the Dodger float in the Tournament of Roses Parade in Pasadena — the Los Angeles Dodgers entered their 50th year on the West Coast. Thus began a year-long celebration of Dodgers past and present. The 80-year-old Scully sat with 80-year-old Tommy Lasorda in the grandstand section of the float. Carl Erskine, Don Newcombe, Fernando Valenzuela, Steve Garvey, and Wes Parker represented the past. In dugout sections on each side of the float, Nomar Garciaparra, James Loney, Takashi Saito, Hong-Chin Kuo, Brad Penny, and current manager Joe Torre (who was born in Brooklyn) represented the present. A large "Dodgers" sign exploded with fireworks as the float processed along Colorado Boulevard toward the Rose Bowl, the venue that nearly became the Los Angeles Dodgers' first home.[1]

On March 29, 2008, having just ended their 56th and final spring training session at Dodgertown in Vero Beach, Florida, for the first time since 1961 the Dodgers returned to the Los Angeles Memorial Coliseum for an exhibition game with the world champion Boston Red Sox. Approximately 115,300 fans— mostly dressed in blue along with a few conspicuous and brave red people from Red Sox Nation — set a world attendance record for a baseball game. They filled every conceivable space inside and outside the concrete oval on South Figueroa Street, including the 92,000 actual seats, the cement slabs in the peristyle end, and the standing room behind a temporary fence that separated right field from the rest of the grass. For the Dodgers' four years at the Coliseum (1958–1961), a track surrounded the football field, forcing them to construct a baseball field of grotesque dimensions: 250 feet from home plate to the left-field foul pole; 425 feet to center field; 440 feet to the right-field power alley; and 301 feet from home plate to the right-field foul pole. Now with the track gone, it was only 201 feet to the left-field foul pole and 225 feet to straight-away left field. Little League dimensions for sure, but not to worry, the Dodgers had dealt with this problem before. Whereas the 1958 Dodgers had created "The Thing," a 42-foot screen above the left-field wall, on this night they erected a new 60-foot Thing.[2]

Two days later on Opening Day at Dodger Stadium, number 4 startled a capacity crowd of 56,000 when he suddenly appeared from behind a blue outfield wall and began to walk toward second base under the noon-day sun. An 81-year-old Duke Snider was wearing his Brooklyn jersey, but when he stopped at his former position in center field, he ignited the crowd when he ripped it off to reveal another jersey with the blue letters, "Los Angeles." Over the next 15 minutes, some 40 former Dodgers emerged one by one from behind the fences in left, center, and right field to take their old positions on the field. Perhaps the largest roar was elicited by Vin Scully in the press box when he announced the ceremonial first pitch thrown by a trio of Dodger icons: Don Newcombe, Carl Erskine, and Sandy Koufax. And no other than the San Francisco Giants would be on hand to "help" them open their 50th year on the West Coast. With a 5–0 shutout, the Dodgers avenged their humiliating 8–0 loss to the San Francisco Giants in the first major league game on the West Coast 50 years earlier at Seals Stadium.[3] The second 50 years had begun.

Chapter Notes

Prologue

1. Roger Kahn, *The Boys of Summer* (New York, Harper & Row, 1972), 349.
2. Kahn, 344.

Chapter 1

1. "Film Star James Dean Killed in Auto Crash," *Los Angeles Times*, Oct. 1, 1955, 9 A.M. Final, 1.
2. John Drebinger, "Dodgers Beat Yanks, 8–5, for 2–2 World Series Tie," *New York Times*, Oct. 2, 1955, late city ed., sec. 5, 1.
3. Al Wolf, "Dodgers Beat Yankees, 5 to 3; Take Series Lead," *Los Angeles Times*, Oct. 3, 1955, 9 A.M. Final, 1.
4. John Drebinger, "Yanks Tie the Series, Downing Dodgers 5–1 at Stadium," *New York Times*, Oct. 4, 1955, late city ed., 1.
5. "128 Pitches Do It; Ford Threw 76 Strikes, 52 Balls in Halting Brooks," *New York Times*, Oct. 4, 1955, late city ed., 41.
6. John Drebinger, "Dodgers Capture 1st World Series; Podres Wins, 2–0," *New York Times*, Oct. 5, 1955, late city ed., 1.
7. "Southpaw's 'Wows' Show His Joy After He 'Wows' Brooklyn Fans," *New York Times*, Oct. 5, 1955, late city ed., 42.
8. "Feat of Witherbee's Most Famous Son Starts Celebration in Up-State Hamlet," *New York Times*, Oct. 5, 1955, late city ed., 42.
9. Meyer Berger, "About New York — and Brooklyn, Dodger Fans Have Their Innings," *New York Times*, Oct. 5, 1955, late city ed., 1.
10. "All Brooklyn Busts Loose at Big News," *Los Angeles Times*, Oct. 5, 1955, 9 A.M. Final, Part IV, 1.
11. Ibid, 44.
12. "Calling All Cars! Nab That Dodger Fan," *Los Angeles Times*, Oct. 5, 1955, 9 A.M. Final, Part IV, 1.
13. "Who's a Bum!," *New York Daily News*, Oct. 5, 1955, late ed., 1.
14. "Podres' Adirondack Neighbors Turn Out 3,000 Strong to Hail Series Hero," *New York Times*, Oct. 9, 1955, late city ed., 57.
15. "Buses Boycotted Over Race Issue," *New York Times*, Dec. 6, 1955, late city ed., 31.
16. E.R. Shipp, "Rosa Parks, 92, Founding Symbol of Civil Rights Movement, Dies," *New York Times*, Oct. 25, 2005, late city ed., 1.
17. Robert A. Rosenbaum, *The Penguin Encyclopedia of American History* (New York, Penguin Reference, 2003), 235.
18. Roscoe McGowen, "Dodgers Will Play 7 League Games at Jersey City in 1956," *New York Times*, Dec. 2, 1955, late city ed., 33.
19. John Drebinger, "Podres, World Series Hero of Dodgers, Is Reclassified 1-A by Draft Board," *New York Times*, Dec. 28, 1955, late city ed., 29.
20. "Johnny Podres Now Member of U.S. Navy," *Los Angeles Times*, March 20, 1956, 9 A.M. Final, Part IV, 1.

Chapter 2

1. "Snider and Fan Clash," *New York Times*, July 18, 1956, late city ed., 30.
2. Clifton Daniel. ed., *The 20th Century Day by Day* (New York, DK, 1999), 786.
3. John Drebinger, "Dodgers' Maglie Beats Yanks, 6–3, in Series Opener," *New York Times*, Oct. 4, 1956, late city ed., 1.
4. John Drebinger, "Dodgers Triumph Over Yanks, 13–8, for 2nd Straight," *New York Times*, Oct. 6, 1956, late city ed., 1.
5. "Dodgers Now Favored," *New York Times*, Oct. 6, 1956, late city ed., 25

6. John Drebinger, "Yanks Triumph, 5–3, Cut Dodgers' Series Lead to 2–1," *New York Times,* Oct. 7, 1956, late city ed., S1.

7. John Drebinger, "Yanks Defeat Dodgers, 6–2; Series in 2–2 Tie," *New York Times,* Oct. 8, 1956, late city ed., 1.

8. John Drebinger, "Larsen Beats Dodgers in Perfect Game; Yanks Lead, 3–2, on First Series No-Hitter," *New York Times,* Oct. 9, 1956, late city ed., 1.

9. John Drebinger, "Dodgers Defeat Yanks in 10th, 1–0, and Even Series," *New York Times,* Oct. 10, 1956, late city ed., 1.

10. John Drebinger, "Yanks Champions; Kucks' 3-Hitter Tops Dodgers, 9–0," *New York Times,* Oct. 11, 1956, late city ed., 1.

11. Edward Prell, "Maglie Feels That Big Newk Overpitched," *Chicago Daily Tribune,* Jan. 31, 1957, Spt.-Bus., 2.

12. Walter H. Stern, "Ebbets Field Sold for Housing; Dodgers Can Stay Five Seasons," *New York Times,* Oct. 31, 1956, late city ed., 1.

13. Daniel, *The 20th Century Day by* Day, 789.

14. Peter N. Stearns, ed., *The Encyclopedia of World History,* 6th ed. (New York, Houghton Mifflin, 2001), 966.

15. James F. Lynch, "Jackie Robinson Quits Baseball; Trade is Voided," *New York Times,* Jan. 6, 1957, late city ed., S1.

16. Ibid.

17. George Barrett, "Bus Integration in Alabama Calm," *New York Times,* Dec. 22, 1956, late city ed., 1.

Chapter 3

1. "Podres Handles Yanks as Bums Triumph, 2–1," *Los Angeles Times,* April 15, 1957, Part IV, 1.

2. Peter Morris, *A Game of Inches, The Stories Behind the Innovations That Shaped Baseball—The Game Behind the Scenes* (Chicago, Ivan R. Dee, 2006), 333.

3. Daniel, *The 20th Century Day by Day,* 805.

4. Anthony Lewis, "President Sends Troops to Little Rock," *New York Times,* Sept. 25, 1957, late city ed., 1.

5. Michael Korda, *IKE: An American Hero* (New York, HarperCollins, 2007), 698.

6. Rosenbaum, *Penguin Encyclopedia of American History,* 212.

7. Roscoe McGowen, "Dodgers Defeat Pirates in Ebbets Field Finale," *New York Times,* Sept. 25, 1957, late city ed., 33.

8. Doris Kearns Goodwin, *Wait Till Next Year* (New York, Simon & Schuster Paperbacks, 1997), 225.

9. McGowen, "Dodgers Defeat Pirates," 33.

10. Goodwin, *Wait Till Next Year,* 226.

11. Peter C. Bjarkman, "Brooklyn Dodgers–Los Angeles Dodgers, From Daffiness Dodgers to the Boys of Summer and the Myth of America's Team," *Encyclopedia of Major League Baseball—National League,* ed. (Westport, CT, Meckler, 1991), 101.

12. Roger Craig, personal interview, June 30, 2007.

13. Ibid.

14. Bjarkman, "Brooklyn Dodgers–Los Angeles Dodgers," 101.

15. Roscoe McGowen, "Snider Hits 39th, 40th Homers as Dodgers Halt Phils," *New York Times,* Sep. 23, 1957, late city ed., 32.

16. Milton Bracker, "The New York Giants, 1883–1957," *New York Times,* Sept. 30, 1957, late city ed., 1.

17. Bill Becker, "Giants Will Shift to San Francisco for 1958 Season," *New York Times,* Aug. 20, 1957, late city ed., 1.

18. "Trend Reversed Too Late," *New York Times,* Sept. 30, 1957, late city ed., 36.

19. Emanuel Perlmutter, "Dodgers Accept Los Angeles Bid to Move to Coast," *New York Times,* Oct. 9, 1957, late city ed., 1.

20. Neil J. Sullivan, *The Dodgers Move West* (New York, Oxford University Press, 1987), 136.

21. "O'Malley Tells Reasons For Leaving," *Los Angeles Times,* Oct. 9, 1957, Part IV, 2.

22. Paul Zimmerman, "Bums' Move Climaxes Years of Hard Work," *Los Angeles Times,* Oct. 9, 1959, Part IV, 1.

23. "O'Malley Tells Reasons For Leaving," *Los Angeles Times,* Oct. 9, 1957, Part IV, 2.

24. Zimmerman, "Bums' Move Climaxes Years of Hard Work," 2.

25. "O'Malley Tells Reasons For Leaving," *Los Angeles Times,* Oct. 9, 1957, Part IV, 2.

26. Zimmerman, "Bums' Move Climaxes Years of Hard Work," 2.

27. Ibid.

28. Paul Crowell, "Rockefeller Bid to Help Dodgers Ends in Failure," *New York Times,* Sept. 21, 1957, late city ed., 38.

29. Ibid, 1.

30. Perlmutter, "Dodgers Accept Los Angeles Bid," 1.

31. Joseph M. Sheehan, "Fans Added Zest to Lore of Bums," *New York Times,* Oct. 9, 1957, late city ed., 37.

32. Perlmutter, "Dodgers Accept Los Angeles Bid," 1.

33. Zimmerman, "Bums' Move Climaxes Years of Hard Work," 1.

34. Ibid, 2.

35. Ibid.

36. Korda, *IKE,* 700.

37. Ibid.

38. Rosenbaum, *Penguin Encyclopedia of American History,* 361.

39. Robert G. Whalen, "The Year in Review, Treads in Time of Increased Tension," *New York Times*, Dec. 29, 1957, late city ed., 8E.
40. Solomon, 553.

Chapter 4

1. Emanuel Perlmutter, "Dodgers Accept Los Angeles Bid to Move to Coast," *New York Times*, Oct. 9, 1957, late city ed., 37.
2. Frank Finch, "O'Malley Still Hopes to Play in Rose Bowl," *Los Angeles Times*, Dec. 31, 1957, Part IV, 2.
3. "Pasadena Prepares Rose Bowl Contract," *Los Angeles Times*, Dec. 31, 1957, Part IV, 2.
4. "Dodgers' Future is Not All Roses," *New York Times*, Jan. 8, 1958, late city ed., 93.
5. Frank Finch, "Rose Bowl Proposal Rejected," *Los Angeles Times*, Jan. 14, 1958, Part IV, 1.
6. Lawrence S. Ritter, *Lost Ballparks* (New York, Penguin, 1992), 198.
7. Ibid.
8. Ibid, 199.
9. "Frick Says Wrigley Field a Cow Pasture," *Los Angeles Times*, Jan. 12, 1958, 9 A.M. Final, Part III, 1.
10. Frank Finch, *The Los Angeles Dodgers, The First Twenty Years* (Los Angeles, Jordan & Company, 1977), 14.
11. Gladwin Hill, "Dodgers Will Play Home Games in L.A. Coliseum," *New York Times*, Jan. 18, 1958, late city ed., 19.
12. Casey Stengel, "Chicago is What You'd Call Stagnant," *Life*, Oct. 19, 1959, 132.
13. Finch, *The Los Angeles Dodgers*, 23.
14. "Screen Goes up in Left Field at Coliseum," *Los Angeles Times*, Apr. 5, 1958, 9 A.M. Final, Part II, 2.
15. Peter C. Bjarkman, "Brooklyn Dodgers–Los Angeles Dodgers, From Daffiness Dodgers to the Boys of Summer and the Myth of America's Team," 102.
16. Will Grimsley, "Pitchers Blast Short Coliseum Fence," *Los Angeles Times*, Jan. 21, 1958, 9 A.M. Final, Part IV, 1.
17. Ibid.
18. Ibid.
19. Ibid.
20. Roger Craig, personal interview, July 7, 2007.

Chapter 5

1. Frank Finch, "Dodgers Hunt For First-line Catcher," *Los Angeles Times*, Jan. 29, 1958, Part IV, 1.
2. Craig, personal interview, July 7, 2007.
3. Roy Silver, "Roy Campanella Paralyzed in Crash; Broken Neck is Expected to Heal," *New York Times*, Jan. 29, 1958, late city ed., 1.
4. Ibid.
5. Ibid.
6. Craig, personal interview, July 7, 2007.
7. Finch, "Dodgers Hunt For First-line Catcher," 1.
8. Ibid.

Chapter 6

1. John W. Finney, "U.S. Satellite is 'Working Nicely,'" *New York Times*, Feb. 2, 1958, late city ed., 1.
2. Kahn, *The Boys of Summer*, 1.
3. Craig, personal interview, July 7, 2007.
4. Frank Finch, "Dodgers Win in Exhibition Finale," *Los Angeles Times*, April 14, 1958, 9 A.M. Final, Part IV, 2.
5. Paul Zimmerman, *The Los Angeles Dodgers* (New York, Coward-McCann, 1960), 121.
6. Ibid.
7. Ibid, 116.
8. Ibid, 117.
9. Craig, personal interview, July 7, 2007.
10. Ibid.
11. Staff Writer, "Tab Bavasi Big Success as Official," *Los Angeles Times*, April 14, 1958, 9 A.M. Final, Part V, 6.
12. Ibid.
13. Ibid.
14. Ibid.
15. Ibid.
16. Ibid.
17. Ibid.
18. Braven Dyer, "Dream Lives For O'Malley," *Los Angeles Times*, April 14, 1958, 9 A.M. Final, Part V, 3+.
19. Ibid, 3.
20. Ibid, 20.
21. Ibid.
22. Ibid, 18.
23. Ibid, 20.
24. Ibid, 18.
25. Ibid.
26. Brent Shyer, "Vin Scully," *Dodger History, Hall of Famers, Vin Scully*, http,//www.walteromalley.com/Vin Scully.
27. "Dodger Workouts Open in Florida," *Los Angeles Times*, Feb. 21, 1958, 9 A.M. Final, Part IV, 1.
28. "Bum Won't Hit the Road," *New York Times*, March 19, 1958, late city ed., 37.
29. Daniel, *The 20th Century Day by Day*, 811.
30. Frank Finch, "Dodgers Win in Exhibition Finale," 1.

Chapter 7

1. Max Frankel, "U.S. Pianist, 23, Wins Soviet Contest,'" *New York Times*, April 14, 1958, late city ed., 1.

2. "Tall at the Keyboard," *New York Times*, April 14, 1958, late city ed., 18.

3. Daniel, *The 20th Century Day by Day*, 812.

4. Ritter, *Lost Ballparks*, 171.

5. Frank Finch, "S.F. Beats Dodgers in Opener, 8–0," *Los Angeles Times*, April 16, 1958, 9 A.M. Final, Part I, 1.

6. Glenn Stout and Richard A. Johnson, *The Dodgers, 120 Years of Dodgers Baseball* (New York, Houghton Mifflin, 2004), 248.

7. Art Byon, "78,672 See Dodgers Beat Giants, 6 to 5," *Los Angeles Times*, April 19, 1958, 9 A.M. Final, Part I, 1.

8. Ibid.

9. Ibid, A.

10. Ibid.

11. Al Wolf, "Players Complain But Fans Happy," *Los Angeles Times*, April 19, 1958, 9 A.M. Final, Part II, 1.

12. *Times* Staff, "Dodgers Take Breath Away From Fans," *Los Angeles Times*, April 19, 1958, 9 A.M. Final, Part I, A.

13. *Times* Sports Staff, "Ceremonies at Coliseum Thrill Throng," *Los Angeles Times*, April 19, 1958, 9 A.M. Final, Part II, 4.

14. Jeane Hoffman, "Star-studded Crowd Sees Opener," *Los Angeles Times*, April 19, 1958, 9 A.M. Final, Part II, 2.

15. Ibid.

16. Al Wolf, "Davenport Admits Skull at Third Base," *Los Angeles Times*, April 19, 1958, 9 A.M. Final, Part II, 1.

17. Frank Finch, "Daffy Running Costly to Giants," *Los Angeles Times*, April 19, 1958, 9 A.M. Final, Part II, 1.

18. Wolf, "Players Complain But Fans Happy," 1.

19. Ibid.

20. Ibid.

21. Ibid.

22. Ross Newhan, "The Coliseum Was Not 'Real Baseball,'" *Los Angeles Times*, March 29, 2008.

23. Ibid.

24. Ibid.

25. Byon, "78,672 See Dodgers Beat Giants, 6 to 5," 1.

26. Ibid.

Chapter 8

1. Frank Finch, "Dodgers Routed Again, 16–9," *Los Angeles Times*, May 14, 1958, 9 A.M. Final, Part IV, 1.

2. Frank Finch, "Desperate Dodgers Call Up 2 Rookies," *Los Angeles Times*, May 15, 1958, 9 A.M. Final, Part IV, 1.

3. Craig, personal interview, June 30, 2007.

4. Ibid.

5. Tad Szulc, "Nixon Cuts Tour Short,'" *New York Times*, May 15, 1958, late city ed., 1.

6. Daniel, *The 20th Century Day by Day*, 813.

7. Al Wolf, "Dodgers Wonder What's Wrong With the Dodgers?" *Los Angeles Times*, May 14, 1958, 9 A.M. Final, Part IV, 1.

8. Ross Newhan, "The Coliseum Was No 'Real Baseball,'" *Los Angeles Times*, March 29, 2008.

9. Frank Finch, "Bavasi Hits at Snider's Indifference," *Los Angeles Times*, May 20, 1958, 9 A.M. Final, Part IV, 1.

10. Steve Springer, "Former Dodgers Reflect on Coliseum," *Los Angeles Times*, March 25, 2008.

11. Finch, "Bavasi Hits at Snider's Indifference," 3.

12. Springer, "Former Dodgers Reflect on Coliseum.."

13. Wolf, "Dodgers Wonder What's Wrong With the Dodgers?" 1.

14. Frank Finch, "Cubs Hand Double Loss to Dodgers," *Los Angeles Times*, May 31, 1958, 9 A.M. Final, Part II, 1.

15. Frank Finch, "Bavasi Slaps $300 Fine on Newcombe," *Los Angeles Times*, June 1, 1958, 9 A.M. Final, Part III, 1.

Chapter 9

1. "Issues in Referendum," *New York Times*, June 1, 1958, late city ed., 25.

2. "Referendum Petitions Filed on Dodgers," *Los Angeles Times*, November 15, 1957, 9 A.M. Final, Part I, 2.

3. "Referendum Vote Slated for June 3," *Los Angeles Times*, December 31, 1957, 9 A.M. Final, Part IV, 1.

4. Sullivan, *The Dodgers Move West*, 138.

5. Ibid.

6. "Second Suit Fights Chavez Ravine Deal," *Los Angeles Times*, October 15, 1957, 9 A.M. Final, Part I, 5.

7. Sullivan, *The Dodgers Move West*, 153.

8. Ibid.

9. Ibid.

10. "O'Malley Worried by Giles," *Los Angeles Times*, May 23, 1958, 9 A.M. Final, Part IV, 1.

11. Sullivan, *The Dodgers Move West*, 156.

12. "O'Malley Vows Fight for Dodgers," *Los Angeles Times*, May 27, 1958, 9 A.M. Final, Part I, 1.

13. Ibid.

14. Henry Giniger, "De Gaulle Shuns Assembly Debate,'" *New York Times*, June 2, 1958, late city ed., 1.

15. Daniel, *The 20th Century Day by Day*, 814.

16. "De Gaulle Viewed With Hope, Fear,"

Los Angeles Times, June 1, 1958, 9 A.M. Final, Part I, 1.

17. Eric Avila, Popular *Culture in the Age of White Flight: Fear and Fantasy in Suburban Los Angeles* (Berkeley, University of California Press, 2006), 165.

18. "Notables Back Prop. B on TV," *Los Angeles Times*, June 2, 1958, 9 A.M. Final, Part I, 1.

19. "Referendum Vote Slated for June 3," *Los Angeles Times*, December 31, 1957, 9 A.M. Final, Part IV, 1.

20. "Notables Back Prop. B on TV," 7.

21. Ibid.

22. Ibid.

23. Ibid.

24. Ibid.

25. Ibid.

26. Ibid.

27. Staff Writer, "24,293-Vote Victory Won For Baseball," *Los Angeles Times*, June 6, 1958, 9 A.M. Final, Part I, 1.

28. Robert C. Doty, "De Gaulle Wins Reform Power After He Threatens to Resign," *New York Times*, June 3, 1958, late city ed., 1.

29. Sullivan, *The Dodgers Move West*, 152.

Chapter 10

1. "Soviet Diplomat Expelled by U.S.," *New York Times*, June 8, 1958, late city ed., 1.

2. "28 U.S. Navy Men Due to be Freed by Cuban Rebels," *New York Times*, June 30, 1958, late city ed., 1.

3. Felix Belair, Jr., "Eisenhower Sends Marines into Lebanon" *New York Times*, July 16, 1958, late city ed., 1.

4. Daniel, *The 20th Century Day by Day*, 816.

5. Ibid, 817.

6. Stout and Johnson, *The Dodgers*, 249.

7. "Judge Issues Injunction Blocking Chavez Plans," *Los Angeles Times*, June 7, 1958, 9 A.M. Final, Part I, 1.

8. Frank Finch, "Dodgers Route Braves, Sweep Series," *Los Angeles Times*, June 9, 1958, 9 A.M. Final, Part IV, 1.

9. Frank Finch, "Newcombe Swapped," *Los Angeles Times*, June 16, 1958, 9 A.M. Final, Part I, 1.

10. Al Wolf, "Newk Takes Slump Blame," *Los Angeles Times*, June 17, 1958, 9 A.M. Final, Part IV, 1.

11. "Chavez Project Upset Sought by Fourth Suit," *Los Angeles Times*, June 18, 1958, 9 A.M. Final, Part III, 1.

12. "Chavez Oil Claims Given up by Dodgers," *Los Angeles Times*, June 20, 1958, 9 A.M. Final, Part I, 1.

13. Gene Blake, "Decision on Chavez Ravine Suits Seen Within Ten Days," *Los Angeles Times*, June 26, 1958, 9 A.M. Final, Part III, 1.

14. Frank Finch, "Dodgers Win 7th in Row From Braves," *Los Angeles Times*, June 28, 1958, 9 A.M. Final, Part II, 1.

15. Frank Finch, "Aaron, Braves Destroy Dodgers," *Los Angeles Times*, June 30, 1958, 9 A.M. Final, Part IV, 1.

16. "Suits Hold up Certification of Chavez Vote," *Los Angeles Times*, July 3, 1958, 9 A.M. Final, Part I, 2.

17. Frank Finch, "Dodgers Route Braves, Sweep Series," *Los Angeles Times*, July 4, 1958, 9 A.M. Final, Part III, 1.

18. Al Wolf, "Koufax Now 21st Dodger Casualty," *Los Angeles Times*, July 4, 1958, 9 A.M. Final, Part III,1.

19. Jack Walsh, "Baseball's Big Names Testify Here Today," *Washington Post*, July 9, 1958, Part A, 19.

20. W.H. Lawrence, "Stengelese is Baffling to Senators," *New York Times*, July 10, 1958, late city ed., 1.

21. Ibid, 33.

22. Ibid.

23. Ibid.

24. Ibid.

25. Ibid.

26. Ibid.

27. Ibid.

28. "Dodgers' Chavez Deal Held Void," *Los Angeles Times*, July 15, 1958, 9 A.M. Final, Part I, 1.

29. "Court Voids Dodger Contract for Chavez Ravine," *New York Times*, July 15, 1958, late city ed., 29.

30. Al Wolf, "O'Malley Confident Despite Ruling," *Los Angeles Times*, July 15, 1958, 9 A.M. Final, Part IV, 1.

31. John Drebinger, "One Storm After Another," *New York Times*, July 27, 1958, late city ed., Sec. 5, S2.

32. John Drebinger, "How Low Can You Get?" *New York Times*, July 28, 1958, late city ed., 19.

33. Finch, "Aaron, Braves Destroy Dodgers," 1.

34. John Drebinger, "Walter (O'Malley) Is at It Again," *New York Times*, July 30, 1958, late city ed., 21.

35. Ibid.

36. Ibid.

37. Sullivan, *The Dodgers Move West*, 171.

38. Frank Finch, "Dodgers Rehire Alston For Next Year," *Los Angeles Times*, Aug. 14, 1958, 9 A.M. Final, Part IV, 1.

39. "Dodgers Hail Alston," *New York Times*, Aug. 15, 1958, late city ed., 25.

40. Craig, personal interview, July 7, 2007.

41. Braven Dyer, "Drysdale Homers Twice, Beats Braves," *Los Angeles Times*, Aug. 24, 1958, 9 A.M. Final, Part III, 1.

42. Frank Finch, "Giants Trample Dodgers,

14–2," *Los Angeles Times*, Sept. 1, 1958, 9 A.M. Final, Part IV, 1.

Chapter 11

1. Finch, "Giants Thump Dodgers, 13–3," 1.
2. Ibid.
3. Frank Finch, "Phillies Defeat Dodgers," *Los Angeles Times*, Sept. 12, 1958, 9 A.M. Final, Part IV, 1.
4. Rosenbaum, *The Penguin Encyclopedia of American History*, 212.
5. Finch, "Giants Trample Dodgers, 14–2," 1.
6. Frank Finch, "Snider Hurt; L.A. Loses 2," *Los Angeles Times*, Sept. 17, 1958, 9 A.M. Final, Part IV, 1.
7. Frank Finch, "Dodgers Close Year With 7–4 Loss, Finish 7th," *Los Angeles Times*, Sept. 28, 1958, 9 A.M. Final, Part III, 1.
8. Stout and Johnson, *The Dodgers*, 248.
9. Newhan, "The Coliseum Was No 'Real Baseball.'"

Chapter 12

1. Lowell Reidenbaugh, *The Sporting News Selects Baseball's 25 Greatest Teams* (St. Louis, Sporting News Publishing Co., 1988), 125.
2. Morris Eckhouse, "More Woes Than Wahoos for Baseball's Wonderers," *Encyclopedia of Major League Baseball— National League*, Peter C. Bjarkman, ed. (Westport, CT, Meckler, 1991), 42.
3. Ibid, 43.
4. Ibid, 44.
5. "Schoendienst Deal Rated Cheer That Made Milwaukee Famous," *New York Times*, Sept. 24, 1957, late city ed., 44.
6. Ibid, 45.
7. Bob Buege, *The Milwaukee Braves: A Baseball Eulogy* (Milwaukee, Douglas American Sports Publications, 1987), 169.
8. Eckhouse, "More Woes Than Wahoos," 45.
9. "Schoendienst Deal Rated Cheer," 44.
10. Ibid.
11. Ibid.
12. Ibid, 46.
13. Buege, *The Milwaukee* Braves, 186.
14. Ibid, 185.
15. Ibid, 192.
16. Edwin L. Lake, Jr., "Russians Resume Nuclear Testing in Arctic Region," *New York Times*, Oct. 1, 1958, late city ed., 21.
17. Frank Finch, "Braves Edge Out Yankees in 10th, 4–3," *Los Angeles Times*, Oct. 2, 1958, 9 A.M. Final, Part IV, 1.
18. John Drebinger, "Braves Win, 13–5, Scoring 7 in First; Lead Series, 2 to 0," *New York Times*, Oct. 3, 1958, late city ed., 1.
19. John Drebinger, "Yanks Win, 4–0, and Cut Braves Lead to 2–1" *New York Times*, Oct. 5, 1958, late city ed., sec. 5, 1.
20. John Drebinger, "Spahn Stops Yanks, 3–0, With 2-Hitter; Braves Lead, 3–1" *New York Times*, Oct. 6, 1958, late city ed., 1.
21. Eckhouse, "More Woes Than Wahoos," 46.
22. John Drebinger, "Yankees Win, 7–0; Cut Braves' Lead in Series to 3–2" *New York Times*, Oct. 7, 1958, late city ed., 1.
23. Buege, *The Milwaukee Braves*, 220.
24. Ibid, 221.
25. Robert Creamer, "Breaking up the Braves," *Sports Illustrated*, Oct. 20, 1958, 73.
26. Eckhouse, "More Woes Than Wahoos," 46.
27. Buege, *The Milwaukee Braves*, 216.

Chapter 13

1. Daniel, *The 20th Century Day by Day*, 823.
2. Paul Zimmerman, "L.A. Fans Entitled to Stronger Team," *Los Angeles Times*, Sept. 29, 1958, Part IV, 1.
3. "Schoendienst Has Tuberculosis and Appears Lost to Braves for Next Year," *New York Times*, Nov. 19, 1958, late city ed., 46.
4. J. Ronald Oakley, *Baseball's Last Golden Age, 1946–1960* (Jefferson, McFarland, 1994), 280.
5. Walter Bingham, "A Good Man Gets Bad News," *Sports Illustrated*, Dec. 1, 1958, 32.
6. "Braves' Schoendienst Has Lung Surgery to Hasten Recovery from Tuberculosis," *New York Times*, Feb. 20, 1959, late city ed., 32.
7. Eckhouse, "More Woes Than Wahoos," 47.
8. Craig, personal interview, July 7, 2007.
9. "Schoendienst Has Tuberculosis," 46.
10. Zimmerman, *The Los Angeles Dodgers*, 147.
11. Buzzie Bavasi and Jack Olsen, "The Secret of Trading," *Sports Illustrated*, June 5, 1967, 53.
12. Zimmerman, *The Los Angeles Dodgers*, 146.
13. Ibid.
14. Bavasi and Olsen, "The Secret of Trading," 54.
15. Ibid, 53.
16. Craig, personal interview, July 7, 2007.
17. Zimmerman, *The Los Angeles Dodgers*, 81.
18. Ibid, 162.
19. Frank Finch, "Dodgers Swap Cimoli to Land Cards' Moon," *Los Angeles Times*, Dec. 5, 1958, Part IV, 1.
20. Ibid, 1.
21. Zimmerman, *The Los Angeles Dodgers*, 165.

22. Craig, personal interview, July 7, 2007.
23. Zimmerman, *The Los Angeles Dodgers*, 162.
24. L.A. Times Staff, "Reese Finally Retires, Takes Coaching Job," *Los Angeles Times*, Dec. 19, 1958, 9 A.M. Final, Part IV, 1.
25. Stout and Johnson, *The Dodgers*, 249.
26. R. Hart Phillips, "Bautista and Regime Flee Cuba; Castro Moving to Take Power," *New York Times*, Jan. 2, 1959, late city ed., 1.
27. R. Hart Phillips, "Castro Heads Cuba's Armed Forces," *New York Times*, Jan. 4, 1959, late city ed., 1.
28. Maitland A. Edey, ed., *Time Capsule/1959* (New York, Time-Life Books, 1968), 89.
29. Daniel, *The 20th Century Day by Day*, 822.
30. Frank Finch, "Dodgers Cut Distances in Coliseum Diamond," *Los Angeles Times*, Jan. 10, 1959, 9 A.M. Final, Part II, 1.
31. Ibid.
32. Gene Blake, "High Court Approves Dodgers Chavez Pact," *Los Angeles Times*, Jan. 14, 1959, 9 A.M. Final, Part I, 1.

Chapter 14

1. Daniel, *The 20th Century Day by Day*, 824, 829.
2. "None of 50 Experts Picked Dodgers First," *Los Angeles Times*, Sept. 28, 1959, Part IV, 2.
3. John Drebinger, "Yankees Favored in Junior Circuit," *New York Times*, April 5, 1959, sec, 5, 1.
4. Leslie Lieber, "The Radar Brain Picks the Pennant Winners, " *Los Angeles Times*, April 26, 1959, THIS WEEK Magazine, 10.
5. Ibid.
6. Ibid, 12.
7. R. Hart Phillips, "Castro Takes Oath as Premier of Cuba," *New York Times*, Feb. 17, 1959, late city ed., 1+.
8. Frank Finch, "Alston Declines Flag Prediction," *Los Angeles Times*, Feb. 19, 1959, 9 A.M. Final, Part IV, 1.
9. Ibid.
10. Ibid.
11. Frank Finch, "Fairly and Baxes to Face Cubs," *Los Angeles Times*, April 9, 1959, 9 A.M. Final, Part IV, 1.
12. Ibid.
13. Craig, personal interview, June 30, 2007.
14. Frank Finch, "Gentile, 4 Others Sent Down," *Los Angeles Times*, April 3, 1959, 9 A.M. Final, Part IV, 1.

Chapter 15

1. "Crowd Hails Castro as He Reaches U.S. for an 11-Day Visit," *New York Times*, April 16, 1959, late city ed., 1.
2. Edey, *Time Capsule/1959*, 94.
3. Ibid, 95.
4. Frank Finch, "Neal Keeps Promise With .338," *Los Angeles Times*, May 1, 1959, Part IV, 2.
5. Ibid.
6. Frank Finch, "Braves Shade Dodgers, 3–2, in 16th," *Los Angeles Times*, May 6, 1959, Part IV, 1.
7. Frank Finch, "78,898 See Braves Beat Dodgers, 6–0," *Los Angeles Times*, May 6, 1959, Part III, 1.
8. Frank Finch, "49,347 See Braves Route Dodgers, 8–3," *Los Angeles Times*, May 7, 1959, Part IV, 1.
9. Frank Finch, "Dodgers Top Giants, 2–1, Take Third," *Los Angeles Times*, May 8, 1959, Part IV, 1.
10. John Drebinger, "93,103 See Dodgers Bow to Yanks After Halting Giants in Afternoon," *New York Times*, May 8, 1959, late city ed., 30.
11. Frank Finch, "93,103 Watch Yanks Defeat Dodgers, 6–2," *Los Angeles Times*, May 8, 1959, Part I, 1+.
12. Finch, "93,103 Watch Yanks Defeat Dodgers, 6–2," 1.
13. John Drebinger, "93,103 See Dodgers Bow to Yanks," 30.
14. Ibid.
15. Ibid.
16. Frank Finch, "Grand Slam Nips Dodgers" *Los Angeles Times*, May 27, 1959, Part IV, 1
17. Oakley, *Baseball's Last Golden Age*, 296.
18. Buege, *The Milwaukee Braves*, 239.
19. Ibid.
20. Ibid, 241.
21. Ibid.
22. Ibid.
23. Ibid.
24. Donald Honig, *Baseball in the '50s* (New York, Crown, 1987), 211.
25. Buege, *The Milwaukee Braves*, 239.
26. Henry Aaron with Lonnie Wheeler, *I Had a Hammer* (New York, HarperCollins, 1991), 140.
27. F. Scott Fitzgerald, *The Great Gatsby* (New York, Charles Scribner's Sons, 1925), 162.
28. Edey, *Time Capsule/1959*, 26.
29. Ibid, 23.
30. Daniel, *The 20th Century Day by Day*, 826.
31. "John Foster Dulles, The President's Tribute," *New York Times*, May 25, 1959, late city ed., 1.
32. Frank Finch, "Alston Shakes Up Dodgers After Loss," *Los Angeles Times*, May 29, 1959, Part IV, 1.
33. Frank Finch, "Cubs' 8-Run 4th Inning Ruins Dodgers," *Los Angeles Times*, May 30, 1959, Part II, 1.

Chapter 16

1. James Reston, "A Debate of Politicians," *New York Times*, July 25, 1959, late city ed., 3.
2. Harrison E. Salisbury, "Nixon and Khrushchev Argue in Public as U.S. Exhibit Opens; Accuse Each Other of Threats," *New York Times*, July 25, 1959, late city ed., 1+.
3. Daniel, *The 20th Century Day by Day*, 828.
4. Rosenbaum, *The Penguin Encyclopedia of American History*, 82.
5. Korda, *IKE*, 708.
6. "Dodgers Trade Lillis for Spokane Shortstop Wills," *Los Angeles Times*, June 2, 1959, Part IV, 1.
7. Frank Finch, "Maury Wills From Spokane Joins L.A.," *Los Angeles Times*, June 6, 1959, Part II, 1.
8. Zimmerman, *The Los Angeles Dodgers*, 143.
9. Buzzie Bavasi and Jack Olsen, "May Have Been a Headache But They Never Were a Bore," *Sports Illustrated*, May 29, 1967, 32.
10. Zimmerman, *The Los Angeles Dodgers*, 140.
11. Frank Finch, "Carl Erskine Calls It Quits as a Pitcher," *Los Angeles Times*, June 16, 1959, Part IV, 1.
12. Ibid.
13. Ibid.
14. Frank Finch, "Dodgers Acquire Roger Craig to Replace Erskine on Roster," *Los Angeles Times*, June 17, 1959, Part IV, 3.
15. Frank Finch, "Roger Craig Optimistic, Eager to Start," *Los Angeles Times*, June 19, 1959, Part IV, 4.
16. Al Wolf, "Craig's Comeback Cheers Boss Alston," *Los Angeles Times*, June 20, 1959, Part II, 3.
17. Bavasi and Olsen, "The Secret of Trading," 50.
18. Ibid.
19. Buege, *The Milwaukee Braves*, 237.
20. John de la Vega, "Sherry Tamed Wild Streak on Way Up," *Los Angeles Times*, Sept. 29, 1959, Part IV, 2.
21. Ibid.
22. Ibid.
23. Ibid.
24. Ibid.
25. Paul Zimmerman, "Sherry Performs Under Pressure," *Los Angeles Times* Sept. 29, 1959, Part IV, 2.
26. Zimmerman, *The Los Angeles Dodgers*, 140.
27. Craig, personal interview, June 30, 2007.
28. "White Sox Defeat Red Sox, 5–4," *New York Times*, July 23, 1959, late city ed., 20.
29. Oakley, *Baseball's Last Golden Age*, 290.
30. "Red Sox Officials Are Called to Discrimination Inquiry," *New York Times*, April 15, 1959, late city ed., 38.
31. "Racial Charge Is Denied," *New York Times*, April 22, 1959, late city ed., 38.
32. "McCovey's 4-for-4 Debut Awakens Giants," *Los Angeles Times*, July 31, 1959, Part IV, 3
33. "Giants Take Lead, Defeat Phils, 7–2," *Los Angeles Times*, July 31, 1959, Part IV, 3
34. "Rookie Hurls Card Victory," *Los Angeles Times*, July 31, 1959, Part IV, 3
35. Frank Finch, "L.A. Sweeps Phils, 4–3, Takes 2nd," *Los Angeles Times*, Aug. 3, 1959, Part IV, 1.
36. Frank Finch, "A.L. Home Run Barrage Beats N.L., 5–3," *Los Angeles Times*, Aug. 4, 1959, Part IV, 1.
37. Frank Finch, "Essegian, Local Boy, Comes Home," *Los Angeles Times*, Aug. 5, 1959, Part IV, 2.
38. Frank Finch, "Reds Ruin L.A., 4–1," *Los Angeles Times*, Aug. 5, 1959, Part IV, 1.
39. Rosenbaum, 13.
40. Robert G. Whalen, "Fifty Important Dates of 1959," *New York Times*, Dec. 27, 1959, late city ed., 48.
41. Frank Finch, "Dodgers Drop Pair, Tumble to Third" *Los Angeles Times*, Aug. 24, 1959, Part IV, 1.
42. Frank Finch, "Dodgers' Homers Defeat Phils, 5–2" *Los Angeles Times*, Aug. 26, 1959, Part IV, 1
43. "Phillies Cut Giants' Lead to 2 Games," *Los Angeles Times*, Aug. 28, 1959, Part IV, 1.
44. Jane Leavy, *Sandy Koufax: A Lefty's Legacy* (New York, HarperCollins, 2002), 48.
45. Ibid, 49.
46. Ibid, 50.
47. Ibid, 57.
48. Craig, personal interview, June 30, 2007.
49. Stout and Johnson, *The Dodgers*, 255.
50. Richard Whittington, *The Los Angeles Dodgers:, An Illustrated History* (New York, Harper & Row, 1982), 80.
51. Frank Finch, "Koufax Fans 18 For Record; L.A. Wins," *Los Angeles Times*, Sept. 1, 1959, Part IV, 2.
52. Mal Florence, "'Best Game and Luckiest I Ever Pitched,' Says Koufax," *Los Angeles Times*, Sept. 1, 1959, Part IV, 3.

Chapter 17

1. Korda, *IKE*, 708.
2. Robert T. Hartmann, "Mr. K's Reception Cool But Polite," *Los Angeles Times*, Sept. 16, 1959, Part I, 1.
3. Frank Finch, "Dodgers Win Two, Trail by Half Game," *Los Angeles Times*, Sept. 12, 1959, Part II, 1.
4. Frank Finch, "Dodgers Beat Braves, 8–7,

in Thriller," *Los Angeles Times*, Sept. 16, 1959, Part IV, 1.

5. Buege, *The Milwaukee Braves*, 251.
6. Ibid.
7. Ibid, 252.
8. Ibid.
9. Robert T. Hartmann, "Khrushchev Asks Full Disarming in 4 Years," *Los Angeles Times*, Sept. 19, 1959, Part I, 1.
10. Edey, *Time Capsule/1959*, 137.
11. Lindsay Parrott, "Delegates at U.N. Reserved on Plan," *New York Times*, Sept. 19, 1959, late city ed., 1.
12. Honig, *Baseball in the '50s*, 209.
13. Marvin Miles, "Hollywood Greets Premier in Star-Studded Welcome," *Los Angeles Times*, Sept. 20, 1959, Part I, 1.
14. Edey, *Time Capsule/1959*, 36.
15. Zimmerman, *The Los Angeles Dodgers*, 142.
16. Ibid.
17. Ibid.
18. Craig, personal interview, July 7, 2007.
19. Frank Finch, "Hodges Homer in 11th Drops Cubs," *Los Angeles Times*, Sept. 26, 1959, Part I, 1.
20. Paul Zimmerman, "Phillies Upset Milwaukee, 6–3, as Rain Falls," *Los Angeles Times*, Sept. 26, 1959, Part I, 1.
21. Frank Finch, "Cubs Drub L.A. by 12–2; Flag at Stake Today," *Los Angeles Times*, Sept. 27, 1959, Part I, 1.
22. Paul Zimmerman, "Milwaukee 3–2 Victor Over Philadelphia," *Los Angeles Times*, Sept. 27, 1959, Part I, 1.
23. Al Wolf, "Giants Win on Jones' 7-Inning No-Hit Hurling," *Los Angeles Times*, Sept. 27, 1959, Part I, 1.
24. Craig, personal interview, June 30, 2007.
25. Ibid.
26. Ibid.
27. Frank Finch, "Dodgers, Braves Tie For Pennant — Dodgers Clobber Cubs, 7–1," *Los Angeles Times*, Sept. 28, 1959, Part I, 1.
28. Ibid.
29. Al Wolf, "Glum Giants Lose Pair to Cardinals," *Los Angeles Times*, Sept. 28, 1959, Part IV, 4.
30. Craig, personal interview, June 30, 2007.
31. W.H. Lawrence, "Khrushchev Off With 21-Gun Pomp," *New York Times*, Sept. 28, 1959, late city ed., 1.
32. Robert T. Hartmann, "Deadlock No Berlin Ended, President Says," *Los Angeles Times*, Sept. 29. 1959, Part I, 1.

Chapter 18

1. Lindsay Parrott, " Khrushchev Takes Off For Moscow," *Los Angeles Times*, Sept. 28, 1959, Part I, 1.
2. Stout and Johnson, *The Dodgers*, 253.
3. Paul Zimmerman, "Didn't Feel the Pressure Says Sherry," *Los Angeles Times*, Sept. 27, 1959, Part IV, 1.
4. Ibid.
5. Buege, *The Milwaukee Braves*, 238.
6. Zimmerman, *The Los Angeles Dodgers* 46.
7. Buege, *The Milwaukee Braves*, 233.
8. Aaron and Wheeler, *I Had A Hammer*, 142.
9. Craig, personal interview, June 30, 2007.
10. Mal Florence, "Torre Says Furillo Would Have Been Out but For Crazy Bounce," *Los Angeles Times*, Sept. 30, 1959, Part IV, 1.
11. Ibid.
12. Ibid.
13. Craig, personal interview, June 30, 2007.
14. Craig, personal interview, July 7, 2007.

Chapter 19

1. Richard C. Lindberg, "Chicago White Sox, Second Class in the Second City," *Encyclopedia of Major League Baseball — American League*, Peter C. Bjarkman, ed. (Westport, CT, Meckler, 1991), 76.
2. Honig, *Baseball in the '50s*, 211.
3. Ibid.
4. Casey Stengel, "Ol' Case Figures the Series," *Life*, Oct. 12, 1959, 128.
5. Stengel, "Ol' Case Figures the Series," 133.
6. Times Staff Representative, "White Sox Boast Great Defense," *Los Angeles Times*, Oct. 1, 1959, Part IV, 2.
7. Solomon, 570.
8. Honig, *Baseball in the '50s*, 213.
9. Donald Dewey and Nicholas Acocella, *The Biographical History of Baseball* (New York, Carroll & Graf, 1995), 518.
10. Ibid.
11. Lindberg, "Chicago White Sox," 76.
12. "Indians' Colavito Hits 4 Homers Against Orioles," *New York Times*, June 11, 1959, late city ed., 41.
13. Lindberg, "Chicago White Sox," 76.
14. Ibid, 77.
15. Ibid.
16. "White Sox 'Glad it's Over,'" *Los Angeles Times*, Sept. 23, 1959, Part IV, 5
17. Lindberg, "Chicago White Sox," 77.
18. Oakley, *Baseball's Last Golden Age*, 289.
19. Ibid, 76.
20. Honig, *Baseball in the '50s*, 214.
21. "Veeck Nears Deal," *Chicago Daily Tribune*, Dec. 23, 1958, Part III, 1.
22. Lindberg, "Chicago White Sox," 77.
23. Ritter 33.

Chapter 20

1. Don Shannon, "Talks in Steel Strike Resumed," *Los Angeles Time*, Oct. 1, 1959, Part I, 1.
2. Edey, *Time Capsule/1959*, 71.
3. Craig, personal interview, July 7, 2007.
4. John Drebinger, "White Sox Rout Dodgers in Series Opener, 11 to 0," *New York Times*, Oct. 2, 1959, late city ed., 1+.
5. Stengel, "Ol' Case Figures the Series," 133.
6. "Chi Sox Got Kluszewski Just In Time," *Los Angeles Times*, Oct. 2, 1959, Part IV, 2.
7. "Big Klu Does a Real Cadillac Job," *Sports Illustrated*, Oct. 12, 1959, 17.
8. Craig, personal interview, July 7, 2007.
9. "Roger Craig 'Owned' by Kluszewski," *Los Angeles Times*, Oct. 2, 1959, Part IV, 4.
10. Craig, personal interview, July 7, 2007.
11. "Big Klu Does a Real Cadillac Job," 17.
12. Drebinger, "White Sox Rout Dodgers in Series Opener, 11 to 0," 32.
13. Frank Finch, "Dodgers Lose Opener 11–0," *Los Angeles Times*, Oct. 2, 1959, Part IV, 2.
14. Stengel, "Ol' Case Figures the Series," 128.
15. Ibid.
16. "Two Homers Klu's Biggest Thrill," *Los Angeles Times*, Oct. 2, 1959, Part IV, 2.
17. Finch, "Dodgers Lose Opener 11–0," 1.
18. Craig, personal interview, July 7, 2007.
19. "Game 1—Wow! That White Sox Power!," *Sports Illustrated*, Oct. 12, 1959, 16–17.
20. Ibid.
21. Al Wolf "We're Not Dead Yet Vow Dodgers," *Los Angeles Times*, Oct. 2, 1959, Part IV, 1.
22. "Game 1—Wow! That White Sox Power!," 16–17.
23. "Game 2—Dodger Homers, White Sox Goof," *Sports Illustrated*, Oct. 12, 1959, 18–19.
24. Al Wolf, "Neal's Bat + Spirit + Fight = 4–3 Dodger Victory," *Los Angeles Times*, Oct. 3, 1959, Part II, 1.
25. Stengel, "Ol' Case Figures the Series," 133.
26. "Game 2—Dodger Homers, White Sox Goof," 18.
27. Wolf, "Neal's Bat + Spirit + Fight = 4–3 Dodger Victory," 1.
28. Louis Effrat "Cuccinello Takes Blame for Waving Lollar Home on Key Play of 2nd Game," *New York Times*, Oct. 3, 1959, late city ed., 11.
29. "Game 2—Dodger Homers, White Sox Goof," 19.
30. Craig, personal interview, July 7, 2007.
31. Stengel, "Ol' Case Figures the Series," 128.
32. Wolf, "Neal's Bat + Spirit + Fight = 4–3 Dodger Victory," 1.
33. Stengel, "Ol' Case Figures the Series," 133.
34. Craig, personal interview, July 7, 2007.
35. "Game 2—Dodger Homers, White Sox Goof," 19.
36. Wolf, "Neal's Bat + Spirit + Fight = 4–3 Dodger Victory," 1.
37. John Drebinger, "92,294 See Dodgers Win, 3–1, and Take Series Lead," *New York Times*, Oct. 5, 1959, late city ed., 1+
38. Arthur Daley, "In a California Cauldron," *New York Times*, Oct. 5, 1959, late city ed., 38.
39. Drebinger, "92,294 See Dodgers Win, 3–1, and Take Series Lead," 38.
40. Al Wolf, "Confidence in Furillo Gives Alston Big Hit," *Los Angeles Times*, Oct. 5, 1959, Part IV, 1.
41. Frank Finch, "92,294 See Dodgers Win, 3–1," *Los Angeles Times*, Oct. 5, 1959, Part I, 1+.
42. Wolf, "Confidence in Furillo Gives Alston Big Hit," 1.
43. Arthur Daley, "In a California Cauldron," 38.
44. "Game 3—92,294 People and One Furillo," *Sports Illustrated*, Oct. 12, 1959, 20.
45. Ibid.
46. Finch, *The Los Angeles Dodgers, The First Twenty Years*, 25.
47. Craig, personal interview, July 7, 2007.
48. Ibid.
49. Frank Finch, "Dodgers Make it Third in a Row With 5–4 Win on Hodges' Homer," *Los Angeles Times*, Oct. 6, 1959, Part I, 1+.
50. Arthur Daley, "A Game Called Screeno," *New York Times*, Oct. 6, 1959, late city ed., 47.
51. Frank Finch, "Finch's Report of Dodgers' 3rd Series Win," *Los Angeles Times*, Oct. 6, 1959, Part IV, 2.
52. Ibid.
53. Braven Dyer, "Dodgers Again Come Through in the Clutch," *Los Angeles Times*, Oct. 6, 1959, Part IV, 1+.
54. "Sherry, Sherry Everywhere," *Sports Illustrated*, Oct. 12, 1959, 21
55. Craig, personal interview, July 7, 2007.
56. Finch, *The Los Angeles Dodgers*, 25.
57. "White Sox Change Luck with White Stockings," *New York Times*, Oct. 7, 1959, late city ed., 53.
58. Frank Finch, "92,706 See Chisox Edge Dodgers, 1–0," *Los Angeles Times*, Oct. 7, 1959, Part I, 1+.
59. John Drebinger, "White Sox Win, 1–0, Cut Dodger Lead for Series to 3–2," *New York Times*, Oct. 7, 1959, late city ed., 1+.
60. Drebinger, "White Sox Win, 1–0," 53.
61. Frank Finch, "Finch's Report of 5th Series Game," *Los Angeles Times*, Oct. 7, 1959, Part IV, 5.
62. Bill Becker, "Lopez Happy After Strategy Succeeds," *New York Times*, Oct. 7, 1959, late city ed., 53.
63. Finch, "Finch's Report of 5th Series Game," 5.
64. Drebinger, "White Sox Win, 1–0," 53.
65. Ibid.

66. Zimmerman, *The Los Angeles Dodgers,* 33.
67. Finch, *The Los Angeles Dodgers,* 25.
68. Frank Finch, "Podres to Face Wynn in Sixth Game," *Los Angeles Times,* Oct. 8, 1959, Part I, 1+.
69. Casey Stengel, "Chicago is What You'd Call Stagnant," *Life,* Oct. 19, 1959, 135.
70. Finch, "Podres to Face Wynn in Sixth Game," 1.
71. Zimmerman, *The Los Angeles Dodgers,* 118.
72. Stengel, "Chicago is What You'd Call Stagnant," 135.
73. Finch, *The Los Angeles Dodgers,* 25.
74. Craig, personal interview, July 7, 2007.
75. Edey, *Time Capsule/1959,* 74.
76. Bill Becker, "Jubilant Throng of 3,500 Greets Dodgers at Los Angeles Airport," *New York Times,* Oct. 10, 1959, late city ed., 16.

Chapter 21

1. Stengel, "Chicago is What You'd Call Stagnant," *Life* 19 Oct. 1959, 132.
2. Craig, personal interview, July 7, 2007.
3. Stengel, "Chicago is What You'd Call Stagnant," 133.
4. Stengel, "Chicago is What You'd Call Stagnant," 132.
5. Zimmerman, *Los Angeles Dodgers,* 27.
6. Stengel, "Chicago is What You'd Call Stagnant," 135.
7. Ibid.
8. Ibid.
9. Craig, personal interview, July 7, 2007.
10. Al Wolf "'Greatest Team, it Never Quit,' Says Walt Alston," *Los Angeles Times,* Oct. 9, 1959, Part IV, 1.
11. Stengel, "Chicago is What You'd Call Stagnant," 131.
12. Ibid., 132.
13. Ibid.
14. Buege, *The Milwaukee Braves,* 238.
15. Craig, personal interview, July 7, 2007.
16. Bjarkman, "Brooklyn Dodgers–Los Angeles Dodgers, From Daffiness Dodgers to the Boys of Summer and the Myth of America's Team," 104.
17. Zimmerman, *The Los Angeles Dodgers,* 15.
18. Finch, *The Los Angeles Dodgers,* 25.
19. Bjarkman, "Brooklyn Dodgers–Los Angeles Dodgers, From Daffiness Dodgers to the Boys of Summer and the Myth of America's Team," 104.
20. Craig, personal interview, July 7, 2007.
21. Ibid.
22. Wolf, "'Greatest Team, It Never Quit,' Says Walt Alston," 1.
23. Sullivan, *The Dodgers Move West,* 188.

Chapter 22

1. Craig, personal interview, July 7, 2007.
2. Oakley, *Baseball's Last Golden Age,* 325.
3. Mark Newman, "Finding Ways to Get 100 Series," MLB.com, Sept. 21, 2003.
4. Oakley, *Baseball's Last Golden Age,* 326.
5. Steve Gietschier, ed., *The Complete Baseball Record & Fact Book* (St. Louis, The Sporting News, 2006), 468.
6. John M. Carroll, "Houston Colt .45s–Astros, From Showbiz to Serious Baseball Business," *Encyclopedia of Major League Baseball — National League,* Peter C. Bjarkman, ed. (Westport, CT, Meckler, 1991) 243.
7. Carroll, "Houston Colt .45s–Astros," 243–244.
8. "Lewis Dismissed as Baseball Players' Lawyer," *New York Times,* March 25, 1959, late city ed., 29.
9. "Players O.K. New Counsel," *Chicago Sunday Tribune,* Dec. 6, 1959, Part II, 1
10. Carroll, "Houston Colt .45s–Astros," 201.
11. Joseph Wallace, Neil Hamilton, and Marty Appel, *Baseball, 100 Classic Moments in the History of the Game* (New York, Dorling Kindersley, 2000), 158.
12. Geoffrey C. Ward and Ken Burns, *Baseball: An Illustrated History* (New York, Knopf, 1994), 443.
13. Wallace, Hamilton, and Appel, *Baseball, 100 Classic Moments,* 173.
14. Oakley, *Baseball's Last Golden Age,* 321.
15. Ibid., 322.
16. Ibid., 330.
17. Ibid.
18. Ward and Burns, *Baseball,* 421.

Chapter 23

1. Oakley, *Baseball's Last Golden Age,* 301.
2. Bjarkman, "Brooklyn Dodgers–Los Angeles Dodgers, From Daffiness Dodgers to the Boys of Summer and the Myth of America's Team," 107.
3. Frank Finch, "Dodgers Boot Chance to Wrap it Up," *Los Angeles Times,* Sept. 30, 1962, Sec. D, 1.
4. Frank Finch, "Cards Slam Back Door on Dodgers," *Los Angeles Times,* Oct. 1, 1962, Part III, 1.
5. Dan Hafner, "Stunned Dodgers Can't Believe it," *Los Angeles Times,* Oct. 1, 1962, Part III, 4.
6. Frank Finch, "Dodgers Throw Away Flag to Giants," *Los Angeles Times,* Oct. 4, 1962, Part III, 1.
7. Kahn, *The Boys of Summer,* 333.
8. Ibid, 334.

9. Ibid.
10. Ibid, 327.
11. Ibid, 336.
12. Ibid.
13. "At Last! Early Wynn Captures No. 300," *Chicago Tribune*, July 14, 1963, Sec. 2, 1.
14. Rosenbaum, *The Penguin Encyclopedia of American History*, 101.

Epilogue: 50 Years On

1. Ben Platt, "Dodgers Parade into New Year's Day," MLB.com, Jan. 1, 2008.
2. Bill Shaikin, "Huge Crowd for a Tiny Field, *Los Angeles Times*, March 30, 2008.
3. Bill Plaschke, "Boys of Spring Thrill Dodger Fans," *Los Angeles Times*, March 31, 2008.

Bibliography

Books

Aaron, Henry, and Lonnie Wheeler. *I Had a Hammer*. New York: HarperCollins, 1991.

Alston, Walter, and Si Burdick. *Alston and the Dodgers*. New York: Doubleday, 1966.

Avila, Eric. *Popular Culture in the Age of White Flight: Fear and Fantasy in Suburban Los Angeles*. Berkeley: University of California Press, 2006.

Bjarkman, Peter C., ed. *Encyclopedia of Major League Baseball Team Histories— American League*. Westport, CT: Meckler, 1991.

_____, ed. *Encyclopedia of Major League Baseball Team Histories— National League*. Westport, CT: Meckler, 1991.

Buege, Bob. *The Milwaukee Braves: A Baseball Eulogy*. Milwaukee: Douglas American Sports, 1988.

Cepeda, Orlando, and Herb Fagen. *Baby Bull: From Hardball to Hard Time and Back*. Dallas: Taylor, 1998.

Daniel, Clifton, ed. *The 20th Century Day by Day*. New York: DK Publishing, 1999.

Delsohn, Steve. *True Blue: The Dramatic History of the Los Angeles Dodgers, Told by the Men Who Lived It*. New York: HarperCollins, 2001.

Dewey, Donald, and Nicholas Acocella. *The Biographical History of Baseball*. New York: Carroll & Graf, 1995.

Drysdale, Don, and Bob Verdi. *Once a Bum, Always a Dodger*. New York: St. Martin's Press, 1990.

Edey, Maitland A., ed. *Time Capsule/1959*. New York: Time-Life Books, 1968.

Finch, Frank. *The Los Angeles Dodgers: The First Twenty Years*. Los Angeles: Jordan & Company, 1977.

Fitzgerald, F. Scott. *The Great Gatsby*. New York: Charles Scribner's Sons, 1925.

Gietschier, Steve, ed. *The Complete Baseball Record & Fact Book*. St. Louis: Sporting News, 2006.

Goodwin, Doris Kearns. *Wait Till Next Year*. New York: Simon & Schuster, 1997.

Honig, Donald. *Baseball in the '50s*. New York: Crown Publishers, 1987.

Kahn, Roger. *The Boys of Summer*. New York: Harper & Row, 1972.

Korda, Michael. *IKE: An American Hero*. New York: HarperCollins, 2007.

Leavy, Jane. *Sandy Koufax: A Lefty's Legacy*. New York: HarperCollins, 2002.

Leventhal, Josh. *The World Series: An Illustrated Encyclopedia of the Fall Classic*. New York: Black Dog & Leventhal, 2001.

Mays, Willie, and Charles Einstein. *Willie Mays: My Life In and Out of Baseball.* New York: E.P. Dutton, 1966.
McNeil, William F. *The Dodgers Encyclopedia.* 2nd ed. Champaign, IL: Sports Publishing, 2003.
Morris, Peter. *A Game of Inches: The Stories Behind the Innovations That Shaped Baseball— The Game Behind the Scenes.* Chicago: Ivan R. Dee, 2006.
Oakley, J. Ronald. *Baseball's Last Golden Age, 1946–1960.* Jefferson, NC: McFarland, 1994.
Reidenbaugh, Lowell. *The Sporting News Selects Baseball's 25 Greatest Teams.* St. Louis: Sporting News Publishing Co, 1988.
Ritter, Lawrence S. *Lost Ballparks.* New York: Penguin Books, 1992.
Rosenbaum, Robert A. *The Penguin Encyclopedia of American History.* New York: Penguin Reference, 2003.
Snider, Duke, and Bill Gilbert. *The Duke of Flatbush.* New York: Zebra Books, 1988.
Solomon, Burt. *The Baseball Timeline.* New York: DK Publishing, Inc., 2001.
Stearns, Peter N., ed. *The Encyclopedia of World History.* 6th ed. New York: Houghton Mifflin, 2001.
Stein, Fred, and Nick Peters. *Giants Diary: A Century of Giants Baseball in New York and San Francisco.* Berkeley, CA: North Atlantic Books, 1987.
Stout, Glenn, and Richard A. Johnson. *The Dodgers: 120 Years of Dodgers Baseball.* New York: Houghton Mifflin, 2004.
Sullivan, Neil J. *The Dodgers Move West.* New York: Oxford University Press, 1987.
Ward, Geoffrey C., and Ken Burns. *Baseball: An Illustrated History.* New York: Knopf, 1994.
Whittington, Richard. *The Los Angeles Dodgers: An Illustrated History.* New York: Harper & Row, 1982.
Wills, Maury, and Mike Celizic. *On the Run: The Never Dull and Often Shocking Life of Maury Wills.* New York: Carroll & Graf, 1991.
Zimmerman, Paul. *The Los Angeles Dodgers.* New York: Coward-McCann, 1960.

Articles

Bavasi, Buzzie, and Olsen, Jack. "They May Have Been a Headache But They Never Were a Bore." *Sports Illustrated*, May 29, 1967: 30–44.
Bavasi, Buzzie, and Olsen, Jack. "The Real Secret of Trading." *Sports Illustrated*, June 5, 1967: 47–54.
"Big Klu Does a Real Cadillac Job." *Sports Illustrated*, Oct. 12, 1959: 17.
Bingham, Walter. "A Good Man Gets Bad News." *Sports Illustrated*, Dec. 1, 1958: 32.
Creamer, Robert. "Breaking up the Braves." *Sports Illustrated*, Oct. 20, 1958: 73.
"Game 1— Wow! That White Sox Power!" *Sports Illustrated*, Oct. 12, 1959: 16–17.
"Game 2 — Dodger Homers, White Sox Goof." *Sports Illustrated*, Oct. 12, 1959: 18–19.
"Game 3 — 92,294 People and One Furillo." *Sports Illustrated*, Oct. 12, 1959: 20.
"Sherry, Sherry Everywhere." *Sports Illustrated*, Oct. 12, 1959: 21.
Stengel, Casey, "Ol' Case Figures the Series." *Life*, Oct. 12, 1959: 125–128.
Stengel, Casey. "Chicago is What You'd Call Stagnant." *Life*, Oct. 19, 1959: 131–137.

Newspapers

Chicago Daily Tribune
Los Angeles Times
New York Times

Index

Numbers in ***bold italics*** refer to pages with photographs.